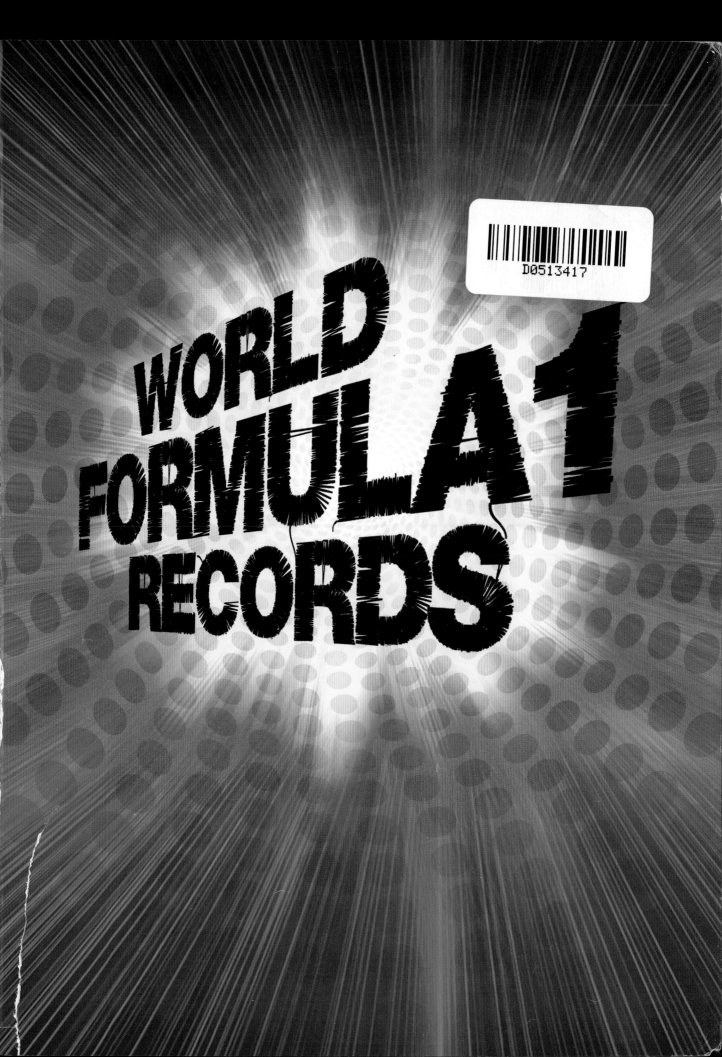

WORLD
FORMULA1
RECORDS

This edition published in 2016
by Carlton Books Limited
20 Mortimer Street
London W1T 3JW

Previous editions published by Carlton Books Limited in 2011, 2012, 2013, 2014, 2015

A CIP catalogue record for this book is available from the British Library

10 9 8 7 6 5 4 3 2 1

ISBN 978-1-78097-840-6

Editor: Martin Corteel
Project Art Editor: Stephen Cary
Designer: Katie Baxendale
Picture Research: Paul Langan
Production: Lisa Cook

Printed in Dubai

NOTE: All statistics are up to date as of the end of 2015.

Right: Off to a flier: With his victory
at the 2016 Chinese GP, Nico Rosberg
became the first driver to start a
season with a hat-trick of world
championship wins since Michael
Schumacher in 2004.

WORLD FORMULA 1 RECORDS

SIXTH EDITION

BRUCE JONES

CARLTON
BOOKS

CONTENTS

Contents pages **Mexican wave:**
(*main image*) Mexico returned to the
F1 calendar in 2015, offering fans a
great view through this new stadium
section towards the end of the lap.
(*inset top left*) Ayrton Senna in 1989;
(*inset top right*) Sebastian Vettel
leads the way for Red Bull in the
2013 Canadian GP; (*inset bottom left*)
Michael Schumacher wins the 2004
Japanese GP at Suzuka for Ferrari;
(*inset bottom right*) Jim Clark leads
the 1968 South African GP.

Overleaf: Hunting for another title: Both McLaren
and Jenson Button have won titles before, but they
need a return to form with Honda power.

INTRODUCTION

All sports produce record and statistics galore, from goals scored to matches won to titles collected, and motor racing has its own measures of excellence, whether it's races won, pole positions collected, fastest laps, races started or even laps led.

Examine the tables of who has done what, or which team, and you will be looking at a list of the best of the best. However, as you go through this book you will find anomalies aplenty, such as the greatest names from the early days of the Formula One World Championship languishing far further down the lists than you might expect. That's simple to explain, as they contested far fewer races each year in the 1950s, sometimes as few as six per year and, sadly, they also had a tendency to be killed in action as cars and circuits were far less safe back then. That's why Juan Manuel Fangio, a five-time World Champion, has just 24 grand prix wins to his name, leaving him only 10th in the all-time list at the start of 2016. Mind you, that was 24 wins from just 51 starts, whereas Rubens Barrichello has more than six times that number of starts and fewer than half of the number of wins, emphasising how Fangio's hit rate, at 47 per cent, is something that will probably never be matched.

Such was the longevity and success of Michael Schumacher's career – first with Benetton and then, chiefly, with Ferrari before his swansong return with Mercedes – that he tops pretty much every category of records. Indeed, even if Sebastian Vettel or Lewis Hamilton, the most successful of today's heroes, start winning every grand prix from 2016 on, it will be midway through the 2018 World Championship at the earliest before they will be able to topple the German's remarkable tally of 91 wins.

What leapt out as I complied the figures and wrote the stories for this book is just how much the tide has flowed between success and failure across the years as the World Championship accelerates into its seventh decade. For example, teams that once had the world at their feet, such as Cooper and Brabham, have long since shut their doors for the final time and even McLaren is now struggling.

I've had fun compiling this book and hope you enjoy wallowing in the statistics!

BRUCE JONES
June 2016

Right: It's celebration time in the Mercedes garage after victory at the Circuit of the Americas – his 10th of the season – enabled Lewis to claim his third F1 title.

PART 1

F1 ALL-TIME RECORDS

Formula One, the world's fastest-moving sport, has been exciting and entertaining fans around the globe since the World Championship began in 1950. The drive to win is as strong as ever, but Formula One has changed dramatically over the past 65 years. The cars have been transformed into high-tech missiles with incredible acceleration, cornering and braking capabilities. The circuits are bigger, better and considerably safer. So, with every grand prix, the records keep on being added to in a blaze of glamour and speed.

Below **All eyes on Turn 1:** *It's Mercedes in control as poleman Nico Rosberg holds off his team-mate Lewis Hamilton by occupying the inside line into the first corner on F1's return to Mexico in 2015. Sebastian Vettel can be seen between them in his Ferrari. Yet victory here came too late for Rosberg to prevent Hamilton landing his third title.*

DRIVERS

Michael Schumacher's dominance of Formula One from 2000 to 2004 means that his name is at the top of almost every list of driver achievement. But some of his rivals and those who raced before him certainly made huge contributions to the colourful history of Formula One, including greats such as Alberto Ascari, Juan Manuel Fangio, Stirling Moss, Jack Brabham. Jim Clark, Jackie Stewart, Niki Lauda, Nelson Piquet, Alain Prost, Ayrton Senna, Nigel Mansell, Fernando Alonso, Sebastian Vettel and Lewis Hamilton.

Below **A man on a mission:** Juan Manuel Fangio produced one of his greatest performances to chase, catch and pass the Ferraris to win the 1957 German GP at the Nurburgring for Maserati, en route to his fifth F1 title.

CHAMPIONS

WINNER BY A FRACTION

IIIIIIIIIIIIIIIIIIIIIIIIIIIIIIIIIIIII

Some champions win by a clear margin, others just scrape home. Lewis Hamilton (2008), Kimi Räikkönen (2007), James Hunt (1976) and Mike Hawthorn (1958) all edged home by one point, but Hawthorn's championship required an act of fair play from Stirling Moss who stopped Hawthorn from being disqualified from the Portuguese GP, verifying that Hawthorn's Ferrari hadn't been given a push-start. The closest championship finish was in 1984, when Niki Lauda beat his McLaren teammate Alain Prost by half a point.

WINNING FOR YOURSELF

To win the Formula One drivers' title is a huge honour. To win it in a car bearing your name is doubly so, and the late Jack Brabham is the only person to have managed this, in 1966. Teammate Denny Hulme then became champion for Brabham in 1967.

BRITISH DRIVERS COME OUT ON TOP

British drivers, teams and engine suppliers top many tables of F1 statistics, which is a fact that would have amazed onlookers in the 1950s as the dark green cars made up the numbers behind the best from Italy and Germany. Yet Britain has claimed more drivers' titles than any other country, 15, and more world champions too, 10, namely Mike

Above **British drivers come out on top:** Jackie Stewart claimed his third F1 title with Tyrrell in 1973. *Below* **Winner by a fraction:** McLaren's James Hunt took the 1976 drivers' title by a solitary point after an epic fight with Ferrari's Niki Lauda.

Hawthorn, Graham Hill, Jim Clark, John Surtees, Jackie Stewart, James Hunt, Nigel Mansell, Damon Hill, Lewis Hamilton and Jenson Button.

THE LION'S SHARE

Every now and again, a team or a driver dominates F1. Take Michael Schumacher's run at the beginning of the 21st century, when he was world champion from 2000 to 2004. Ferrari won a record-equalling 15 grands prix, both in 2002 and 2004, to match McLaren's record from 1988. Of those, Michael won 11 in 2002 and 13 in 2004. McLaren's wins were split seven to eight between Alain Prost and Ayrton Senna. Then, in 2014, Mercedes won 16, albeit from 19 rounds with Lewis Hamilton winning 11 to Nico Rosberg's five.

Above **Privateers strike a blow:** Jack Brabham celebrates after winning the 1959 British GP at Aintree as Cooper came good.
Below **Playing dirty:** Michael Schumacher's Benetton is flipped on to two wheels after turning in on Damon Hill's Williams.

TOP WORLD CHAMPIONSHIP-WINNING DRIVERS

1	Michael Schumacher	7
2	Juan Manuel Fangio	5
3	Alain Prost	4
=	Sebastian Vettel	4
5	Jack Brabham	3
=	Lewis Hamilton	3
=	Niki Lauda	3
=	Nelson Piquet	3
=	Ayrton Senna	3
=	Jackie Stewart	3
11	Fernando Alonso	2
=	Alberto Ascari	2
=	Jim Clark	2
=	Emerson Fittipaldi	2
=	Mika Hakkinen	2
=	Graham Hill	2
17	Mario Andretti	1
=	Jenson Button	1
=	Giuseppe Farina	1
=	Mike Hawthorn	1
=	Damon Hill	1
=	Phil Hill	1
=	Denis Hulme	1
=	James Hunt	1
=	Alan Jones	1
=	Nigel Mansell	1
=	Kimi Räikkönen	1
=	Jochen Rindt	1
=	Keke Rosberg	1
=	Jody Scheckter	1
=	John Surtees	1
=	Jacques Villeneuve	1

 ## BREAK CLEAR

Sebastian Vettel recorded the largest title-winning margin in F1 World Championship history in 2013, beating Fernando Alonso by 155 points to outstrip his 2011 margin of 122 over Jenson Button. These tallies were helped by the 2010 change to 25 points for a win rather than 10, outstripping Michael Schumacher's then record 67-point margin over Ferrari teammate Rubens Barrichello in 2002.

 ## PRIVATEERS STRIKE A BLOW

Jack Brabham and Cooper struck a blow for the little guys when they won both the 1959 World Drivers' and Constructors' Championships together. This made Cooper the first specialist racing-car manufacturer to beat the established automotive marques such as Alfa Romeo, Ferrari, Mercedes and Maserati, which ran their F1 teams alongside their established road-car business.

PLAYING DIRTY

Damon Hill had every reason to feel aggrieved in the season-ending finale in Adelaide in 1994. Michael Schumacher seemed to have left a gap; Hill dived for it, not knowing that the German had just damaged his car against the wall. Schumacher then turned his Benetton across into Hill's Williams and the resulting clash caused irreparable damage to Hill's car and he had to retire from the race. Schumacher claimed the World Championship by a point. Damon's father Graham also lost a title through dastardly deeds. This happened at Mexico in 1964 when Ferrari's John Surtees beat him to the title by a point after his teammate Lorenzo Bandini tipped Hill into a spin.

HOP, SKIP AND A JUMP

Aside from Giuseppe Farina's record in winning the inaugural World Championship in 1950, the smallest total number of grands prix contested by a driver before becoming world champion is Juan Manuel Fangio, who won the title in 1951 for Alfa Romeo after competing in just 12 grands prix. Drivers these days contest many more grands prix than that in just one season alone.

FROM GOOD TO BAD

World Champions can't win year in, year out, for a variety of reasons. Juan Manuel Fangio, Mike Hawthorn, Jochen Rindt, Nigel Mansell and Alain Prost have failed to do so due to injury, death or retirement, but the following drivers failed to win a race in the year after claiming the title: Alberto Ascari (1954), Fangio (1958), Jack Brabham (1961), Phil Hill (1962), John Surtees (1965), Mario Andretti (1979), Jodi Scheckter (1980), Nelson Piquet (1988), Damon Hill (1997), Jacques Villeneuve (1998) and Sebastian Vettel (2014).

JUST ONE WILL DO

Anyone who watched Keke Rosberg race will know that he was a driver who raced to win, a driver full of on-the-limit aggression, yet he claimed his world title for Williams in 1982 with just one win. That was Mike Hawthorn's tally too when he was crowned in 1958. Jack Brabham (1959), Phil Hill (1961), John Surtees (1964) and Denny Hulme (1967) all managed to win the title with just two victories.

KEEP IT IN THE FAMILY

The Hill family has a proud boast. Despite F1 being littered with sons following their fathers into the sport, Graham and Damon are the only father and son to both win the F1 title. Graham won in 1962 for BRM and in 1968 for Lotus while Damon was crowned with Williams in 1996. The Andrettis and Scheckters failed to match their feat, while the Piquet and Rosberg dynasties have since aimed to emulate them.

WORLD CHAMPION PAIRINGS

The pairing of Lewis Hamilton and Jenson Button at McLaren from 2010 to 2012 made it 10 seasons in which a team has run two world champions after Alberto Ascari and Giuseppe Farina at Ferrari in 1953 and 1954; Jim Clark and Graham Hill at Lotus in 1967 and 1968; Emerson Fittipaldi and Denny Hulme at McLaren in 1974; Alain Prost and Keke Rosberg at McLaren in 1986; and Alain Prost and Ayrton Senna at McLaren in 1989. The record extended to 11 in 2014 when Ferrari fielded Fernando Alonso and Kimi Räikkönen.

TWO WHEELS TO FOUR

John Surtees – who was the world champion for Ferrari in 1964 – has the distinction of being the only motorcycle world champion to hit world title-winning heights after transferring to car racing. Fellow motorcycle world champions Mike Hailwood and Johnny Cecotto also made the move to four wheels, but "Mike the Bike" peaked with a best finish of second place in the 1972 Italian GP, ironically racing for Surtees's team, while Cecotto's best result was a sixth position at Long Beach for Theodore in 1983.

Above **From good to bad:** Alberto Ascari struggled in 1954, failing to finish a single race despite winning titles in both 1952 and 1953. He's shown here in his Ferrari 625 in the Italian GP at Monza. *Top* **Keep it in the family:** In 1996, Damon Hill, son of Graham, leads Williams teammate Jacques Villeneuve, son of Gilles, during the year he became the first second-generation world champion.

WITH ROOM TO SPARE

The driver who clinched the World Championship with the most races still to be run was Michael Schumacher during his runaway success for Ferrari in 2002. There were 17 rounds that year and the German was world champion by the 11th race, the French GP at Magny-Cours, which he won.

I'LL TAKE THE FASTEST CAR

Juan Manuel Fangio was undoubtedly a maestro behind the wheel, but he was also a master at making sure he had the right machinery beneath him and he moved teams to ensure this, which explains why he won the World Championship with more teams than any other driver. He was champion with Alfa Romeo, Mercedes, Ferrari and Maserati.

THE FIRST WORLD CHAMPION

Giuseppe Farina was the first F1 world champion in 1950 at the age of 44. The Italian achieved his final win three years later just a few months short of his 47th birthday and, in so doing, became the second-oldest F1 race winner ever. These days, most of the drivers' fathers are younger than that.

COMING BACK FROM RETIREMENT

Niki Lauda had two World Championship titles to his name when he quit before the end of the 1979 season. Like many before and after him he couldn't stay away and was back in 1982, racing for McLaren. In winning the title in 1984 he set the record for the longest gap between titles – seven years.

ADDING TITLES TO TITLES

Sebastian Vettel became the youngest double world champion in 2011 at the age of just 24 years and 98 days. Then in 2013, he became the youngest quadruple world champion, at 26 years and 116 days, beating Alain Prost's record by a comprehensive 12 years.

Right The first World Champion: Mario Andretti took 80 races to be champion, but Nigel Mansell took 100 more. **Below** I'll take the fastest car: Juan Manuel Fangio smiles with delight as he wins the 1957 German GP after hunting down the Ferraris in his Maserati.

DRIVERS WHO COMPETED IN MOST RACES BEFORE WINNING FIRST WORLD CHAMPIONSHIP

1	Nigel Mansell	180
2	Jenson Button	170
3	Kimi Räikkönen	121
4	Mika Hakkinen	112
5	Jody Scheckter	97
6	Alain Prost	87
7	Mario Andretti	80
=	Alan Jones	80
9	Ayrton Senna	77
10	Fernando Alonso	67
=	Damon Hill	67

RUNNERS-UP

FIRST OF THE LOSERS

Nobody wants to finish second in a grand prix. In F1 it's referred to as "the first of the losers". So, imagine how drivers gnash their teeth at ending the year as the championship runner-up. It's even worse if they trip up in the final round and let the title slide from their grasp. The most extreme example of this was when Lewis Hamilton blew his chance of winning the title at his first attempt in 2007 at the Brazilian GP when gearbox problems affected his race and he could only finish seventh. Ferrari's Kimi Räikkönen powered to a race victory and the title.

LAUDA PIPS PROST

Being faster and scoring more wins is one thing, but master tactician Niki Lauda taught his McLaren teammate Alain Prost a lesson in consistency in 1984. Prost settled in quickly after joining from

Renault and won the opening round, then added six more wins, including three of the final four races. However, Lauda kept racking up the points, including five race wins. Lauda won the World Championship by half a point, courtesy of only half the points being awarded when the Monaco GP was stopped prematurely because of a heavy rainstorm when Prost was leading.

CHASING THE DREAM

Rubens Barrichello – runner-up in 2002 and 2004 – ran second behind Ayrton Senna in the 1993 European GP at Donington Park in his Jordan when a month short of his 21st birthday. It was only his third grand prix and yet he would end up contesting the most grands prix without clinching a World title, having raced 325 times by the end of the 2011 season. He then lost his ride for 2012 and turned to IndyCar racing.

Above **Instant impact:** An oil leak stopped Jacques Villeneuve from winning on his F1 debut for Williams in 1996, but he was soon triumphant, winning fourth time out at the Nurburgring. *Below* **If at first you don't succeed...:** Nigel Mansell had his first title in his sights in 1986, but had to wait to 1992 to claim it.

POINTS DON'T MEAN PRIZES

When he finished 2015 as runner-up to Mercedes teammate Lewis Hamilton for the second year in a row, Nico Rosberg had 14 wins to his name but no title. It left him second behind Stirling Moss in the table of race wins without being champion. Rosberg has the most points without a title: 1,209.5.

INSTANT IMPACT

Jacques Villeneuve and Lewis Hamilton are the only drivers to finish their debut seasons as World Championship runners-up. Villeneuve achieved this for Williams behind Damon Hill in 1996 and Hamilton for McLaren in 2007. However, both drivers did win the title a year later.

IF AT FIRST YOU DON'T SUCCEED...

Nigel Mansell would have been world champion in 1986 but for his blowout in the Adelaide finale that left him ranked second behind Alain Prost. But he persevered and was runner-up twice more, in 1987 and 1991, before it all came good and he finally landed his World Championship crown for Williams in 1992.

DRIVERS WITH MOST CAREER RACE WINS
WITHOUT WINNING WORLD CHAMPIONSHIP

1	Stirling Moss	16
2	Nico Rosberg	14
3	David Coulthard	13
4	Carlos Reutemann	12
5	Rubens Barrichello	11
=	Felipe Massa	11
7	Gerhard Berger	10
=	Ronnie Peterson	10
9	Mark Webber	9
10	Jacky Ickx	8

Above **Drivers with most career race wins without winning World Championship:** Nico Rosberg won the final three rounds in 2015, taking his wins total to 14, but he has yet to claim the F1 drivers' title. *Below* **Always the bridesmaid:** Stirling Moss won four races in the 1958 World Championship – including the British GP – but lost the title to Mike Hawthorn, who won but once.

⫸ A RECORD NOT WANTED

Not only does Stirling Moss have the most years as runner-up to his name – four – but he also tops the chart for the driver with the most F1 wins without a title, at 16. David Coulthard is next on 13 and Carlos Reutemann is third on 12, with Gerhard Berger and Ronnie Peterson having won 10 times each.

⫸ IS SEVEN A LUCKY NUMBER?

Three drivers who became or had been world champion hold an unwanted record in that they managed to win the most races in a season, seven, without taking the title. Alain Prost did it in 1984 and 1988, Kimi Räikkönen in 2005 and Michael Schumacher in 2006.

ALWAYS THE BRIDESMAID

Stirling Moss will be remembered as the best driver never to have been world champion. Four times he finished as runner-up, three of those behind Juan Manuel Fangio, his one-time mentor at Mercedes. On the fourth occasion he lost out by a single point to Mike Hawthorn, despite winning more races that year. Alain Prost was also runner-up four times, but he could balance those against his four World Championships.

WINS

FERRARI TO THE FORE

Combine the fact that Ferrari has been racing in F1 for longer than any other marque (going back to the inaugural season in 1950) with the fact that the most garlanded winner, Michael Schumacher, scored the bulk of his 91 wins with them, and it's not surprising that it tops the charts for the most wins, with a tally of 224 wins by the end of 2015. McLaren lags 43 wins behind, but it did fleetingly nose in front in the late 1990s before Schumacher and Ferrari dominated.

MR CONSISTENCY

Perhaps the most impressive of Michael Schumacher's many, many records is that once he started winning in 1992 he kept going, claiming at least one grand prix win in all of the next 14 World Championship seasons through to 2006, but he wasn't able to add any in his return in 2010.

13: UNLUCKY FOR EVERYONE ELSE

Michael Schumacher wasn't the sort of driver troubled by superstition. There were no habits such as always getting into the car from the same side or wearing odd boots or a lucky pair of underpants or gloves. But 13 was a lucky number for him, as his 13 wins from 18 grands prix in 2004 gave him his seventh and final title. Sebastian Vettel also bagged 13, in 2013, for his fourth title.

RULE BRITANNIA

Not only are British drivers the most successful in landing World Championships, they've also won the most grands prix. They have 248 wins shared between 19 of them, with Lewis Hamilton at the top of the pile with 43. This is good only for third in the overall wins table, though, far behind Michael Schumacher's 91. That said, Britain's overall tally is 89 more than the next most successful country, Germany, with Brazil third on 101.

Right **Rule Britannia:** Lewis Hamilton is one of 19 British drivers **to win a** grand prix. *Below* **Mr Consistency:** Michael Schumacher gave Ferrari almost half of its **record-breaking 224 wins**, but Felipe Massa, Fernando Alonso, shown here in the 2011 Chinese GP, **and Sebastien Vettel** have carried on where Schumacher left off.

ON A ROLL

If one win upsets a driver's rivals, just think what a string of wins does. King of the rolling wins was Alberto Ascari, who hit the most vivid of purple patches in 1952 when he won the Belgian GP and carried on winning through the next eight grands prix, with the last of these being the Belgian GP the following year. Not surprisingly, he was world champion both years. This record was broken in 2013 when Sebastian Vettel won the last nine grands prix.

MOST BREAKTHROUGH WINNERS

There were only two breakthrough winners in the inaugural World Championship campaign, but there have seldom been many more first-time winners than that. Indeed, the maximum number in a season is four, in 1975 when Carlos Pace, Jochen Mass, James Hunt and Vittorio Brambilla made their mark on F1. Then in 1982 it was the turn of Riccardo Patrese, Patrick Tambay, Elio de Angelis and Keke Rosberg to make their breakthroughs.

TOO GOOD TO BE A FLUKE

When a driver dominates, a lot of F1 fans point to the merits of the car. So, perhaps one of the best ways to prove that a driver's input is vital is to find the driver who has won for the most different teams. Step forward Stirling Moss, who won for five marques – Mercedes, Maserati, Vanwall, Cooper and Lotus. Juan Manuel Fangio and Alain Prost both won for four teams.

HOME IS WHERE THE HEART IS

With a little help from having two grands prix held in Germany most years during his career, the inimitable Michael Schumacher holds the record for the most wins at a driver's home race, adding five wins in the European GP at the Nürburgring to his three in the German GP. Alain Prost recorded six wins in the French GP.

EVERYONE HAS A GO

The 1982 season was extremely competitive as 11 drivers took at least one win in the 16 grands prix. Keke Rosberg ended the year as world champion ahead of Didier Pironi and John Watson (both of whom scored two wins), with Michele Alboreto, Rene Arnoux (two), Elio de Angelis, Niki Lauda (two), Riccardo Patrese, Nelson Piquet, Alain Prost (two) and Patrick Tambay also enjoying victories.

NO DISCERNIBLE PATTERN

The 1982 World Championship in which 11 drivers won grands prix also produced the longest run of different winning drivers. Riccardo Patrese's surprise win in the sixth round in Monaco triggered a sequence of wins for different drivers that ran through to Keke Rosberg's win in the 14th round in the Swiss GP. There's never been another year like it.

TOP 10 DRIVERS WITH MOST GRAND PRIX WINS

1	Michael Schumacher	91
2	Alain Prost	51
3	Lewis Hamilton	43
4	Sebastian Vettel	42
5	Ayrton Senna	41
6	Fernando Alonso	32
7	Nigel Mansell	31
8	Jackie Stewart	27
9	Jim Clark	25
10	Niki Lauda	25

Left **Top 10 drivers with most grand prix wins:** Michael Schumacher got used to lifting the winner's trophy, doing so 91 times in all. *Above* **No discernible pattern:** With his victory at Monaco in 1982, Riccardo Patrese started a historic run of nine grands prix with a different winner each time.

Above **Winning nation:** The first Briton to win a World Championship round was Mike Hawthorn (left), who pipped Juan Manuel Fangio at the 1953 French GP.
Below **When overtaking is essential:** John Watson in fine form in a spectacular US West GP at Long Beach in 1983 when he drove his McLaren from 22nd to first.

THE LAP THAT COUNTS

Jochen Rindt was an expert at leading the final lap rather than the first one, and he pulled off the trick to the greatest effect at Monaco in 1970 when he hunted down Jack Brabham and pressured him into a mistake at the first corner of the final lap. Poor Brabham was pipped in another last-lap changeover later that year at Brands Hatch, when again Rindt demoted him as he coasted to the finish line, out of fuel.

A WONDERFUL YEAR'S WORK

Six wins in any World Championship campaign is an impressive and seldom achieved tally. However, World Championships were considerably shorter in the early 1950s and Alberto Ascari's six wins in his first title-winning year for Ferrari, 1952, came from just seven grands prix, giving him a winning rate of 86 per cent – the best ever. Michael Schumacher's 13 wins from 18 races in 2004 represented a 72 per cent return.

FIRST IMPRESSIONS

Jacques Villeneuve and Lewis Hamilton share the record for the most grand prix wins in their maiden F1 seasons. Their tally is four apiece, with Villeneuve scoring the first of these with Williams on his fourth outing, at the Nurburgring in 1996, and Hamilton taking his McLaren first past the chequered flag at his sixth attempt, in Canada in 2007. Juan Manuel Fangio and Giuseppe Farina both won three grands prix in 1950, the inaugural year of the F1 World Championship.

DOMINANT PAIRINGS

Michael Schumacher led home Rubens Barrichello on 19 occasions when they raced together at Ferrari. When he had a particular year's World Championship in the bag, Michael would ease off and let Rubens through to head home giving another Ferrari one-two. He did this five times, although one of these was a fumble when he tried to stage a dead heat at Indianapolis in 2002 and failed.

WINNING NATION

Drivers from 21 nations have won in F1, but the British have the greatest number of winning drivers, with 19 of them sharing a table-topping 248 victories. The first of these wins was by Mike Hawthorn, when his Ferrari edged out Juan Manuel Fangio's Maserati to win the French GP at Reims in 1953 by one second. Germany rank as runners-up, in most part due to seven-time world champion Michael Schumacher's tally of 91 wins. Only six of his compatriots have added to the haul.

COMETH THE HOUR, COMETH THE MAN

There are 23 drivers who have won just one solitary grand prix. How did it all go so right just the once then never again? In the case of Jean-Pierre Beltoise, a former French motorcycle racing champion who showed immense promise, he won in extremely wet conditions at Monaco in 1972. His BRM lacked the regular power of the other cars on the grid, but the rain negated this disadvantage and he never again had the equipment to add to that tally.

WHEN OVERTAKING IS ESSENTIAL

With overtaking becoming increasingly difficult, the possibility of a driver advancing from the rear of the grid is becoming less likely. Therefore, John Watson's record, set at the 1983 US West GP at Long Beach, California, of winning from 22nd on the grid is probably guaranteed its place in the history books for ever. He also holds the record for the third best charge, from 17th to 1st at Detroit in 1982.

FIRST TO TEN

As F1 found its feet through the 1950s, drivers started to lay down markers of their excellence. The first to achieve 10 wins was not five-time champion Juan Manuel Fangio but Alberto Ascari, who had the good fortune to be leading Ferrari's attack when it had the pick of the cars. His victory in the 1953 Dutch GP made him the first driver to double figures.

HIT THE GROUND RUNNING

Nigel Mansell enjoyed the best start to a season when he and his Williams-Renault FW14B won the first five grands prix in 1992. It could have been the first six but for a wheel weight coming loose at Monaco and his subsequent charge just failed to overhaul Ayrton Senna's McLaren. Michael Schumacher matched this feat in 2004.

Below **No one shall pass:** Jim Clark celebrates at Silverstone in 1967 after the 11th of his 13 wins from pole for Lotus. *Bottom* **By the skin of his teeth:** Peter Gethin noses his BRM past Ronnie Peterson's March (25) for the closest grand prix finish ever.

STARTING OFF FAST

Drivers from Italy and Argentina shared the wins through the first three World Championships from 1950 to 1952, with Giuseppe Farina, Luigi Fagioli, Alberto Ascari and Piero Taruffi making Italy proud and Juan Manuel Fangio and Jose Froilan Gonzalez doing the same for Argentina. Amazingly, despite Fangio winning five F1 titles, only one other driver from Argentina – Carlos Reutemann – has won since, whereas a further 11 Italians have done so.

TOP 10 COUNTRIES WITH MOST GRAND PRIX WINS

1	Great Britain	248
2	Germany	159
3	Brazil	101
4	France	79
5	Finland	46
6	Italy	43
7	Austria	41
8	Argentina	38
=	Australia	38
10	Spain	32

BY THE SKIN OF HIS TEETH

A last-lap lead change in the Italian GP at Monza in 1971 produced the closest finish in F1 history. Peter Gethin nosed his BRM to the front of a five-car pack after a slipstreaming dash out of the final corner, doing his best to gain the stewards' confidence that he'd secured victory by punching the air ostentatiously as he crossed the line. His margin of victory was 0.01 seconds over March's Ronnie Peterson, with the first five covered by just 0.61 seconds.

NO ONE SHALL PASS

Ayrton Senna started from pole 65 times and he made the most of them as he holds the record for leading the most grands prix from start to finish. He did this 19 times, with Jim Clark next on the list with 13, and Michael Schumacher, Jackie Stewart and Sebastian Vettel on 11 each.

STARTING WITH A BANG

Two drivers hold the almost unbelievable record of winning a grand prix on their World Championship debut. Giuseppe Farina achieved this in 1950, in the first ever World Championship (he went on to win the title), but the more significant achievement was by Giancarlo Baghetti. Having been promoted through the Ferrari ranks in their search for a young Italian driver, in 1961 he won two non-championship races and then won a slipstreamer by 0.1 secs from Dan Gurney on his World Championship debut in the French GP at Reims. He never won again. Since then, only Jacques Villeneuve has come close to the same achievement, finishing as runner-up in Australia in 1996.

⏵⏵⏵ TAKING THEIR TIME

In 2009 Mark Webber usurped Rubens Barrichello to become the holder of the record for the most grands prix contested before scoring a win. He had 130 races under his belt before he and his Red Bull triumphed at the Nürburgring. Barrichello's 2009 teammate, Jenson Button (113 starts before winning), ranks fourth in this list behind Jarno Trulli (119).

⏵⏵⏵ WHO'D HAVE THOUGHT IT?

Throughout F1 history there have been wins that have surprised everyone. Jo Bonnier's victory in the 1959 Dutch GP is a good example as no one thought that a BRM would ever win. Vittorio Brambilla's win in Austria in 1975 came as a shock as no one expected that the wild Italian would be the one to stay on the track in the wet. However, Giancarlo Baghetti's win on his World Championship debut in France in 1961 was the most surprising as he had to work his way forward from 13th to do it, and it required his teammates to retire to aid his progress.

⏵⏵⏵ WINNING BY A COUNTRY MILE

Jackie Stewart was always an exponent of "winning at the lowest speed possible". Risks weren't something he considered worthwhile but the policy paid off as he won 27 grands prix and three World Championships. Stewart also holds the record for the largest winning margin in F1 history– two laps. At the 1969 Spanish GP at Montjuich Park he won by 4.711 miles. Damon Hill also won by two laps in the 1995 Australian GP at Adelaide, but his winning margin was 4.698 miles.

Above **Taking their time:** Victory at last for Mark Webber at the Nürburgring in 2009 after 130 previous attempts *Below* **Starting with a bang:** Ferrari's Giancarlo Baghetti holds off Dan Gurney to win on his debut in the 1961 French GP at Reims.

SMALLEST WINNING MARGIN

Margin	Winner	Runner-up	GP	Year
0.010 sec	Peter Gethin	Ronnie Peterson	Italian	1971
0.011 sec	Rubens Barrichello	Michael Schumacher	US	2002
0.014 sec	Ayrton Senna	Nigel Mansell	Spanish	1986
0.050 sec	Elio de Angelis	Keke Rosberg	Austrian	1982
0.080 sec	Jackie Stewart	Jochen Rindt	Italian	1969
0.100 sec	Juan Manuel Fangio	Karl Kling	French	1954
0.100 sec	Giancarlo Baghetti	Dan Gurney	French	1961
0.174 sec	Michael Schumacher	Rubens Barrichello	Canadian	2000
0.182 sec*	Michael Schumacher	Rubens Barrichello	Austrian	2002
0.200 sec*	Stirling Moss	Juan Manuel Fangio	British	1955

* The win was donated to a teammate due to team orders or benevolence

Below **Winning by a country mile:** Master of precision Jackie Stewart won the 1969 Spanish GP at Montjuich Park for Matra by two laps (4.711 miles). *Right* **Beat the clock:** Stirling Moss was in a class of his own in his Vanwall in the 1958 Portuguese GP, winning by more than five minutes.

BEAT THE CLOCK

In terms of time, rather than laps, Stirling Moss holds the record for the greatest margin of victory. He took the chequered flag with his Vanwall 5 mins and 12.75 secs clear of Mike Hawthorn in the Portuguese GP at Oporto in 1958. Hawthorn half spun on the final lap and Moss, not wanting to embarrass his title rival by lapping him, slowed to let him rejoin, as he himself ambled around his slowing-down lap.

TAKING ON SCHUEY'S MANTLE

When Sebastian Vettel scored his first victory at the 2008 Italian GP for Scuderia Toro Rosso, he became the first German driver other than a Schumacher (Ralf six, Michael 91) to win a grand prix since Heinz-Harald Frentzen beat Ralf to the finish for Jordan in the 1999 Italian GP at Monza.

A LITTLE HELP FROM YOUR FRIENDS

Shared wins were allowed until 1957, when a team's lead driver might realize that something was wrong with his car and commandeer one of his teammates' cars to complete the race. The points would be split between them. This happened three times for wins, and many more times for lower placings. Juan Manuel Fangio took over Luigi Fagioli's Alfa Romeo to win the 1951 French GP and did the same to Ferrari teammate Luigi Musso in Argentina in 1956.

LA BELLE FRANCE

Michael Schumacher seemed to have an affinity with the French GP, as he won the race on eight occasions. This is the most times that any driver has won any grand prix. His first win in France came in 1994 at Magny-Cours and his last in 2006.

HE CERTAINLY TRIED

The unwanted record for the most grands prix without a win belongs to Andrea de Cesaris, who entered 214 races (208 starts) between 1980 and 1994. His best results were two second-place finishes in 1983.

THEY ARE ALL MINE

Fernando Alonso is the most famous Spanish Formula One racer, as he should be with two World Championships and several near misses. However, he alone carries their flag, as none of his compatriots have managed to win a grand prix and his tally of 32 wins boosted Spain to 10th in the chart of winners by nation.

A HAT-TRICK OF HAT-TRICKS

A grand slam is when a driver starts a grand prix from pole position, leads every lap and sets the fastest lap en route to victory. Twenty drivers have achieved this, but three stand out for managing it three times in a single season: Alberto Ascari, Jim Clark and Nigel Mansell, and they all achieved this remarkable feat in a world-championship-winning campaign. Ascari did it for Ferrari, in 1952, at Rouen-les-Essarts, the Nurburgring and Zandvoort. Clark was next in 1963, at Zandvoort, Reims and Mexico City. Then Mansell matched them in 1992 by winning at Kyalami, Catalunya and Silverstone for Williams.

POLE POSITIONS

THE PERFECT SCORE

Winning from pole position and also setting the race's fastest lap is just a dream for all but a few. The driver who achieved this most recently was Nico Rosberg for Mercedes in the 2015 Mexico Grand Prix. However, the ultimate is to achieve the grand slam – pole, fastest lap, lead every lap and win. Sebastian Vettel was the last driver to achieve this, when he drove an exemplary race for Red Bull in the 2013 Korean GP. Jim Clark achieved the grand slam a record eight times.

Above **Turn up, take pole:** Juan Manuel Fangio, shown here in 1950, achieved the greatest pole to race average, taking 29 from 51. *Below* **Lucky seven:** Ayrton Senna leads from pole for the last time at Imola, in 1994.

AS EASY AS ONE, TWO, THREE

Achieving pole position, setting the race's fastest lap and then winning the race shows a certain style, and guess who has achieved this clean sweep the most times? Yes, Michael Schumacher, on 22 occasions. Jim Clark is next, on 11, meaning that Clark achieved this feat close to one in every six grands prix he entered.

A QUARTER CENTURY

Juan Manuel Fangio knew that the best place from which to start a grand prix was from pole. The value of that was shown when he took his first F1 pole at Monaco in 1950 and so was first to come across the wreckage of an opening lap accident and was able to thread his way through. Fittingly, he became the first driver to reach 25 poles, doing so at the same venue seven years later.

HE WAS THE MAN

Michael Schumacher tops the list for the most pole positions, but his pole to starts ratio is nowhere near as good as Ayrton Senna's. The Brazilian was really the man when it came to a banzai lap. The 1988 Monaco GP is a perfect example as he was on pole by 1.4 secs. His 65 poles, just three fewer than Schumacher, gave him a 40 per cent hit rate compared to the German's 27 per cent. Sebastian Vettel was on 29.1 per cent at the end of 2015.

TOP 10 DRIVERS WITH MOST POLE POSITIONS

1	Michael Schumacher	68
2	Ayrton Senna	65
3	Lewis Hamilton	49
4	Sebastian Vettel	46
5	Jim Clark	33
=	Alain Prost	33
7	Nigel Mansell	32
8	Juan Manuel Fangio	29
9	Mika Hakkinen	26
10	Niki Lauda	24
=	Nelson Piquet	24

NIGEL MANSELL'S GOLDEN YEAR

Armed with the dominant Renault-powered Williams FW14B, Nigel Mansell took pole after pole after pole in 1992. In all he claimed pole at 14 of the season's 16 grands prix, for an 87.5 per cent average, missing out only at the Canadian GP and the Hungarian GP. Senna achieved 13 poles from 16 in both 1988 and 1989, as did Alain Prost in 1993, while Sebastian Vettel qualified fastest at 14 of 2011's 19 grands prix for Red Bull Racing.

DESIGNED TO FLY

Red Bull Racing technical chief Adrian Newey has long been called a design genius, and he must have done something right in shaping the Red Bull RB6 as the team's drivers Sebastian Vettel and Mark Webber claimed 18 of 2011's 19 pole positions. And you can't manage that without a car that handles…

LUCKY SEVEN

Ayrton Senna clearly loved Imola as he qualified on pole position there for seven years in a row between 1985 and 1991, three times for Lotus and four for McLaren. He put his Williams on pole there in 1994, in the race that was to be his last.

Left **Pole at the first attempt:** Jackie Stewart gave March pole on its debut at Kyalami in 1970. *Below* **It's Senna again:** Ayrton Senna was king of the pole position and led into Turn 1 at Phoenix in 1989, from his eighth pole in a row. *Bottom* **A shooting star:** Sebastian Vettel scored the fourth of his poles at Silverstone in 2009.

POLE AT THE FIRST ATTEMPT

Alfa Romeo had one of its cars qualify on pole position for its first World Championship grand prix, as the Italian team dominated the inaugural event. So too then did Brawn, in Australia in 2009, after being salvaged from Honda Racing. More impressive was March filling the first two grid slots on its World Championship debut in South Africa in 1970, with Jackie Stewart ahead of Chris Amon.

STARTING FROM THE FRONT

Michael Schumacher edges out Ayrton Senna at the top of the all-time number of pole positions table by three, but his advantage is greater when front-row starting positions are considered. Schumacher qualified first or second 116 times, 29 more than Senna. Alain Prost is one behind the Brazilian.

IT'S SENNA AGAIN

Ayrton Senna emphasized his outstanding ability to qualify faster than anyone else when he claimed pole position for a record eight grands prix in a row in his McLaren. The run started at the 1988 Spanish GP and continued through to the 1989 US GP at Phoenix.

FOUR IN A ROW

British fans had every reason to expect a home driver to be on pole at the British GP in the 1950s and 1960s. Stirling Moss was on pole for four straight years, 1955–58, as the race alternated between Aintree and Silverstone. Then Jim Clark matched that feat between 1962–65, at Aintree, twice at Silverstone and Brands Hatch. The Scottish Lotus driver didn't manage pole in 1966, but was at the front of the grid in 1967.

THERE'S NO PLACE LIKE HOME

Ayrton Senna seemed fated never to win his home grand prix, although he finally managed it on his eighth attempt in 1991. But setting pole in Brazil came to him far more easily and he holds the record for the most number of times that a driver has qualified on pole for his home race. He did so six times, in 1986, from 1988 to 1991 inclusive and in 1994. The first three came at Rio de Janeiro's Jacarepagua circuit and the others at Interlagos in his home city of São Paulo.

A FRENCH AFFAIR

Jim Clark qualified his Lotus on pole position for the French GP four years straight from 1962–65 (matching his achievement at the British GP). He achieved this on three markedly different circuits – Rouen-les-Essarts (twice), Reims and Clermont-Ferrand.

A SHOOTING STAR

|||||||||||||||||||||||||||||||||||||||||

Sebastian Vettel holds the record for being the youngest pole-sitter, when he secured his place at the front of the grid at the 2008 Italian GP at the age of 21 years and 73 days. The previous holder of this record was Fernando Alonso, who outqualified the rest of the pack at the 2003 Malaysian GP at the age of 21 years and 236 days.

FASTEST LAPS

FASTER, FASTER

Michael Schumacher's all-round excellence is shown by the fact that he doesn't just top the record tables in race wins, pole positions, laps led and points scored, he also occupies first place for the most fastest laps set too, a career total of 76. He holds the record by some margin, as Kimi Raikkonen, who passed Alain Prost in 2015 is the second-placed driver on the list with 42 fastest laps.

HITTING DOUBLE FIGURES

Michael Schumacher and Kimi Räikkönen both gave Ferrari a return of 10 fastest laps in a single season, with the German achieving this impressive tally in 2004 and

the Finn doing the same in 2008, both from 18 starts. Räikkönen also claimed 10 fastest laps for McLaren in 2005, although this percentage is slightly lower because there were 19 grands prix that season.

Above **Top 10 fastest laps by driver nationality:** Nico Rosberg has been helping to boost Germany's tally of fastest laps since his first, on his F1 debut, in the 2006 Bahrain GP at Sakhir. *Below* **Ascari's dominance:** Alberto Ascari drove his Ferrari to the fastest lap in every grand prix he contested in 1952.

TOP 10 FASTEST LAPS BY DRIVER NATIONALITY

1	Great Britain	213
2	Germany	129
3	Brazil	87
=	France	86
5	Finland	71
6	Italy	51
7	Austria	49
8	Australia	46
9	Argentina	37
10	USA	25

LOVING THE SMOOTH

David Coulthard demonstrated an affinity for the smooth surface and twisting nature of Magny-Cours as he set the fastest lap of the race there five years in succession for McLaren between 1998 and 2002, albeit coming away as the winner on just one of those occasions, in 2000.

NO ONE'S AN EXPERT

The Jarama circuit outside Madrid hosted nine Spanish GPs between 1968 and 1991, but not one driver was able to take the fastest lap more than once. A record nine different drivers set fastest lap times, starting with Matra's Jean-Pierre Beltoise in 1968 and ending with Williams's reigning world champion Alan Jones in 1981. Rival Spanish circuit Jerez ended up with a similar record, with seven drivers setting fastest laps there on F1's seven visits.

WAS IT REALLY?

Every now and again a fastest lap is set by a driver that no one had expected to be so fast. This often happens when a driver with nothing to lose pits for fresh tyres. The most notorious example was Masahiro Hasemi setting the fastest lap on his F1 debut in the 1976 Japanese GP. There were mitigating circumstances in that he knew Fuji Speedway well and it was F1's first visit. Furthermore, it was incredibly wet and his Kojima chassis was on Dunlop wets that were superior to the Goodyears used by the regulars, but still…

ASCARI'S DOMINANCE

Alberto Ascari's near total dominance of the 1952 World Championship left him with a tally of six fastest laps from seven rounds as he raced to the title for Ferrari. The Indianapolis 500 was also a round of the World Championship then, but he, like other F1 drivers, gave it a miss. So, his tally was even better than the six from eight that some record books show.

AN HONOUR, BUT...

Kimi Räikkönen's 10 fastest laps in 2008 – six of them in succession – reflected well on his ability, but this was at a time of refuelling pit stops and it actually showed his ambition to impress rather than his Ferrari's speed over a race distance, and he ended the year third overall despite his 55.55 per cent strike rate. Jim Clark hit an identical figure for Lotus in 1962, also without becoming world champion.

START AS THEY MEAN TO GO ON

After the inaugural season of 1950, just three drivers have set a fastest lap on their F1 debut. Masahiro Hasemi's amazing 1976 Japanese GP was the first, and it was followed by Jacques Villeneuve in the 1996 opener in Australia. Only Nico Roseberg, at Bahrain in 2006, has achieved a debut fastest lap since then.

ASCARI GOES AHEAD

Saving the machinery was vital in the 1950s when not only were cars more likely to fail but races were run over longer distances. So, setting the fastest lap wasn't always hugely important. However, Juan Manuel Fangio started to change this view and Alberto Ascari's strong run in 1952 and 1953 resulted in him becoming the first driver to 10 fastest laps, clinching this at Bremgarten in 1953.

KEEPING IT ALL GOING

Alberto Ascari set six fastest laps in seven rounds in 1952 – he missed the first race, in Switzerland, so he could compete in the Indianapolis 500 (but didn't set the fastest lap there) – and kept his run going into the 1953 campaign, adding a seventh consecutive fastest lap at the season-opening Argentinian GP. His run was broken by his Ferrari teammate Luigi Villoresi at the Dutch GP.

TOP 10 DRIVERS WHO HAVE SET MOST FASTEST LAPS

1	Michael Schumacher	76
2	Kimi Räikkönen	42
3	Alain Prost	41
4	Nigel Mansell	30
5	Jim Clark	28
=	Lewis Hamilton	28
7	Mika Hakkinen	25
=	Sebastian Vettel	25
9	Niki Lauda	24
10	Juan Manuel Fangio	23

Above **Top 10 drivers who have set most fastest laps:** Michael Schumacher set the first of his 75 fastest laps for Benetton in the 1992 Belgian GP. *Below* **An honour, but...:** Ferrari's Kimi Räikkönen set the most fastest laps in 2008, and his two fastest laps in 2015 took him second overall, ahead of Alain Prost.

POINTS

QUICK NICK, BUT NO WINS

||||||||||||||||||||||||||||||||||||||||

Nick Heidfeld has twice come close to scoring his first grand prix win, most recently in the wet/dry 2009 Malaysian GP, but he has never ascended to the top step of the podium despite notching up a career tally of 259 points by the end of 2011. Martin Brundle is next on the all-time list of points scored without taking a win, with a tally of 98, thus emphasizing Heidfeld's perseverance.

LEADING THE WAY

Michael Schumacher and Alain Prost were, until race-winners collected 25 points from 2010, F1's leading points scorers. Both have been usurped and Schumacher's fourth place is under pressure from Nico Rosberg. Fernando Alonso passed Schumacher in 2013, and although Sebastian Vettel took over at the top in 2015, Lewis Hamilton ended the season in second place, 29 points behind.

KEEP ON SCORING

Kimi Räikkönen's return to F1 proved that he still has the desire to go for glory, as he has not only won grands prix but shown a clear propensity for scoring points. In 2013, he built on his strong first year back with Lotus to beat Michael Schumacher's record of 24 consecutive point-scoring drives, extending it to 27 before he retired from the Belgian GP.

ONCE AND ONCE ONLY

Scoring their first World Championship point is a breakthrough moment for any Formula 1 driver. However, 21 have taken that first point, either for fastest lap in the 1950s, or for sixth place from 1960–2002, then eighth from 2003–09 and for 10th from 2010, and yet never scored again. Lella Lombardi would have joined them, but her point for sixth in the 1975 Spanish GP was halved as the race was stopped before 60 per cent of the planned distance had been covered.

FROM CHAMPION TO SHORT RATIONS

America's first F1 world champion, Phil Hill, had a rapid fall from grace after his 1961 World Championship with Ferrari. Just over a year after winning the title he made a terrible mistake and followed some of Ferrari's staff to ATS, a new Italian team that proved to be a disaster. So, shortly after he peaked, he plummeted and ended up with a career tally of 98 points, the fewest for a world champion.

Right **From champion to short rations:** Phil Hill raced a red car in 1963, but it was an ATS not a Ferrari. *Below* **Quick Nick, but no wins:** Nick Heidfeld scored 259 points in his 12-year Formula One career, with third place for Renault at Sepang in 2011 the last of his podium finishes.

TOP 10 DRIVERS WITH MOST GRAND PRIX POINTS

1	Sebastian Vettel	1,896
2	Lewis Hamilton	1,867
3	Fernando Alonso	1,778
4	Michael Schumacher	1,566
5	Jenson Button	1,214
6	Nico Rosberg	1,209.5
7	Mark Webber	1,047.5
8	Kimi Räikkönen	1,174
9	Felipe Massa	1,071
10	Alain Prost	798.5

Figures are gross, i.e. including scores that were later dropped

A HELPING HAND

The changes to the World Championship points system from the start of the 2010 season, when a win became 25 points (from 10) and the first 10 places scored points (it had been eight), had a dramatic effect on the all-time points table. At the end of 2015, only Alain Prost, who raced mainly when it was nine points for a win, remained in the top 10. Most of Michael Schumacher's 1,566 points came when wins were worth ten points.

ADD THEM TOGETHER

Since British drivers hold the highest cumulative tally of wins, it comes as no surprise that British drivers also hold the record for the most combined points scored. Up to the end of 2015, British drivers had scored 7,630.28 points, with Germany second on 6,758.5, Brazil third on 3,435 and France fourth on 2,807.47. Perhaps most impressive is Finland's tally of 2,306.5 points, despite having ever had only eight drivers compete in F1.

SHARED BY MANY

Almost 300 drivers have scored points in the World Championship since 1950 (excluding 33 others who scored in the nominally included Indianapolis 500 between 1950 and 1960), split between 35 nationalities, with Great Britain producing the most point-scoring drivers – 61. The Italians have had a total of 45 drivers in the points, the French 42 and the Germans 23.

JUST WHAT'S THE POINT?

Prior to the start of the 2009 season, Luca Badoer held an unwanted record: after 49 races he had not scored a single point. He hoped to put a stop to the record getting any worse when he stood in at Ferrari for the injured Felipe Massa midway through the season. Unfortunately he didn't score, and he has extended that record to 51 races without a point. The closest he has come to a points finish was in the 1999 European GP, when he had to retire his Minardi while in fourth place with just 12 laps to go.

MAKING THE MOST OF EACH TIME OUT

With points having been awarded down to 10th place since 2010, it's easier to score now than in F1's early days. McLaren set a record in 2013, when it completed 64 consecutive scoring races before it failed at the Canadian GP, but Ferrari's run continued until the 15th race of the 2014 season, in Japan, a total of 81 races.

POINTS FOR ALL

Even though points were allocated to only the first six finishers back in 1989, a record 29 different drivers made it onto the scoreboard that year, from world champion Alain Prost on 76 points, down to Philippe Alliot, Olivier Grouillard, Luis Perez Sala and Gabriele Tarquini on one point apiece. It was an incredible year, as 39 cars turned up for most races and a system of pre-qualifying had to be used to clear out the slowest before normal qualifying could start.

Left **Gaping chasm:** Jenson Button and Sebastian Vettel were on the podium together a lot in 2011, but Vettel finished far ahead on points. *Above* **Top 10 drivers with most grand prix points:** Mark Webber started his points haul with fifth on his debut in Australia in 2002.

GAPING CHASM

Yet another new record was set in 2013 when Sebastian Vettel improved on his previous record points advantage of 122 over Jenson Button in 2011 to beat Ferrari's Fernando Alonso to the crown by 155.

CAREER DURATION

OLD FATHER TIME

Graham Hill held the record for the longest F1 career in terms of the number of years between his first race – the 1958 Monaco GP – and his last, in Brazil in 1975. Hill's F1 career span was 16 years and 253 days. However, Rubens Barrichello broke that record when he raced for Williams in 2010, then went on to complete 18 years and 258 days as an active F1 driver by the end of the 2011 season.

EVER YOUNGER

Rubens Barrichello was very much the World Championship's old-timer when he started his 19th F1 season in 2011 just short of his 39th birthday. However, he was still only the same age that Graham Hill was when he completed his 10th season. Then again, Hill didn't pass his

Below **Old father time:** Graham Hill raced in Formula One for just short of 17 years. *Bottom* **Silver-haired flier:** Luigi Fagioli was still with Alfa Romeo 18 years after joining it when he raced to his final win in 1951.

driving test to drive on the road until he was 24 and actually did extremely well to get to F1 by the time he was 29.

NEVER GIVE UP!

Some drivers just never want to give up. Witness the haste with which the then 41-year-old Michael Schumacher jumped at the chance to end a three-year spell in retirement to return to F1 with Mercedes in 2010, racing through until the end of 2012. This is nothing compared to Jan Lammers, who returned to F1 in 1992 at the age of 36 after a break of 10 years and 114 days. The Dutchman is still racing in sportscars.

LOOKING DOWN FROM ABOVE

All drivers get a kick out of standing on the podium after a race, having finished first, second or third. The thrill was great for Rubens Barrichello, who holds the record for the longest spell between his first podium place – at the 1994 Pacific GP – and his last appearance on the podium at the 2009 Italian GP. His record spans 15 years and 149 days.

SILVER-HAIRED FLIER

Racer Luigi Fagioli showed that staying power is rewarded. Fagioli raced for Alfa Romeo in 1933, and was still with the team in 1951 when he took his one win in the World Championship, 22 days past his 53rd birthday, making him the oldest person to win an F1 race. The victory came in strange circumstances as he was pulled out of his car when he pitted and was forced to hand it over to team leader Juan Manuel Fangio whose car was having mechanical difficulties. Fangio went on to win, but Fagioli was so unhappy, despite being credited with the win (shared with Fangio), that he quit.

⫸ TRIED AND TESTED

Michael Schumacher clearly believed in sticking with a winning formula, as his stay with Ferrari was the longest of any driver with one team in F1 history. He turned out for the team in 179 grands prix in 11 seasons between 1996 and 2006. And Schumacher's total would have been higher still, except for the fact that he missed six races in 1999 after breaking a leg in the British GP at Silverstone.

⫸ BLINK AND YOU MISSED IT

Marco Apicella was a decent driver, so it's odd that the Italian's spell in F1 remains the shortest on record. He had one crack at F1, with the Jordan team after Thierry Boutsen had been dropped, in his home race at Monza in 1993. He qualified 23rd out of 26 and, unfortunately, was unable to avoid the melee into the first chicane on the opening lap. His distance covered as an F1 racer was around ½ mile.

⫸ EXCELLENCE OVER A DECADE AND MORE

Michael Schumacher holds the record for the most years between his first grand prix victory and his last – 14 years and 32 days. This was between the 1992 Belgian GP at Spa-Francorchamps for Benetton and the 2006 Chinese GP at Shanghai for Ferrari.

⫸ F1: IT'S A CAREER

Graham Hill and Rubens Barrichello are the faces of longevity on the driving front, but their career spans are short next to the number of years put in by those out of the cockpit. Bernie Ecclestone has clocked up 59 years – from his first appearance as a driver-manager to his role as F1's ringmaster.

A PREGNANT PAUSE

||||||||||||||||||||||||||||||||||||||

Riccardo Patrese scored six wins in his lengthy F1 career, but perhaps the most remarkable thing about them is the gap between his second win, for Brabham in the season-closing 1983 South African GP, and his third win in the 1990 San Marino GP at Imola for Williams, a record 6 years and 210 days later.

PAYBACK TIME

Alex Wurz's lengthy period as a test driver was rewarded when he subbed for McLaren in the 2005 San Marino GP at Imola. He was standing in for the injured Juan Pablo Montoya, and he came away with third place. This gave him the record for the longest period of time between podium places, at 7 years and 313 days. However, he didn't get to enjoy his moment in the sun this time as he was promoted to third after the podium ceremony had taken place because Jenson Button was subsequently disqualified.

Left **Payback time:** Alex Wurz spent years as a test driver before returning to racing in 2005 and finishing third at Imola. *Above* **A pregnant pause:** The 1983 South African GP was Riccardo Patrese's second win, but it would be more than six years before he claimed a third victory, as shown here at Imola in 1990.

TOP 10 LONGEST SERVERS

1	Bernie Ecclestone (1957–)	59 years
2	Herbie Blash (1968–)	48 years
3	Frank Williams (1969–)	47 years
4	Ron Dennis (1966–2009, 2014–)	46 years
5	Tyler Alexander (1966–2009)	44 years
6	Luca Montezemolo (1973–2014)	42 years
7	Jo Ramirez (1961–2001)	41 years
=	Giampaolo Dallara (1970–2010)	41 years
9	Max Mosley (1970–2009)	40 years
10	Eric Broadley (1960–1997)	38 years

YOUNGEST AND OLDEST

YOUNG AND KEEN

With drivers having years of kart racing as children, it's not surprising that they are able to climb to F1 ever more quickly. In 2009, Jaime Alguersuari lowered the mark to just 19 years and 125 days when he made his debut for Scuderia Toro Rosso at the Hungarian GP. However, this was beaten comprehensively in 2015 when Max Verstappen made his first outing for the same Italian team at the opening race in Australia, aged just 17 years and 166 days.

AFTER YOU, YOUNG SIR

The youngest driver to lead a grand prix is Sebastian Vettel, who led the 2007 Japanese GP during a pit-stop sequence

when racing for Toro Rosso. He was just 20 years and 89 days old. Later in the race he showed the impetuousness of youth when he took out Red Bull's Mark Webber when circulating behind the safety car, which put an end to the race for both drivers.

RACING IS ONE THING...

Some drivers get the lucky break and make it to F1 while still in their teens, but the next step up to getting a drive that offers the chance to win a grand prix is quite another thing. So Sebastian Vettel's record for being the youngest winner at just 21 years and 73 days is a remarkable one. His victory came in the 2008 Italian GP while driving for Toro Rosso.

A WEALTH OF EXPERIENCE

Luigi Fagioli was just short of 37 when he scored his second to last grand prix win, for Mercedes at Monaco in 1935. So, it must have been for his experience that he was added to Alfa Romeo's line-up at the start of the first World Championship in 1950, in which he ranked third overall. In his one race in 1951, at the French GP, he was forced out of his car mid-race as team leader Juan Manuel Fangio's car had mechanical difficulties. They shared the win. Luigi was aged 53 years and 22 days. Giuseppe Farina was next oldest when he won in Germany in 1953, at 46 years and 276 days.

DELIVERING UNDER PRESSURE

Qualifying has always been an exacting element of a grand prix meeting, and it takes many drivers years to learn how to squeeze the maximum from

themselves and their cars without pushing just that little bit too hard. The mercurial Sebastian Vettel is the youngest ever pole-sitter, being just 21 years and 72 days when he took first place on the grid at the 2008 Italian GP. Ferrari's Giuseppe Farina is the oldest pole-sitter, aged 47 years and 79 days at the 1954 Argentinian GP.

FROM FRESH-FACED TO VETERAN

The inaugural winner of the World Championship in 1950, Giuseppe Farina, was a couple of months short of his 44th birthday. Juan Manuel Fangio topped that, taking his final title in 1957 at 46 years and 41 days, making him the oldest ever World Championship winner. At the other end of the scale, in 2006, Fernando Alonso – at 24 years and 58 days – broke Emerson Fittipaldi's record from 1972 to become the youngest champion. Two years later Lewis Hamilton won the title aged 23 years and 300 days, but his record fell to Sebastian Vettel, aged 23 years and 134 days, in 2010.

Left **Young and keen:** Max Verstappen was still 17 midway through 2015 when he raced in Hungary. *Right* **From fresh-faced to veteran:** Sebastian Vettel beat Lewis Hamilton's record in 2010 to become the youngest ever F1 World Champion.

10 YOUNGEST DRIVERS IN F1

	Name	Team	GP	Year	Age
1	Max Verstappen	Toro Rosso	Australian	2015	17 years 166 days
2	Jaime Alguersuari	Toro Rosso	Hungarian	2009	19 years 125 days
3	Mike Thackwell	Tyrrell	Canadian	1980	19 years 182 days
4	Ricardo Rodriguez	Ferrari	Italian	1961	19 years 208 days
5	Fernando Alonso	Minardi	Australian	2001	19 years 218 days
6	Esteban Tuero	Minardi	Australian	1998	19 years 320 days
7	Chris Amon	Lola	Belgian	1963	19 years 324 days
=	Daniil Kvyat	Toro Rosso	Australian	2014	19 years 324 days
9	Sebastian Vettel	BMW Sauber	US	2007	19 years 348 days
10	Jenson Button	Williams	Australian	2000	20 years 52 days
=	Eddie Cheever	Theodore	South African	1978	20 years 52 days

CHAMPIONS BECOME EVER YOUNGER

One of the greatest differences between the F1 drivers of the 21st century and their forebears is that the drivers in the first decade of the World Championship were so much older. Inaugural champion Giuseppe Farina was 43 in 1950 and it wasn't until Mike Hawthorn lifted the crown in 1958 that F1 had its first champion still in his 20s. He was 29 when he wrapped up his championship at the Moroccan GP, but dead before he turned 30.

STILL A TEENAGER

Max Verstappen was aged 17 years and 130 days when he finished seventh in his second race in F1, the 2015 Malaysian GP, thus becoming the youngest driver ever to score World Championship points. The previous record belonged to Sebastian Vettel, at 19 years and 348 days, who had finished eighth for BMW Sauber in the 2007 US GP, his F1 debut. Philippe Etancelin is the oldest, at 53 years and 249 days, when he finished fifth in his Lago Talbot in the 1950 Italian GP.

10 OLDEST DRIVERS IN F1

	Name	Team	GP	Year	Age
1	Eitel Cantoni	Maserati	Italian	1952	55 years 337 days
2	Louis Chiron	Lancia	Monaco	1955	55 years 292 days
3	Philippe Etancelin	Maserati	French	1952	55 years 190 days
4	Arthur Legat	Veritas	Belgian	1953	54 years 232 days
5	Luigi Fagioli	Alfa Romeo	French	1951	53 years 21 days
6	Adolf Brudes	Veritas	German	1952	52 years 292 days
7	Hans Stuck	AFM	Italian	1953	52 years 260 days
8	Bill Aston	Aston	German	1952	52 years 127 days
9	Clemente Biondetti	Ferrari	Italian	1950	52 years 15 days
10	Louis Rosier	Maserati	German	1956	50 years 273 days

DON'T THEY ALL LOOK YOUNG?

The youngest, most fresh-faced trio to appear on the podium was at the 2008 Italian GP when Sebastian Vettel, Heikki Kovalainen and Robert Kubica finished first, second and third respectively. The trio had an average age of just 23 years and 350 days.

Above **Don't they all look young?:** Sebastian Vettel heads to his first win and the youngest ever podium grouping at Monza in 2008. *Below* **From another century:** Being aged 50 didn't appear to slow Louis Chiron as he raced to third place in his native Monaco in 1950. Alberto Ascari, behind, would go on to finish second.

FROM ANOTHER CENTURY

Apart from Luigi Fagioli, Louis Chiron is the only other driver over 50 to step up on to the podium. He was aged 50 years and 289 days when he finished third for Maserati in his hometown of Monaco in 1950. Both drivers were born in the 19th century.

RACE STARTS

⫸ CHOPPING AND CHANGING

Jo Bonnier and Johnny Claes share the record for driving for the most teams in a World Championship season – four. Claes turned out for Gordini, Ecurie Belge, HWM and Vickomtesse de Walckiers in 1952. Bonnier raced for his own team, Giorgio Scarlatti's, Scuderia Centro Sud and BRM in 1958.

Above **The wrong motto:** Jacques Villeneuve had a torrid time in BAR's much-trumpeted maiden season in 1999. *Below* **F1's centurions:** Rubens Barrichello rounds the La Source hairpin at Spa in 2010 during his 300th grand prix.

⫸ I'VE BEEN HERE BEFORE

Seven-time world champion Michael Schumacher has led no fewer than 142 grands prix for a minimum of one lap. Ayrton Senna is next on the list, albeit way behind on 86 grands prix led, and this is two more than the 84 achieved by his arch-rival, and sometime teammate, Alain Prost. Fernando Alonso matched Prost's tally of 84 in 2014.

⫸ THE WRONG MOTTO

BAR was asking for trouble when the team was launched with the motto "A tradition of excellence". Firstly, it had no tradition. Secondly, its lead driver Jacques Villeneuve's run of retirements in the first 11 grands prix of the team's maiden season in 1999 set a record that is anything but excellent.

⫸ A FLYING START

Two drivers, Tiago Monteiro and Heikki Kovalainen, share the record for the most consecutive races finished from the first race of their F1 careers – 16 grands prix. Monteiro achieved it driving for Jordan in 2005, and Kovalainen repeated the feat as a member of the Renault team two years later.

F1'S CENTURIONS

The first driver to contest 100 grands prix was Jack Brabham, driving for his own team, at the 1968 Dutch GP. The first to break the 200 grands prix barrier was Williams racer Ricardo Patrese, at the British GP in 1990. In 2010 Brazil's Rubens Barrichello duly became the first driver to contest 300 grands prix, achieving it at the Belgian GP when he wore a celebratory helmet livery.

MAKING IT TO THE END

Jenson Button's record of 36 finishes in a row includes all 19 grands prix in 2013. This exceeded the record for finishes in a season set by Tiago Monteiro in 2005 and matched three years later by Nick Heidfeld, Sergio Perez and Max Chilton (right) who also finished all 19 races in 2013, with Sebastian Vettel, Fernando Alonso and Lewis Hamilton all managing 18 finishes from the 19 starts.

STARTING AND FINISHING

Jenson Button set a record at the 2014 Hungarian GP when he achieved his 34th consecutive finish in a run that started at the 2012 Indian GP. This exceeded the record of 33 in a row set previously by Nick Heidfeld between the 2007 Chinese GP and the 2009 Singapore GP. The McLaren racer then added two more finishes before failing to make the finish in the Singapore GP when his McLaren's control unit failed when he was running seventh.

A NATIONAL SPORT

British drivers have the most appearances in grands prix. In total, 144 British drivers have qualified and raced. The next most prodigious country in getting its drivers on to an F1 grid is Italy, with 84 drivers, then France with 71, followed by 51 from Germany and 48 from the USA.

MANY AND FEW

In 1952 a mind-boggling total of 75 drivers contested the seven grands prix that season. In 2008, just 22 drivers went head-to-head in 18 grands prix.

FIRST ON THE START LINE

British drivers have between them racked up a table-topping 3,548 grand prix starts since the World Championship began at Silverstone in 1950. Italy's drivers are next on the all-time starts list with 2,903.

36 AND RISING

By the end of the 2012 Formula 1 World Championship, drivers from 36 nations had taken part since its inception in 1950. Over those 63 seasons, there have been drivers from each and every one of the world's continents, apart from Antarctica.

PODIUMS, BUT NO WINS

Despite starting 185 F1 races across 12 seasons, from 2000 to 2011, Nick Heidfeld never claimed a grand prix victory. He did clock up another podium finish with third at Sepang in 2011 to bring his tally of podiums to 13 without taking a win and so overhaul Stefan Johansson's record for podiums without a win, set between 1985 and 1989.

TOP 10 DRIVERS WITH MOST GP STARTS

	Driver	Starts
1	Rubens Barrichello	325
2	Michael Schumacher	308
3	Jenson Button	284
4	Riccardo Patrese	256
=	Jarno Trulli	256
6	Fernando Alonso	253
7	David Coulthard	247
8	Kimi Räikkönen	231
9	Giancarlo Fisichella	230
10	Felipe Massa	229

Top **Making it to the end:** Jenson Button flies around the 2013 Malaysian GP. *Above* **36 and rising:** Vitaly Petrov became the first Russian F1 driver in 2010, and finished third in Australia in 2011. *Left* **Top 10 drivers with most GP starts:** Jarno Trulli drove his final race for Lotus at the 2011 Brazilian GP.

CLOSE, BUT NO CIGAR

Gabriele Tarquini holds the unenviable record of the most grand prix appearances that didn't result in a start. Forty times he turned up then failed to qualify. This was the price he paid for driving for uncompetitive teams such as Coloni and AGS in the late 1980s, when 39 cars fought for 26 grid spots and a pre-qualifying session was necessary to decide which were even worthy of a chance to qualify. Luckily, he qualified on 38 other occasions.

HIGHEST WIN RATE

Juan Manuel Fangio won 24 times from 51 starts to give him a record win rate of 0.471. Second on the list is Alberto Ascari, who dominated for Ferrari in the early 1950s and ended up with a rate of 0.419 after winning 13 of his 31 races. Jim Clark ranks third on 0.347 and would certainly have ranked higher but for his Lotus often suffering from mechanical problems. After Sebastian Vettel's fourth title in a row pushed him past Michael Schumacher's .295, his strike rate reached 0.325, but it was down to .258 at the end of the 2015 season.

Above **Bang, splutter, phut!:** Ivan Capelli and Leyton House turned retiring into an art form, as evidenced by the shower of sparks at Monaco in 1990. *Below* **How not to do it:** Andrea de Cesaris retired his Brabham from all 16 grands prix in 1987.

BANG, SPLUTTER, PHUT!

So promising early in his career, it all started to go wrong for Ivan Capelli when he retired from the 1990 Italian GP. He retired his Leyton House from the next 15 grands prix, making this the longest run of retirements in F1 history.

NOT FOR WANT OF TRYING

Andrea de Cesaris holds the record for the most grands prix contested without a win. In all, his F1 career stretched from 1980 (with Alfa Romeo) to 1994 (with Sauber), yet he did not produce one win from his 208 starts, not helped by Andrea retiring from 148 of these. His best results were a pair of second-place finishes in 1983.

WHAT'S A CHEQUERED FLAG?

From his 208 starts, Andrea de Cesaris failed to reach the finish of the race 137 times. There were certainly numerous mechanical failures when he raced for Alfa Romeo in the early 1980s, but he was equally responsible as there were many crashes too. Compatriot Riccardo Patrese clocked up 130 retirements from his 256 starts, but at least he scored six wins.

WELL, HE TRIED...

Claudio Langes seldom sported a smile in the paddock and his one and only campaign in F1, in 1990, gave him every reason to look forlorn. The Italian had

stepped up from F3000 to drive for the EuroBrun Racing team. But the car was not up to scratch and he failed to pre-qualify for all 14 races he entered. And that was the end of his F1 career.

NEW SEASON, NEW TEAM

Chris Amon is described as the best driver never to win a grand prix. One look at his F1 career shows that he wasn't worried about changing teams to chase his dream, as he raced for 12: Reg Parnell Racing, Ian Raby Racing, Cooper, his own team, Ferrari, March, Matra, Tecno, Tyrrell, BRM, Ensign and Walter Wolf Racing. In total he drove 13 different makes of car. Andrea de Cesaris, Stefan Johansson, Stirling Moss and Maurice Trintignant raced 10.

HOW NOT TO DO IT

Andrea de Cesaris retired from all 16 grands prix in 1987 while racing for Brabham; a record for F1's hall of shame. He was actually running third in Monaco, but was stationary when the chequered flag fell, his car having run out of fuel; and he was in eighth place in the Adelaide season finale, but spun off with four laps to go.

THE RISKIEST LAP

All the efforts exerted to develop a car through practice and then to qualify it as far up the grid as possible can come to naught on the opening lap, when the cars are racing at their closest. Take the 1978 Italian GP, the worst ever example of wastage, as 10 cars were eliminated before they had reached the first corner. Sadly, Lotus ace Ronnie Peterson died of his injuries.

TRY, TRY AND TRY AGAIN

While Italy's Andrea de Cesaris holds the record for the most starts without a win for a driver (208 starts between 1980 and 1994), Arrows hold the team record. Founded by Jackie Oliver in 1978, the British-based team took part in 383 grands prix without achieving a victory. Arrows ran out of money and bowed out of F1 with five races remaining in the 2002 season.

TOP 10 TEAMS WITH MOST STARTS

1	Ferrari	908
2	McLaren	781
3	Williams	700
4	Toro Rosso (née Minardi)	526
5	Lotus	492
6	Force India (née Jordan – Midland – Spyker)	435
7	Tyrrell	418
8	Prost (née Ligier)	409
9	Brabham	394
10	Arrows	383

MICHAEL LOVES FERRARI

Michael Schumacher made Ferrari a team to fear again in 1996 when he shook it by the scruff of its neck with the Scuderia CEO Jean Todt. Their success triggered the longest stay any driver has had with a team in F1 history and stretched to 201 starts before Schumacher retired at the end of 2006. It would have been six more had he not broken a leg at the 1999 British GP. David Coulthard has the next longest stay, racing 150 times for McLaren.

Below **Michael loves Ferrari:** Jean Todt (left) and Michael Schumacher returned Ferrari to the top. *Below* **That's how to do it!:** Jody Scheckter gave Wolf a dream start by winning the 1977 season-opener in Argentina.

THAT'S HOW TO DO IT!

Jody Scheckter was enticed by Canadian industrialist Walter Wolf to join his new team, Wolf, for 1977. The move paid off immediately as Scheckter won the first race of the season in Argentina and went on to win two more. No team has made such an instant impact since. (Some might suggest Brawn GP in 2009, but this team was developed from Honda Racing, and didn't start from scratch.)

MISCELLANEOUS DRIVER RECORDS

THE DARKEST DAYS

Death was a regular feature of F1 in the early years, with driver safety scarcely considered in the 1950s. Six drivers died at the wheel in both 1957 and 1958, with five being killed in other events and one in F1 testing in 1957. In 1958, Luigi Musso died in the French GP, Peter Collins in the German GP and Stuart Lewis-Evans from burns received in the Moroccan GP, with three others being killed in non-F1 events.

Above **The darkest days:** Peter Collins was victorious for Ferrari in the 1958 British GP, but would perish next time out, in the German GP. *Below* **You don't have to be male:** Lella Lombardi is the only female driver to have scored a point in F1.

TOP 10 DRIVERS WITH MOST LAPS IN LEAD

1	Michael Schumacher	5,111
2	Ayrton Senna	2,931
3	Alain Prost	2,683
4	Sebastian Vettel	2,614
5	Lewis Hamilton	2,424
6	Nigel Mansell	2,058
7	Jim Clark	1,940
8	Jackie Stewart	1,918
9	Fernando Alonso	1,767
10	Nelson Piquet	1,633

THE MOST COSMOPOLITAN YEAR

The 1970s proved to be the decade when the most different nations had drivers competing in F1, with 18 countries being represented in 1978. They were: Argentina, Australia, Austria, Brazil, Canada, Finland, France, Germany, Great Britain, Holland, Ireland, Italy, Mexico, South Africa, Spain, Sweden, Switzerland and the USA.

NOT AHEAD WHEN IT COUNTED

Neither Jean Behra nor Chris Amon won a grand prix, but they both led races seven times. Nick Heidfeld equalled their record tally then exceeded it by leading eight, but his situation is more easily explained as racing in the 21st century is peppered with pit stops and different race strategies mean that a driver can have a moment of glory before dropping out of the reckoning.

VARIETY AT THE TOP

On five occasions, the world champion and runner-up have been of the same nationality. However, the most cosmopolitan year at the top of the table is shared by 1974 and 1977 when you get to 10th in the table before finding two drivers of the same nationality. In 1974, Mike Hailwood matched fellow Briton James Hunt (eighth), then in 1977 Jacques Lafitte matched French compatriot Patrick Depailler (eighth).

LET'S ALL TAKE TURNS

In the days before tyre and fuel pit stops, a driver leading the race really was leading the race, not just leading for a short period until the "two-stoppers" made their next pit call. In the light of this the 1971 Italian GP stands out as it holds the record for the number of race leaders on merit – eight. They were Clay Regazzoni, Ronnie Peterson, Jackie Stewart, François Cevert, Mike Hailwood, Jo Siffert, Chris Amon and winner, Peter Gethin.

YOU DON'T HAVE TO BE MALE

Only five female racers have entered World Championship grands prix, and only Lella Lombardi and Maria-Teresa de Filippis managed to qualify. Giovanna Amati, Divina Galica and Desire Wilson failed to make it on to the starting grid. Lombardi scored too, finishing sixth for March in the 1975 Spanish GP at Montjuich Park. The race was stopped after 29 laps (out of 75) because of a major accident.

SHOWING WHO'S BOSS

Sebastian Vettel's 2013 world title-winning campaign was one of dominance as he outscored his closest rival, Ferrari's Fernando Alonso, by 155 points. Such was his speed in his Red Bull that Vettel led 18 of the year's 19 grands prix, with only Nico Rosberg's dominance of the Monaco GP from pole position spoiling a clean sweep. Vettel spent 692 laps (2,097 miles) in front, which equates to 58 per cent of all the laps raced that year.

TOP 10 DRIVERS WITH MOST MILES IN LEAD

1	Michael Schumacher	15,002
2	Sebastian Vettel	8,543
3	Ayrton Senna	8,345
4	Alain Prost	7,751
5	Lewis Hamilton	7,666
6	Jim Clark	6,282
7	Nigel Mansell	5,905
8	Juan Manuel Fangio	5,789
9	Jackie Stewart	5,692
10	Fernando Alonso	5,369

CHOPPING AND CHANGING

The most lead changes in a grand prix came in one of the cut and thrust races at Monza, where drivers slipstreamed the car in front down the long straights then dived out to overtake. The record isn't from the classic 1971 encounter in which the lead changed 25 times, but the race in 1965 in which the lead changed a staggering 41 times.

NO BROTHERLY LOVE

Quite a few brothers have competed in F1 at the same time, such as the Fittipaldis, the Scheckters, the Villeneuves and the less well-known Whiteheads. However, the Schumachers are the best known, with Michael taking 91 wins and Ralf six. Michael never cut Ralf any slack on track and was once accused of "trying to kill" him when he edged Ralf towards the wall.

FEW FLAGS TO WAVE

The lowest number of different driver nationalities competing in a season was in 1954, 1966, 1999, 2008 and 2013 when just 10 were represented. This is less surprising in recent years, as despite the fact that the sport is global, drivers tended to stay with their teams throughout the season rather than changing.

THE LONG AND WINDING ROAD

Sebastian Vettel's third world title season of 2012 comprised 20 grands prix, for a total distance of 3,783 miles. The next highest total was achieved by Lotus racer Kimi Raikkonen who completed the same number of laps as Vettel did bar one, losing out at the final grand prix in Brazil for a season's tally of 3,780 miles. In 2010, when there were 19 grands prix, Alonso set the previous record, managing 3,564 in his Ferrari, spoiled by a crash in the Belgian GP.

HE LOOKS A LITTLE FAMILIAR

From the early 1990s to the mid-2000s, it felt odd if Michael Schumacher wasn't grinning down from the podium. He was usually second or third if he didn't win and so made 156 podium appearances in his 308 starts. He was on the podium at all the races in 2002, completing a record run of 19 podium appearances that began at Indianapolis in 2001.

Above **No brotherly love:** There was a clear fraternal order between Michael and Ralf Schumacher. *Below* **Chopping and changing:** Monza's long straights offered plenty of chances to slipstream, and it led to a record 41 lead changes in the 1965 Italian Grand Prix. John Surtees is shown leading for Ferrari.

FAMILY MATTERS

There are many familiar family names in F1. Brothers, fathers and sons have competed, with Graham and Damon Hill the only father and son to have become world champions. Other world champions – Mario Andretti, Jack Brabham, Nelson Piquet and Keke Rosberg – have had sons who have raced in F1, as did race winner Gilles Villeneuve. There have also been uncles, nephews and brothers-in-law.

CONSTRUCTORS

Alfa Romeo, Maserati, Vanwall, Cooper, BRM, Lotus, Tyrrell, Brabham, Benetton and Honda have all shone then disappeared. McLaren, Williams and Red Bull Racing are still in there competing, with Lotus racing again in a different guise. Yet, however the F1 landscape changes, Ferrari continues to win grands prix and attracts support the world over. It is the only team to have been racing since F1 began.

Note: The Renault statistics listed are based on the team that evolved from Benetton in 2002, plus stats from Renault's first spell in F1 between 1977 and 1985. The figures for Benetton include those of Toleman; stats for Red Bull include Stewart and Jaguar Racing teams; Force India's stats include Jordan and Midland Spyker; Scuderia Toro Rosso figures include Minardi; and Mercedes GP's those of BAR, Honda Racing and Brawn GP.

Below **Mercedes:** *Hamilton holds off Rosberg in Spain to make it four wins from the first five rounds in 2014.*

TEAM WINS

FERRARI – TITLES AND MORE TITLES

The team with the most constructors' titles to its name is Ferrari. It has 16, compared with Williams's nine and McLaren's eight. Ferrari would have had a couple more, but the Constructors' Cup wasn't awarded until 1958, therefore its dominant seasons in 1952 and 1953 don't count.

McLAREN'S FIRST XI

McLaren holds the record for the most successive grand prix wins, with a run of 11 in the first 11 races of the 1988 season. Ayrton Senna and Alain Prost dominated, but they tripped up when Ferrari came good at the place that mattered most to them, Monza, with Gerhard Berger winning the Italian GP. McLaren closed the season by winning the final four races.

FERRARI HITS ITS STRIDE

Although Ferrari were beaten by Alfa Romeo in 1950 and 1951, it became dominant once the championship switched to F2 regulations, from 1952. A rash of wins, mainly by Alberto Ascari, made it no surprise that, despite the efforts of Maserati and Mercedes-Benz, Ferrari was the first to 25 wins when Juan Manuel Fangio won the 1956 German GP.

DECADE BY DECADE

If you add up team grand prix wins and look at them decade by decade the 1950s belonged to Ferrari with 29 wins, the 1960s to Lotus with 36 wins, the 1970s to Ferrari with 37 wins, the 1980s to McLaren with 56 wins, the 1990s to Williams with 61 wins and the 2000s to Ferrari with a huge 85 wins. After six years of the 2010s (2010–15), Red Bull had won 43 and Mercedes had won 36.

HOME ADVANTAGE

Ferrari has scored the most wins at its home grand prix, its drivers winning the Italian GP 17 times since Alberto Ascari's win at Monza in 1951 and Fernando Alonso's in 2010. Ferrari has also won Italy's second race, the San Marino GP, eight times.

Below **McLaren's First XI:** Ayrton Senna's win in the 1988 Belgian GP made it 11 wins in a row for McLaren. *Bottom* **Clean sweeps are as rare as hens' teeth:** Nino Farina (10) leads Alfa Romeo teammate Juan Manuel Fangio (18) in the 1950 Italian Grand Prix, a race the former won to claim the first World Championship.

CLEAN SWEEPS ARE AS RARE AS HENS' TEETH

Only two teams have achieved 100 per cent win rates across a season. Alfa Romeo was the first to achieve this, winning all six grands prix in the first World Championship in 1950. Two years later Ferrari matched its national rivals, who quit after 1951, and won seven from seven. The closest any team has come since is when McLaren won 15 from 16 in 1988.

MOST WINS IN ONE SEASON

No.	Team	Year
16	Mercedes GP	2014
=	Mercedes GP	2015
15	Ferrari	2002
=	Ferrari	2004
=	McLaren	1988
13	Red Bull	2013
12	Red Bull	2011
=	McLaren	1984
=	Williams	1996
11	Benetton	1995
10	Ferrari	2000
=	McLaren 1989/2005	
=	Williams 1992/1993	

TOP 10 TEAMS WITH MOST GRAND PRIX WINS

1	Ferrari	224
2	McLaren	181
3	Williams	114
4	Lotus	79
5	Red Bull (née Stewart)	50
6	Lotus*	49
7	Mercedes GP	45
8	Benetton	27
9	Tyrrell	23
10	BRM	17

Lotus* stats are for team that was Toleman, then became Benetton, Renault and Lotus in 2012.

» A HUNGRY WOLF

Walter Wolf had backed Williams in 1976, but he wanted his own team and set one up for the following year. What an impact his team made when the 1977 World Championship opened in Argentina. After front-row starters James Hunt and John Watson faltered, Jody Scheckter came through to take the only maiden team win in F1 history.

» THE JOY OF SIX

It's debatable whether Brawn GP can be viewed as a new team in 2009, as it was effectively a continuation of Honda Racing after the Japanese manufacturer quit at the end of 2008. Even if it was more of a new team name rather than a new team, its six wins were the best haul from a team in its first season.

» WINNING FOR YOUR COUNTRY

Looking at stats in terms of the nationality of the team, or the country out of which it operated, there can be no denying that Britain is the home of F1, with an "arc of excellence" around London from Cambridgeshire to Surrey. The majority of F1 teams have long been based in Britain, even if the owners are not British. As a result of this, British-based teams had won 646 of the 935 grands prix held by the end of 2014, with Italy next, almost entirely thanks to Ferrari, on 240 wins. French teams are third, having claimed 24 victories.

» PERSEVERANCE PAYS OFF

Scuderia Toro Rosso holds the record for the most races contested by a team before scoring its first win. It started life in 1985 as Minardi and never looked likely to score points on a regular basis let alone have its drivers mount the podium or take a win. It took a change of ownership in 2007 and an injection of money into its coffers to turn its fortunes around. Young flyer Sebastian Vettel did the rest, winning in the wet in the Italian GP at Monza in 2008, the team's first victory out of 372 starts.

» MANY WINS, NO PRIZE

As the Constructors' Championship was not contested until 1958, Alfa Romeo goes down in the history books as the marque with the most grand prix wins without a title. It dominated the 1950 and 1951 seasons, taking 10 wins. Mercedes-Benz, with five of its nine wins coming in 1955, and Maserati, four of its nine in 1957, were also denied official recognition. In the post-Constructors' Cup era, Ligier, who ran from 1976 to 1996, also scored nine wins, three of which came in 1979, its best season, is third overall.

Above **Most wins in one season:** Riccardo Patrese leads Nigel Mansell in Brazil in 1992, when Williams won 10 races. *Top* **Top 10 teams with most grand prix wins:** Lewis Hamilton claimed McLaren's 164th win in Singapore in 2009. *Below* **The *Tifosi's* favourite:** Michael Schumacher did a lot of celebrating with Ferrari, including in 2003, after he had taken his sixth title.

THE TIFOSI'S FAVOURITE

Michael Schumacher was admired rather than liked by the *Tifosi* when he joined Ferrari in 1996, but they soon warmed to him when he and the team started winning on a regular basis. He is by far the most successful Ferrari driver, having won 72 times for the Scuderia. The next most successful is Niki Lauda on 15, just ahead of another Ferrari double champion, Alberto Ascari, who took 13 wins.

TEAM POLE POSITIONS

FOR THE TIFOSI

It almost feels like a birthright that a Ferrari should take pole position in the Italian GP and the team has achieved this on 19 occasions, rising to the challenge even in years when its form has been patchy elsewhere. After Ferrari's qualifying glories at Monza, the next most pole positions set by a team at an individual circuit is shared by a group of three: Ferrari at the Nürburgring; McLaren at Hockenheim and Monaco; and Williams at Silverstone.

CHARGING UP THE ORDER

Red Bull's flurry of pole positions in 2010 (its title breakthrough campaign), with 15 shared between Sebastian Vettel and Mark Webber, was followed by 18 more in 2011 and eight in 2012 to fire the team from Milton Keynes ahead of Brabham into fifth place in the all-time poles table.

ALBORETO HITS A CENTURY

One hundred is always a landmark figure and Ferrari became the first team to claim 100 pole positions. Michele Alboreto helped the team achieve this century at Spa-Francorchamps in 1984. As this was in the team's 35th year of F1, its average was three per year.

ALL BUT PERFECT

Between 1988 and 1993, there were four occasions when a team took pole position 15 times in 16 races: McLaren, in 1988 and 1989, and Williams, in 1992 and 1993. That record was beaten by Red Bull, who set a new mark with 18 from 19 races in 2011 (Sebastian Vettel 15, Mark Webber three) and it was matched by Mercedes in 2015 (Lewis Hamilton 11, Nico Rosberg seven).

FROM ZERO TO HERO

A number of teams have taken their first win without having previously achieved a pole position, including debutants Alfa Romeo in 1950, Mercedes in 1954 and Wolf in 1977, plus others who'd been racing a while, such as Cooper, Honda, Matra, McLaren and Porsche. Some teams, including BRM, Ferrari, Lotus, Toro Rosso, Vanwall and Williams, hit form and claimed their first pole and first win at the same race.

- -

Below **A three-way tie for pole:** Michael Schumacher just missed out on pole at Jerez in 1997 but in the end he still got the jump on the Williams duo to lead away.
Opposite **And, at last...:** Alan Jones gave the Shadow team its one and only grand prix victory, at the Osterreichring in 1977.

A THREE-WAY TIE FOR POLE

The 1997 World Championship came to a crescendo at Jerez with the title being fought over by Ferrari's Michael Schumacher and Williams' Jacques Villeneuve. Then, at the end of qualifying for the race, Formula One was faced with a situation it had never witnessed before – the first three qualifying times were identical. Villeneuve claimed pole from Schumacher and his own teammate Heinz-Harald Frentzen, all on 1m21.072s.

McLAREN MOVES AHEAD

When Lewis Hamilton claimed pole then raced to victory at the 2010 Canadian GP, he moved McLaren ahead of Ferrari at the top of the table for teams with the most pole/win doubles. It was McLaren's 37th race victory from pole position. It had 40 by the end of 2012. Lotus was third in this category, largely due to the efforts of Ayrton Senna in 1986, but were recently passed by Red Bull Racing moving on to 32.

INCREDIBLE TREBLE

Taking pole then winning is an achievement, but even more prestigious than that is adding the fastest lap to make it a treble. With one driver doing the hat-trick, Ferrari has achieved this an incredible 82 times, with Michael Schumacher the main driving force. Williams is next up on 50, edging McLaren out by one. Lotus is ranked fourth on 26, with Renault fifth on 11.

Above **The more the merrier:** Both Brawn (top at the Australian GP) and Toyota (above at the Bahrain GP) claimed their first pole positions in 2009.

AND, AT LAST...

The most pole positions achieved by a team before its first victory is just three. Shadow was on pole three times in 1975 through Jean-Pierre Jarier (twice) and Tom Pryce. However, the first win, in fact the team's only win, came two years later when Alan Jones raced from 14th to first on a damp track in the Austrian GP.

TOP 10 TEAM POLES

1	Ferrari	208
2	McLaren	154
3	Williams	128
4	Lotus	107
5	Red Bull	58
6	Mercedes GP	53
7	Brabham	39
8	Lotus*	34
9	Renault	31
10	Tyrrell	14

Lotus* stats are for team that was Toleman, then became Benetton, Renault and Lotus in 2012.

THE MORE THE MERRIER

The record for the greatest number of different teams to achieve pole position in one season is six. The ever-increasing number of rounds favours teams competing in recent years over those who raced in the early 1950s when there were sometimes only seven races in a season, in addition to the fact that there were only a handful of competitive teams in the early years. So the record was first set in 1972, but then matched in 1976, 1981, 1985, 2005 and in 2009.

In 2009 Brawn and Red Bull led the way in terms of the number of poles achieved, ahead of McLaren, Force India, Renault and Toyota.

TEAM FASTEST LAPS

SPEED OVER RESULTS

Ferrari has set the most fastest laps of any team at any circuit, with 17 at Monaco, but it would gladly swap that record for McLaren's table-topping figure of 15 wins around the street circuit. McLaren's drivers, it seems, have kept the cooler heads and delivered what every team boss wants most, especially in front of friends and sponsors on the yachts in the harbour.

WHO'S FASTEST?

Since the 1960s most of the F1 teams have been British or based in Britain, so it's not surprising that their combined tally of 571 fastest laps exceeds the best that Italy (largely Ferrari) and other countries have managed. Italy's combined attack includes Ferrari, Alfa Romeo, Maserati and Lancia, with a total of 264.

FERRARI LEADS THE WAY

Ferrari has been competing in the World Championship since it began in 1950 and has been competitive in the vast majority of seasons since. So it's no surprise that Ferrari tops the table as the team that has set or equalled the most fastest laps at 52 of the 71 circuits used up to the end of 2015. McLaren is the next most successful in its spread of fastest laps, being top or equal top at 47 circuits.

FERRARI FLIES

Michael Schumacher was peerless in 2004, setting 10 fastest laps from 18 rounds. But Ferrari's number-two driver, Rubens Barrichello, was also able to reel off fastest laps in his F2004, helping the Italian team to a record 14 fastest laps in a season. This is one more than its 2008 line-up of Felipe Massa (3) and Kimi Räikkönen (10) managed. Mercedes achieved 12 in both 2014 and 2015.

ONE HUNDRED FOR THE FANS

Michele Alboreto was the driver to give Ferrari its 100th pole in 1984 and he took the legendary Italian team to its century of fastest laps the following year. He achieved this landmark at the San Marino GP at Imola, but ended the day without any points as he retired with electrical failure. Elio de Angelis raced on to take maximum points for Lotus.

Right **Ferrari flies:** Michael Schumacher collected more than just trophies in 2004, as he picked up 10 fastest laps. *Bottom* **Renault's glory days:** René Arnoux set fastest lap for Renault at Dijon-Prenois, with teammate Jean-Pierre Jabouille taking its first win in the same race.

A BRITISH BONANZA

Italian teams started F1 with a bang, with Alfa Romeo, Ferrari or Maserati setting the fastest lap at each of the first 30 grands prix. However, this is no longer the record for the most successive fastest laps set by teams from one country. It was finally bettered between 1991 and 1995 when the British teams of Williams, McLaren, Benetton and Jordan set fastest laps for an incredible 62 races in a row.

RENAULT'S GLORY DAYS

Renault struggled when it arrived in the World Championship midway through 1977. The team had F1's first turbocharged engine, and while power wasn't a problem, reliability was. However, within two years the team's yellow and black cars were flying. Jean-Pierre Jabouille took the marque's first win at Dijon-Prenois and René Arnoux set the race's fastest lap. Renault again bagged the fastest lap on its return visit to the circuit in 1981.

TOP 10 TEAMS WITH THE MOST FASTEST LAPS

1	Ferrari	232
2	McLaren	152
3	Williams	133
4	Lotus	71
5	Lotus*	54
6	Red Bull	47
7	Brabham	40
8	Mercedes GP	32
9	Tyrrell	22
10	Renault	18

⟫⟫ A YEAR OF VARIETY

The 1975 World Championship offered the greatest number of teams that set fastest laps across the 14 grands prix in the season. Eight teams got in on the act: Ferrari (six fastest laps), McLaren (two), Brabham, Hesketh, March, Parnelli, Shadow and Tyrrell (all with one).

⟫⟫ STRONG ON THE DAY

A host of teams have had drivers who have been experts at qualifying – such as Ayrton Senna, who took 65 poles from his 161 starts – but unless the car is resilient enough to last the race this speed does not necessarily translate into a race win. Across the first 63 years of F1, Ferrari holds the record for the most wins/fastest lap doubles, at 53. McLaren is the next most successful team, with 39, and Williams is in third place, having achieved it on 22 occasions.

Below **Favouring America:** Graham Hill added to Lotus's collection of fastest laps in the United States GP in 1967. *Bottom* **Red racers:** Rubens Barrichello controlled the 2004 Italian GP, also bagging another Monza fastest lap for Ferrari.

FAVOURING AMERICA

With a need to sell road-going sports cars as well as its range of racing cars, Lotus boss Colin Chapman was always delighted that his F1 cars seemed to shine in North America. The team has the most or equal most fastest laps at Detroit, Riverside and, most importantly, Watkins Glen in New York State.

RED RACERS

An ample supply of horsepower has been a feature of Ferrari's engines over the years, and this is evident in the stats for which team has set the most fastest laps at an individual circuit. The Italian team tops the table with 18 at its home circuit of Monza, where the long, long straights require plenty of grunt.

TEAM POINTS

 ### RAKING THEM IN

The change of the World Championship points system – awarding points from first place to 10th from 2010, with 25 for a win whereas it had previously been 10 – meant that Red Bull Racing set a record of 498 points, then beat that in 2011 when Sebastian Vettel took the title with 392 points and teammate Mark Webber backed him up by ranking third for a joint tally of 650 points. This worked out at an average of 34.21 points at each of the campaign's 19 grands prix.

ONE AND TWO

F1's most successful teams aren't always at the top, but they all have periods when they manage to have the best chassis, the best engine, the best tyres and the best drivers at the same time. In 2015, Mercedes beat McLaren's record of 10 one-two finishes from 16 starts in 1988 when Lewis Hamilton and Nico Rosberg were first and second to the finish in 15 of the 19 rounds.

POINTS ALL THE WAY

Several teams have scored points in every single grand prix of the year. The most recent teams to achieve this feat of excellence was Mercedes in 2015 after Mercedes, Williams and Ferrari, all managed to score in each of the 19 grands prix held in 2014. Ferrari scored in 20 from 20 in 2012 and 2011, McLaren in 2010 and Brawn GP in 2009, in its only season under that branding before becoming Mercedes GP.

MAXIMUM POINTS HAULS

The quickest way for a team to rack up points is to have its cars finish in first and second places in a grand prix and Ferrari is the best at this, having achieved it 76 times, starting all the way back at the Italian GP in 1951. McLaren, the next most successful team in taking one-two results, with 44, didn't score its first one until 17 years later in Canada when Denny Hulme led home team owner Bruce McLaren.

TOP 10 TEAMS WITH MOST POINTS

#	Team	Points
1	Ferrari	6,244.5
2	McLaren	5,017.5
3	Williams	3,338
4	Red Bull (née Stewart)	3,140.5
5	Lotus*	2,457.5
6	Mercedes (née BAR–Honda–Brawn)	2,788
7	Lotus	1,514
8	Force India	919
9	Brabham	854
10	Sauber	767

Lotus* stats are for team that was Toleman, then became Benetton, Renault and Lotus in 2012.

BY THE THOUSANDS

British and British-based teams lead the way in points accrued, with their combined tally being 21,985.5 at the end of 2015. Italian teams rank second, on 6,643.5 points, with French teams on 777 and Swiss-based Sauber and BMW Sauber accumulating 808 points between them.

Above **One and two:** Ayrton Senna leads Alain Prost towards yet another one-two finish in 1988, this time in Hungary. *Below* **Perseverance pays off:** Benetton team boss Flavio Briatore and Michael Schumacher had plenty to smile about in 1995.

COMING GOOD IN THE END

Benetton scored the most points before landing its first constructors' title. This came in 1995, by which time it had scored 663.5 points across 15 campaigns since starting life as the Toleman team back in 1981. Ironically, the team later became Renault in 2002 after being taken over by the French manufacturer, which had actually started its bid for a title back in 1977.

SCORING AT HOME

Not only because of its speed and success, but also its longevity, Ferrari is the team that has scored the most points at its home race. From 1958, the first year of the Constructors' Cup, to 2015, Ferrari collected 464 points from the Italian GP at Monza. Ferrari's record in Italy's second race, the San Marino GP that ran from 1981 to 2006, is not as strong, although it did record eight victories.

LOOKING DOWN FROM ABOVE

||||||||||||||||||||||||||||||||||||||||||||

Ferrari holds the record for the most consecutive top-three finishes which, largely thanks to the might of Michael Schumacher, resulted in podium finishes at an incredible 53 straight grands prix between the 1999 Malaysian GP and the final grand prix of 2002 in Japan. The team kept the stream of points flowing into 2003, but only for the next two grands prix. Disaster struck in the third race of the season at Interlagos when Ferrari went home empty-handed as both Michael Schumacher (crashed) and Rubens Barrichello (fuel shortage) retired. It bounced back to finish first and third next time out.

CLOSEST TO PERFECTION

The scoring system has changed four times since the World Championship began in 1950* but, even taking this into account, Alfa Romeo achieved the highest points average ever in that inaugural season, as its drivers finished first and second in every race, except two. This gave the Italian marque a points score of 90.476 per cent of the maximum. In modern times, Mercedes recorded an amazing 86.047 per cent strike rate in 2015 (703 out of 817 points). McLaren's 1988 tally is the next best with 82.917 per cent.

Points from 1950–57 counted only towards the drivers' tally, but have been added here for comparative purposes.

SO LITTLE REWARD

You could never criticize Minardi for its effort, but a lack of finance left it struggling to be competitive. The team's record of 38 points from 340 starts is poor, equal to a return of 0.112 points per race. Still, that is impressive compared to both the Zakspeed, which accumulated just two points in 53 starts (0.0377), and Osella, five points from 132 (0.0379). Needless to say, none of the teams managed a single podium finish.

TOP 10 TEAMS WITH MOST ONE-TWO FINISHES

1	Ferrari	76
2	McLaren	47
3	Williams	32
4	Mercedes GP	28
5	Red Bull	15
6	Brabham	8
=	Tyrrell	8
8	Lotus	7
9	BRM	5
10	Alfa Romeo	4
=	Brawn	4

Below **Something for almost everyone:** Lola – this is Philippe Alliot at Monaco – was one of 16 teams to score points in 1989. **Bottom** **Looking down from above:** Michael Schumacher and race winner Eddie Irvine started Ferrari's run of podium finishes at Sepang in 1999.

SOMETHING FOR ALMOST EVERYONE

In 1989 16 different teams scored points in the World Championship, the most ever. This statistic is even more remarkable when you note that points were awarded down to only sixth rather than eighth place, as was the situation from 2003. The scoring teams were, in points order: McLaren, Williams, Ferrari, Benetton, Tyrrell, Lotus, Arrows, Dallara, Brabham, Onyx, Minardi, March, Rial, Ligier, AGS and Lola. Only the Coloni, EuroBrun, Osella and Zakspeed teams failed to score.

TEAM TITLES

FORZA FERRARI

Ferrari's head start in the 1950s and its incredibly strong run of success from 2000 onwards – with Michael Schumacher leading the way – ensure that the Italian team has more constructors' titles than any other, with 16 to Williams's nine and McLaren's eight. Had the constructors' title been awarded before 1958, Ferrari would be closer to 20.

GLORY IS HARD TO COME BY

British or British-based teams rule in terms of race wins, with 625 to Italy's 244. In fact, such is the centralization of expertise that teams based in only seven countries have won a grand prix. France's Renault (in its first iteration), Ligier and Matra help the country rank third on 33, while Mercedes won 10 for Germany. At the foot of the table on one win apiece are the Netherlands,

home of the Honda team from 1964–66, and Switzerland, with BMW Sauber's one and only win coming at Montreal in 2008. The order has changed radically in recent years however, as Austria's Red Bull (43 wins) and Germany's Mercedes (36) have dominated the Constructors' Cup standings.

FERRARI'S FLOP

There's no doubt that the worst follow-up season by a champion team was that of the inaugural constructors' champions, Vanwall, as it scaled down its involvement to almost nothing due to patron Tony Vandervell's ill health. However, of those who returned to defend their titles, Ferrari has had the worst time, scoring just eight points in 1980. As there was no driver change, 1979 world champion Jody Scheckter and Gilles Villeneuve staying on, the blame fell on the car.

CROWNS FOR COUNTRIES

British or British-based teams hold sway in terms of the most constructors' titles won, with their combined forces achieving 42 titles, largely thanks to Williams and McLaren, to Italy's 16. France, the country that hosted the first road races starting in 1894, and the first grand prix in 1906, has three titles (one from Matra and two from Renault), but its claims to titles are debatable as in each case the teams were run out of Great Britain.

TECHNOLOGY DELIVERS

The relentless quest for technological advancement was what made Lotus the team to fear in the 1960s. Team owner Colin Chapman wouldn't rest if there wasn't a new idea that might make his cars the fastest on the grid, introducing changes

faster than the rivals could catch up. This earned the team its first constructors' title in 1963 and when this was backed up titles in 1965, 1968 and 1970, Emerson Fittipaldi helped it to be the first team to five titles in 1972.

WORTH THE LONG WAIT

Mercedes dominated in the mid-1950s, before the Constructors' title was introduced in 1958, but the team's withdrawal at the end of 1955 meant that it wasn't until 2014 that the modern iteration of the team won the title. Then, with Lewis Hamilton and Nico Rosberg dominant, it repeated the feat in 2015, winning 16 of the 19 grands prix to trounce Ferrari by 703 points to 428.

A SIGN OF EXCELLENCE

To win the constructors' title before the final round is a sign of a team in control and 12 teams have managed it since the Constructors' Championship began in 1958. They are: Benetton, Brabham (two), Brawn, Cooper (two), Ferrari (nine), Lotus (five), McLaren (four), Mercedes (two), Red Bull Racing (four), Tyrrell, Vanwall and Williams (eight).

Below **Squeaking home:** Lorenzo Bandini celebrates his only win, in Austria in 1964, to help Ferrari win the title by just three points. *Bottom* **A sign of excellence:** Tyrrell, with Jackie Stewart leading François Cevert to a one-two in Germany, wrapped up the title early in 1973.

SQUEAKING HOME

The narrowest title-winning margin is just three points, which was the result back in 1964 when Ferrari edged out BRM thanks to John Surtees and Lorenzo Bandini getting the better of the British team's Graham Hill and Richie Ginther. However, that season was contested across only 10 rounds, making Ferrari's victory over McLaren by four points after 16 grands prix in 1999 statistically closer.

COME IN NUMBER 15

Demonstrating a clear shuffling of the pack, four constructors have landed their first constructors' title since 2005. First it was Renault (formed from Benetton), duly repeating the feat the following year. Then in 2009 it was Brawn GP (formerly BAR and Honda Racing). In 2010, Red Bull Racing (formerly Stewart Grand Prix then Jaguar Racing) scored its first of four titles. Then, in 2014, Mercedes became the 15th constructor to be crowned.

ECONOMIES OF SCALE

The teams that won the constructors' titles in the early years have the best record in terms of having the fewest race starts to their name before landing the title. The first constructors' champions, Vanwall, had made a total of just 27 starts when it took the 1958 title, only to be trumped by Cooper in 1959, who became champions with just 25 starts.

NEVER AT HOME

Despite the Italian GP taking place towards the end of the F1 racing calendar, not once has the *Tifosi* seen Ferrari claim the constructors' title on home ground, even in the years of Michael Schumacher's dominance. However, in two of those years – 2002 and 2004 – Ferrari had already won the title before heading for Monza, wrapping it up several rounds earlier at the Hungarian GP.

Above **Never at home:** Michael Schumacher gave Ferrari a home win at Monza in 2000, but not the constructors' title. *Below* **Come in number 15:** Nico Rosberg leads Lewis Hamilton at Interlagos in 2015, the year of Mercedes' second title. *Bottom* **Economies of scale:** Jack Brabham won the Monaco GP to help Cooper be crowned after just 25 starts.

MOST CONSTRUCTORS' TITLES

1	Ferrari	16
2	Williams	9
3	McLaren	8
4	Lotus	7
5	Red Bull	4
6	Brabham	2
=	Cooper	2
=	Mercedes GP	2
=	Renault	2
10	Benetton	1
=	Brawn GP	1
=	BRM	1
=	Matra	1
=	Tyrrell	1
=	Vanwall	1

PARTICIPATION

I'LL START, SO I'LL FINISH

Someone always retires, well, except in five of the 935 grands prix between 1950 and 2015. At the 1961 Dutch GP, all 15 starters finished. Then every car finished the 2005 US GP, but that was just six, as the other 14 had pulled off after the formation lap protesting over tyre safety. However, all 20 starters finished at Monza later in 2005, as did all in the 2011 European GP and 2015 Japanese GP, showing how reliability has improved.

YOUR NAME ON THE NOSE

Winning is wonderful, and a handful of drivers have sought to do it in a car bearing their name. Most successful by far is Jack Brabham, who won seven grands prix in 1966 and landed both the drivers' and constructors' titles. His former teammate Bruce McLaren founded a successful dynasty, although it flourished mainly after his death in 1970.

WHY MOVE WHEN YOU'RE WINNING?

Michael Schumacher turned Ferrari back into a winning machine and so saw no reason to move elsewhere. He landed 72 of his 91 grand prix wins and five of his seven world titles while driving for the Italian team, before retiring from racing after a record 162 grands prix for the

Above **Your name on the nose:** Bruce McLaren founded his eponymous team, but was killed before it really thrived. *Below* **I'll start, so I'll finish:** All 15 cars that started the 1961 Dutch GP reached the finish, with Wolfgang von Trips (3) beating pole-sitting Ferrari teammate Phil Hill.

team from Maranello. David Coulthard is the next most long-staying driver, clocking up 150 races for McLaren.

GOING ALL THE WAY

The 2013 World Championship was far from McLaren's greatest season since entering F1 in 1966, but it at least set a new record. This was for getting closest to completing the total racing distance across the season's 19 grands prix, managing a 99.17 per cent completion rate in covering

TEAMS THAT HAVE LED MOST MILES

1	Ferrari	44,982
2	McLaren	31,291
3	Williams	21,902
4	Lotus	16,263
5	Red Bull Racing	15,777

7,138 of the 7,198 miles. This beat BMW Sauber's 2008 tally of 98.30 per cent. Despite this, McLaren could only rank fifth.

TEAMS THAT HAVE LED MOST LAPS

1	Ferrari	13,911
2	McLaren	10,578
3	Williams	7,588
4	Lotus	5,498
5	Red Bull	3,075

▶ TO FINISH FIRST, FIRST YOU HAVE TO FINISH

The 1996 Monaco GP was an odd one. The Minardis took each other out before the first corner; Michael Schumacher took himself out further around the lap; and Rubens Barrichello spun out in his Jordan before the lap was over. At the end of it all, Olivier Panis scored his one and only win, for Ligier, and there were just four classified finishers, only three of which were still running at flag-fall. No race has come close to being as destructive.

▶ LETTING ITS STANDARDS SLIP

Despite being F1's second most successful team, McLaren stumbled in 2013. Its MP4-28 wasn't comptetitive to win. Indeed, Jenson Button and Sergio Perez failed to give the team a podium for the first time

POINTS, BUT NO PRIZES

The Arrows team is no more, but at least it will never extend its record of being the team with the most grand prix starts without winning a grand prix – 382. It came close twice. Riccardo Patrese was leading until 15 laps before the end of the team's third race, in South Africa in 1978, before the engine failed and Damon Hill led the 1997 Hungarian GP until a lap before the finish when Jacques Villeneuve swept past to win and Hill came second.

since 1980. The 2014 season was little better, as Kevin Magnussen and Button finished 2–3 in Australia but failed to win.

▶ COMING AND GOING

There have been teams coming into and leaving F1 since the advent of the World Championship in 1950. By the end of 2014, there had been nigh on 400 teams or individual entrants enter F1 but, due to failing to secure the budget even to remain at the back of the grid, Caterham became the latest to quit. Its five-year run in F1 yielded not a single point since it arrived as Lotus at the start of 2010. With Marussia teetering on the brink of bankruptcy, things weren't looking rosy in the F1 camp.

▶ KEEP IT SHORT

Which is the most successful team if you pit wins against starts? Answer: it is neither Ferrari (0.252) nor McLaren (0.232), but Mercedes, when it raced in F1 first time around for a season and a half in 1954–55. It had a strike-rate of 0.75 – nine wins in 12 starts. Add in the 2010 rebirth, however, and it falls to 0.352 (45 wins in 128 grands prix). Had Alfa Romeo not returned in 1979, its 1950–51 strike rate would have been 0.769: instead it's 0.091 (10 wins in 110 starts).

Above **Points, but no prizes:** At the 1997 Hungarian GP, Damon Hill led for all but the most important lap, the last one. *Right* **Keep it short:** McLaren's wins to starts ratio slid in 2015 when Jenson Button and Fernando Alonso struggled with Honda power. *Right* **Sticking together:** David Coulthard and Mika Hakkinen, on the podium in Barcelona in 1999 with Adrian Newey, raced together 99 times.

STICKING TOGETHER

David Coulthard and Mika Hakkinen raced together more times than any other teammates in the history of F1, totalling 99 grands prix as a duo. They had a six-year stretch together at McLaren between 1996 and 2001 before Hakkinen took what he'd planned to be a sabbatical, which by mid-2002 had become full retirement from F1.

TEAM PRINCIPALS

PASSION HIDDEN BEHIND DARK GLASSES

Enzo Ferrari was drawn to the sport by a desire to compete. In the 1930s, he was put in charge of Alfa Romeo's racing activities. Fired in 1939, Enzo started building his own cars after the Second World War. His team's first World Championship win came at the 1951 British GP and the legend grew from there. Enzo was famously unemotional about his cars, which were broken up after they were superseded. He remained enigmatic in the extreme, and by the end of his career would no longer watch races at the track.

A SHARP BRAIN AND A STERN LOOK

Alfred Neubauer was the man who made the Mercedes team tick during its one-and-a-half-year stint in F1 in the mid-1950s. He joined Mercedes as a racing driver in 1923, but he quit after a teammate was killed at the 1924 Italian GP and turned to team management. He guided the "Silver Arrows" through its glory years of the late 1920s and 1930s. Portly, never without a jacket and tie, and usually with a serious expression, he was still at the helm after the Second World War and he encouraged the team back into racing in 1954 when it set new standards.

A RESTLESS, DRIVEN GENIUS

Colin Chapman probably shaped F1 more than any other team principal through his restless quest to find an engineering advantage. In 1962 his Lotus team was the first to use a monocoque chassis, and Jim Clark started to win. He made ground effects work for the 1978 season and Mario Andretti duly did the same. He tried to introduce a double chassis, but it was banned, infuriating this effervescent character. He died of a heart attack in 1988, leaving memories of a man dressed in black hurling his cap in the air when his drivers won.

TIMBER MERCHANT TURNED CHAMPION CHIEF

Ken Tyrrell was a racing driver, financed by his family's timber business. Following the end of his driving career he ran the Cooper Formula Junior team in 1960, and advanced, with Jackie Stewart, to F2 in 1965. They switched to a Matra chassis for F2 and Ken moved into F1 with his own team in 1968, running a Matra-Ford for Stewart. They won races and improved to win the 1969 title. The first Tyrrell car appeared in 1970, and Stewart won titles in 1971 and 1973, but the team struggled financially after sponsor Elf quit, being taken over by BAR in 1998. Ken died of cancer in 2001.

MID-ENGINES TO MINIS

John Cooper's father Charles got him interested in racing and they started building small chassis powered by motorbike engines after the Second World War. Stirling Moss gave Cooper its first F1 win in 1958 and Jack Brabham claimed the next two drivers' and constructors' titles for the team before Lotus stole its thunder. John took over the running of the team in 1964 after his father died, but was then injured in a car crash and decided to sell the company, moving on to create the high-performance Mini Cooper. John died in 2000.

Top **A sharp brain and a stern look:** Timber merchant Ken Tyrrell and Jackie Stewart formed a great partnership, claiming their third title together in 1973. *Above* **Passion hidden behind dark glasses:** Enzo Ferrari watches over one of Ferrari's mechanics working at the 1966 Italian GP. *Right* **Mid-engines to Minis:** Jack Brabham and John Cooper formed a great partnership.

A DRIVEN MAN

Guy Ligier's first love was rugby and he was a top-class player, but he had an even greater drive to become rich, and he achieved this by building up a successful construction firm. This financed forays into motorcycle racing before Guy tried cars, moving into sports cars before driving in F1 in 1966. His best result was sixth in Germany in 1967. After retiring from driving he turned to building racing sports cars and, in 1976, an F1 car. The team won nine times. Guy sold up in 1992.

CAPTAIN AMERICA

Roger Penske started racing when at university and was competitive enough to enter the US GP in 1961 and 1962, ranking eighth at his first attempt. However, his skills as a businessman soon became more apparent as he built up a chain of car dealerships that is now the second largest in the USA. He also set up a team and ran Mark Donohue to success in TransAm in 1968 before branching into single-seaters. This was mainly in IndyCars, but he tried F1 from 1974–77 and took one win, with John Watson, at the Österreichring in 1976.

FRANCE'S FIXER

Gerard Larrousse came to prominence in rallying, then turned to racing in 1966 and made his name by finishing second in the 1969 Le Mans 24 Hours. He went on to win this race in 1973 and 1974 for Matra. He then set up an F2 team and Jean-Pierre Jabouille won the 1976 crown, after which Gerard became Renault's competitions manager, managing its entry into F1 in 1977. After Renault closed in 1985, he set up his own F1 team for 1987, running Lola chassis. The team's best result was a third place in Japan in 1990 but it folded at the end of 1994.

A TECHNICAL AND TACTICAL BRAIN

Ross Brawn joined March from the atomic industry. From there, he moved to Williams and learnt to be an aerodynamicist. After spells at Beatrice and Arrows, he designed Jaguar's sports cars but returned to F1 and Benetton. Ross started working with Michael Schumacher at Benetton, displaying both tactical and technical skills. The pair moved to Ferrari and won five more titles before Ross took a sabbatical. He came back with Honda, which became Brawn GP for 2009. The team with his name won both titles in 2009, before being renamed as Mercedes GP for 2010. He retired at the end of 2013.

Left **McLaren's meticulous man:** Ron Dennis looks proud rather than happy after Senna and Prost gave McLaren a one-two at Monaco in 1989. *Below* **A technical and tactical brain:** Ross Brawn hugs Jenson Button after he'd won on the team's debut in Australia in 2009.

McLAREN'S METICULOUS MAN

Ron Dennis started as a mechanic with Cooper. He moved to Brabham in 1968, before starting Rondel, with Neil Trundle in 1972. They were successful in F2 and built an F1 car that they had to sell when their sponsor pulled out. Back in F2, Ron gained management experience and, with backing from Marlboro, took over McLaren. Through his legendary attention to detail he turned it into the second most successful team in F1 history. In 2009 he took a step back from F1 to concentrate on the rest of the McLaren Group, before returning to oversee the F1 side from 2014.

ONE BIG TEDDY BEAR

||||||||||||||||||||||||||||||||||||

Lord Hesketh made quite a splash in F1 in the mid-1970s when he rolled in with a plain white car daubed with patriotic red and blue stripes and a teddy bear on the nose. There was no sponsorship to be seen. "The Good Lord", as driver James Hunt called him, was bankrolling his foray into F1 from his considerable inheritance.

They raced a March in 1974, but soon built their own car and had their day of days when Hunt won the Dutch GP at Zandvoort in 1975. Then Hesketh sold the team and moved into politics, leaving F1 all the poorer without his flamboyance.

DRIVEN BY PATRIOTIC FERVOUR

A racer first and foremost, up to F3 level, Frank Williams never had the money to go any higher and turned to running cars for others, most notably for Piers Courage in 1969 and 1970, until Courage died at the Dutch GP. Some lean years followed as Frank fought on in F1, always short of money. In 1977 he formed Williams Grand Prix Engineering with Patrick Head. It developed into F1's third most successful team, winning nine constructors' titles, despite the setback of Frank being paralysed in a car crash in 1986.

FROM RACER TO PRESIDENT

Max Mosley has spent his life being referred to as the son of fascist politician Sir Oswald Mosley, precluding any dreams of a political career. Instead, Max tried racing, reaching F2 before becoming one of the founder members of March in 1969. He quit March in 1977 and moved into helping the teams form a united front through the Formula One Constructors' Association (FOCA), working with Bernie Ecclestone. He then became president of the Fédération Internationale de l'Automobile (FIA) in 1986 and held the position until late 2009 when he stood down and was replaced by the newly elected Jean Todt.

Above **Driven by patriotic fervour:** Frank Williams and partner Patrick Head watch the action at the 1980 British GP. *Below* **One big teddy bear:** Racing was always fun when Lord Hesketh (left with James Hunt and "Bubbles" Horsley) was around.

Left *A racer who turned to management:* Sebastian Vettel and Christian Horner celebrate in the paddock after yet another Vettel win in 2013. **Below** *Ferrari's fierce little Napoleon:* Jean Todt used his nervous energy and piercing brain to achieve great success with Ferrari.

A RACER WHO TURNED TO MANAGEMENT

Christian Horner had hoped to make it as a driver, but wasn't able to progress beyond Formula 3000. At this point, he started his own team, Arden Motorsport, and it would become increasingly competitive until it achieved title success with Bjorn Wirdheim in 2003 and Vitantonio Liuzzi in 2004. Christian's big break came with the formation of Red Bull Racing for 2005 from what had been Jaguar Racing. Installed as team principal, he has run the team for owner Dietrich Mateschitz ever since as it has moved to the top and claimed four drivers' and four constructors' titles.

FLAMBOYANT BUT FLAWED

Flavio Briatore had no love of racing, but became involved through the Benetton family after he'd headed up their clothing chain's push into the USA. He was asked to be commercial director of their team in 1988 and brought in Tom Walkinshaw to help run it. Signing Michael Schumacher was the key to success and titles followed in 1994 (drivers') and 1995 (drivers' and constructors'). He has since been involved with supplying teams with Renault engines and then ran Renault's F1 return until he was banned from the sport in 2009 for his role in "Singaporegate", the race-fixing scandal that arose as a result of the 2008 Singapore GP.

THE ULTIMATE ENTREPRENEUR

Bernie Ecclestone made his first fortune selling motorbike parts. A club-level car racer, Bernie was busier away from the tracks, establishing a multi-pronged business empire. He bought the Connaught F1 team in 1958 and even tried to qualify a car himself at Monaco. His attempt was unsuccessful so he settled for driver management. After the death of charge Jochen Rindt in 1970, he bought Brabham in 1972 and ran that until he sold it in 1987. His role as the F1 rights holder through his Formula One Management company gave him both power and considerable wealth before he sold it to CVC in 2005.

RACER THEN TEAM CHIEF

Jack Brabham landed three F1 drivers' titles and also set new standards by becoming the first F1 driver to win a grand prix in a car bearing his name. Decades later, Christian Horner also transferred to running race teams after starting off as a racing driver. As a driver, he didn't make it to F1, stopping short in F3000, but many feel that it is Christian's insight into a racer's psyche that has helped him take Red Bull Racing forwards after its transformation from Jaguar Racing, including overseeing Sebastian Vettel's three F1 drivers' titles.

A MODEL PROFESSIONAL

Jackie Stewart achieved far more in F1 than winning 27 grands prix and three World Championships. He pushed for driver safety when it was far from fashionable to do so, his efforts no doubt saving many lives. He also sought a more professional level than his contemporaries and, after a spell commentating for American TV, returned to F1 as a team owner in 1997, in conjunction with older son Paul. Stewart GP won once, at the Nürburgring in 1999, but was sold on to Ford, who rebranded it as Jaguar Racing and it later became Red Bull Racing.

THE FACE OF FERRARI

Aristocrat Luca di Montezemolo was a rally driver, but quit to pursue a business career, as every Agnelli family member was expected to do. His family firm – Fiat – snapped up Ferrari in 1969 and he became Enzo Ferrari's right-hand man in 1973. By 1974, he was running Ferrari's F1 team and titles followed quickly from 1975. By 1977, he was in charge of the entire Fiat group. He ran Italy's hosting of the 1990 FIFA World Cup before taking over Ferrari in 1991 and, recently, he became head of the teams' governing body, Formula One Teams' Association (FOTA).

FERRARI'S FIERCE LITTLE NAPOLEON

Jean Todt was a successful rally co-driver through the 1970s before being given his break in management in 1982 when he was asked to set up Peugeot Talbot Sport. Wins and world titles soon followed through Ari Vatanen, before Peugeot sought success in sports car racing, and got it in 1992. After Peugeot declined to enter F1, Todt joined Ferrari in 1993 and stabilized the team, making it more clinical in its approach. The team won its first constructors' title under Todt's leadership in 1999 and then, in conjunction with Michael Schumacher, won title after title from 2000 until 2004. Todt became FIA president in 2009, replacing Max Mosley.

TYRE MANUFACTURERS

MADE TO LAST

Goodyear is the tyre company with the longest F1 association. Its involvement began in 1959 and finished in 1998 after its tyres had been used in just short of 500 grands prix. Bridgestone edged past Michelin (215 grands prix) in 2009, to become the second most-used tyre, with 244 races by the end of 2010. Both were then passed by Pirelli, which quit at the end of 1991 before coming back in 2011, and moving ahead of rival manufacturer Bridgestone in 2013.

GOODYEAR'S BREAKTHROUGH

F1's most successful tyre supplier, Goodyear, had no clue what lay ahead when it did a deal with Honda in 1965 and driver Richie Ginther guided the combination to its first win in the last round of the World Championship in Mexico City. No one then would have predicted that this famous American tyre manufacturer would go on to become F1's leading supplier, achieving a further 367 wins.

NO TREAD REQUIRED

The tyres used in the World Championship have changed in many ways since 1950, but few changes have been as greats as the arrival of slick tyres in 1971, when tread was dispensed with by Firestone and Goodyear in their quest to provide extra grip. These reigned supreme until 1998 when, to slow the

Above **Yet another good year:** Jacques Villeneuve claimed seven wins for Williams in 1997 as he became Goodyear's 24th and most recent F1 World Champion. *Below* **Made to last:** Bridgestone passed Michelin in 2009 to become F1's second most prolific tyre company. Pirelli has been the sole supplier since 2011.

cars, grooved tyres became obligatory. It wasn't until 2009 that slick tyres returned.

YET ANOTHER GOOD YEAR

Cars fitted with Goodyear tyres have started more grands prix than those fitted with any other tyre brand by a factor of two. Goodyear-shod cars have claimed 24 titles between 1966 and 1997, which is also more than twice the tally of its closest rival, Bridgestone, which has 10 titles.

TYRE MANUFACTURER WITH MOST POLE POSITIONS

1	Goodyear	358
2	Bridgestone	168
3	Pirelli	142
4	Michelin	111
5	Dunlop	76
6	Firestone	49
7	Englebert	12
8	Continental	8

SOME MORE NEW TYRES PLEASE

The record number of pit stops made in a single grand prix is an almost unbelievable 88 for the 24 cars contesting the Hungarian GP at the Hungaroring in 2011. With weather conditions changing almost by the lap, the teams just didn't know what sort of tyres to fit. Jenson Button guessed best and won for McLaren after making three pit visits, which was two fewer than several of his rivals.

THEY SHOOT, THEY SCORE

By sheer weight of numbers, Goodyear scored more World Championship points than any other tyre manufacturer, its tally standing at 9,474.5 when it packed up its tyre trucks for the final time after the 1998 Japanese GP, two races after Michael Schumacher gave the American company its final F1 win at Monza. That tally represents just over 19 points for each grand prix that it attended. Don't forget, this would have been much higher still had the current 25-18-15-12-10-8-6-4-2-1 system been in operation in those years when usually only the top six scored.

Above **They shoot, they score:** The tyre manufacturers have their own paddock area, such as Goodyear's.
Top **Some more new tyres please:** Fernando Alonso kept his pit crew on its toes by pitting four times to change tyres in the 2007 European GP.

 ### FORMULA FARCE

The 2005 US GP at Indianapolis remains the biggest farce in F1 history. Following tyre failure on Ralf Schumacher's Toyota as it went through Turn 13, the only high-speed banked turn on an F1 circuit, during Friday practice, Michelin declared that it couldn't guarantee the safety of the identical tyres that it was supplying for BAR, McLaren, Red Bull, Renault, Sauber and Williams. So, the 14 cars on Michelin tyres peeled into the pits after the formation lap and refused to start, leaving just the six cars with Bridgestone tyres to race.

IN THE BLACK CORNER

The most tyre manufacturers to go head-to-head in a World Championship season is six. This happened in 1958 when Avon, Continental, Dunlop, Englebert, Firestone and Pirelli all sought glory. Dunlop took the most wins.

 ### THERE'S A PATTERN

If you look at the records for the number of starts, pole positions, fastest laps and wins, the order is roughly the same in each. Goodyear is top, usually by a factor of roughly two and a half, which equates to its proportional number of starts, followed by Bridgestone, Pirelli and Michelin. Pirelli's recent run, which started with its return in 2011, has boosted it to third in the rankings for the most poles and fastest laps, as well as tying for fourth with Michelin in the list of most wins.

A CHANGING OF THE GUARD

Tyre manufacturers have come and gone through Formula 1's long history and Bridgestone's spell closed at the end of the 2010 season, with Pirelli returning for 2011 after 20 years away. As it is now the World Championship's sole tyre supplier, the Italian company boosted its tally of wins from 44 race wins to 102.

TYRE MANUFACTURER WITH MOST WINS

1	Goodyear	368
2	Bridgestone	175
3	Pirelli	140
4	Michelin	102
5	Dunlop	83
6	Firestone	38
7	Continental	10
8	Englebert	8

ENGINE MANUFACTURERS

GO, GO, GO!

Believe it or not, F1 cars are not the quickest racing cars in the acceleration stakes, as their exposed wheels make them less aerodynamically efficient than larger-engined competition sports-prototype cars with their enclosing bodywork. However, they still hit 100mph from a standstill in around four seconds and keep on accelerating to 200mph and beyond.

MORE THAN JUST A BADGE

Some road cars bore the legend "turbo" on their boot lids, but the engine performance wasn't vastly different. Not so in F1, after Renault's pioneering years in the late 1970s. As more and more horsepower was produced the arbitrary 1.5-litre equivalency allowed against the 3.0-litre normally aspirated engines soon gave the turbo teams a big advantage and they won race after race. Turbos are back for 2014.

STRAIGHT EIGHT OR IN A VEE?

When F1 began in 1950, the dominant Alfa Romeos were powered by supercharged straight-eight engines, with their rivals using straight-six or even four-cylinder engines. Since then, the V8 engine has been most successful, with 353 grand prix wins, with the more recently popular V10 next on 240 wins.

THE MOST BANGS FOR YOUR BUCK

F1 technical regulations have changed constantly since the World Championship began in 1950 and the most recent engines are not the most powerful. That honour goes to the turbocharged engines when their boost was wound up for qualifying for a burst of one lap. The BMW turbo used by Benetton racers Gerhard Berger and Teo Fabi in 1986 is estimated to have pushed out 1400bhp, rather than the 900bhp without the boost cranked up.

TOP 10 ENGINE MANUFACTURERS WITH MOST STARTS

1	Ferrari	889
2	Ford	607
3	Renault	557
4	Mercedes	397
5	Honda	359
6	BMW	269
7	Alfa Romeo	222
8	BRM	189
9	Mugen Honda	147
10	Hart	128

ENDING UP ON TOP

Renault can be delighted by the 165 grand prix wins achieved by cars carrying its engines, but its ability to develop its engines until they are the best of their age is shown by the fact that Renault-powered cars won the final races of the 3.5-litre formula in 1994, the V10 era in 2005 and the 2.4-litre formula in 2013.

Above **The most bangs for your buck:** Teo Fabi's Benetton enjoyed prodigious BMW turbo horsepower in 1986. *Below* **Spinners can be winners:** Williams racer Ralf Schumacher enjoyed an incredible 19,200rpm from his BMW engine in 2003.

SPINNERS CAN BE WINNERS

BMW took peak revolutions per minute to a new level in 2003 when its V10-format P83 engines revved up to 19,200rpm and pushed out more than 900bhp in the back of Juan Pablo Montoya's and Ralf Schumacher's Williams. Within two years, engine capacity was cut back from 3.0 litres to 2.4 to reduce performance in the name of driver safety.

FERRARI LEADS THE WAY

Ferrari's engines have claimed the most wins (225), set the most pole positions (210), fastest laps (230) and scored the most championship points (6,284.5) up to the end of the 2015 World Championship.

THE PACE OF CHANGE

There is no more more testing arena for technical development than F1, it's not surprising there

have been many developments since the World Championship began. The most visible ones have been to the car, but the engines have changed too (see below).

1950 Cars allowed 4500cc normally aspirated or 1500cc supercharged engines.
1952 Engine capacity restricted to 2000cc or 500cc supercharged engines as F2 rules adopted.
1954 Capacity boosted to 2500cc or 750cc supercharged.
1958 Use of commercial fuel made mandatory.
1961 Supercharged engines

banned and engine size reduced to 1500–1300cc.
1966 Engine capacity enlarged to 3000cc.
1972 Maximum of 12 cylinders imposed.
1987 Engine capacity enlarged to 3500cc.
1989 Turbocharged engines banned.
1995 Reduction of maximum engine capacity to 3000cc.
2006 Engines restricted to eight cylinders and 2400cc.
2014 Engines changed to 1600cc turbocharged V6 hybrids.

TOP 10 ENGINE MANUFACTURERS WITH MOST WINS

1	Ferrari	225
2	Ford	176
3	Renault	168
4	Mercedes	129
5	Honda	72
6	Coventry Climax	40
7	Porsche	26
8	BMW	20
9	BRM	18
10	Alfa Romeo	12

Below **The heartbeat of America:** Ferrari's Luigi Musso races towards the first win for a V8, chased by Stirling Moss's Maserati, in Buenos Aires in 1956. *Bottom* **Ferrari powers top drivers:** Kimi Räikkönen was the most recent Ferrari world champion, when he pipped Lewis Hamilton and Fernando Alonso in 2007.

FERRARI POWERS TOP DRIVERS

Ferrari's prancing horses have powered drivers to the most World Championship titles – 15 in all, between Alberto Ascari in 1952 and Kimi Räikkönen's title in 2007. Ford is next on 13, from 1968 to 1994, with the first 12 of those up to 1982 won with the most successful F1 engine ever: the Ford Cosworth DFV.

THE HEARTBEAT OF AMERICA

The V8 engine is still the heartbeat of America, ticking over through the suburbs in Fords and Chevrolets. However, the first winning V8 in F1 was fitted to Luigi Musso's Lancia Ferrari in the 1956 Argentinian GP. That said, Ford put its name to F1's most successful V8 of all, the Cosworth DFV, which claimed a record 155 F1 wins.

TRACKS

The names of the great grand prix circuits flow off the tongue mellifluously: Monaco, Monza, Spa-Francorchamps, Silverstone and Suzuka. They are temples to high speed and their toughest corners a real challenge to the drivers. Most have been changed out of all recognition in the name of safety, but they all retain the soul that marks them out from the bright new facilities that have yet to earn their spurs.

Below **Up hill and down dale:** *Austria's Red Bull Ring is blessed with wonderful topography over which its circuit layout is draped. This is the view back down the mountain from Turn 2, with the pits in the top right of the shot.*

TRACK LENGTHS

⟫ THE CRUELLEST CUT OF ALL

Once it ran for a full 14.189 miles through the Eifel Forest, the second longest circuit ever in the World Championship, but although the Nürburgring went on to host the German GP on alternate years, its Nordschleife lay-out was dropped by F1 after 1976 and when it next hosted a World Championship round in 1985, it had been hacked back to just 3.199 miles, leaving the forest loop to club racers.

⟫ GOING ROUND AND ROUND

The greatest number of laps in a grand prix was the 110 laps covered by the winning entrants in the US GP at Watkins Glen between 1963 and 1965. This equated to a race distance of 258.5 miles. In 1966, maximum race distances were cut back to 248.5 miles.

⟫ NOT THE BEST OF STARTS

The Monaco street circuit had been hosting races since 1929, but its World Championship debut in 1950 was a near disaster as there was an accident at Tabac at the end of the opening lap after Giuseppe Farina lost control and triggered a shunt that eliminated nine cars. The wreckage was spread across the track, but Juan Manuel Fangio was able to thread his way through and race clear to score his first win for Alfa Romeo.

⟫ WILL IT BE OVER SOON?

Grands prix up to 1957 were run to a target time of three hours, although some went on for even longer. The 1954 German GP held at the 14.167-mile-long Nürburgring Nordschleife holds the record as the longest grand prix in terms of time. It took race winner Juan Manuel Fangio 3 hrs 45 mins 45.8 secs to cover the allotted 22 laps, and he was rewarded with victory by 1 min 36.5 secs.

⟫ JUST FOUR LEFT RUNNING

It seems inconceivable, but two grands prix since 1950 have finished with just four cars still running. Less hard to imagine is that both of these were at Monaco, where the walls can bite. The first occasion was in 1966 when Jackie Stewart won for BRM, albeit with two further finishers not being classified as they were so far behind. The second was 30 years later when Olivier Panis won a wet/dry race for Ligier as others crashed out.

⟫ WORST LINE INTO FIRST CORNER

Irish driver Derek Daly will always be remembered for getting his approach to the first corner, Ste Devote, horribly wrong at the start

Above **The cruellest cut:** A gaggle of midfielders climb the sloping approach to Shell Kurve at the Nürgburgring in 1996 with the Dunlop Kehre in the background. *Below* **Hungaroring:** The circuit's endless twists – this is Turn 2 – keep speeds in check.

TRACKS WITH SHORTEST LAP LENGTHS

1	Monaco	1.954 miles
2	Zeltweg (Austria)	1.988 miles
3	Long Beach (USA)	2.020 miles
4	Dijon-Prenois (France)	2.044 miles
5	Jarama (Spain)	2.058 miles

HUNGARORING

Grand prix years: 1986 onwards

No. of grands prix held: 30

Lap length: From 2.494 miles to 2.466 miles to 2.722 miles

Fastest qualifying lap: 1 min 18.773 secs, Sebastian Vettel (Red Bull), 2010

Fastest race lap: 1 min 19.071 secs, Michael Schumacher (Ferrari), 2004

Driver with most wins: Michael Schumacher – four (1994, 1998, 2001, 2004)

of the 1980 Monaco GP. His Tyrrell clipped Bruno Giacomelli's Alfa Romeo under braking, vaulted clean over it and landed on top of the car in front, that of his teammate Jean-Pierre Jarier. None of the drivers was seriously hurt.

OVER ALMOST BEFORE IT STARTED

||||||||||||||||||||||||||||||||||||||||||

Heavy rain made the Adelaide street circuit almost undriveable at the 1991 Australian GP and it had to be called to a permanent halt after just 24 mins 34.899 secs, with 14 laps (32.858 miles) covered. McLaren's pole-starter Ayrton Senna was the winner from Nigel Mansell's Williams, with Gerhard Berger third in the second McLaren.

>>> ARE YOU GOING VERY FAR SIR?

Discounting the 500-mile Indianapolis 500 that was nominally a round of the World Championship from 1950–60, the longest grand prix in terms of distance was the 1951 French GP at Reims, with its 77 laps equating to 373.912 miles. It's no surprise that Juan Manuel Fangio's Alfa Romeo started to fail, forcing him to take over the sister car that started the race in the hands of Luigi Fagioli. Fangio's winning time was 3 hrs 22 mins 11 secs.

>>> GOING ON AND ON

Almost every F1 fan will tell you that the Nürburgring Nordschleife is the longest ever circuit used by F1, at over 14 miles. But the longest is actually the Pescara circuit on Italy's Adriatic coast, which held a grand prix in 1957. The 15.894-mile lap ran uphill, through villages and over level crossings before returning for a blast along the seafront. Stirling Moss beat Juan Manuel Fangio by more than three minutes.

>>> OVER IN A FLASH

Because the Monza circuit produces such a high average speed, it is usually the shortest race on the F1 calendar in terms of duration. Whereas most modern-day grands prix take around 1 hr 30–40 mins, drivers know that, in the Italian GP, if they don't clash and the safety car doesn't have to be involved they can have their afternoon's work completed in just 1 hr 15 mins.

TRACKS WITH LONGEST LAP LENGTHS

1	Pescara (Italy)	15.894 miles
2	Nürburgring (Germany)	14.189 miles
3	Spa-Francorchamps (Belgium)	8.774 miles
4	Monza (Italy)	6.214 miles
5	Sebring (USA)	5.200 miles

Above **Tracks with longest lap lengths:** Masten Gregory points his Maserati around Pescara's 15.894-mile lap in 1957. *Below* **Over almost before it started:** Ayrton Senna blinds the field with his spray as he leads the soon-to-be-stopped 1991 Australian GP.

LOCATIONS

BANKING ON SUCCESS

Racing on banked oval circuits is the domain of American IndyCar racing, but the World Championship has also taken to the banking, at least in sections of five circuits. These are Monza (using the banked section as part of the lap most years between 1955 and 1961), Avus, Interlagos (Turn 1 on the old layout until 1979), Mexico City (the lightly banked Peraltada) and Indianapolis (using the full oval when the Indy 500 was a World Championship round from 1950–60, then just a section combined with an infield loop from 2000–07).

Above **Banking on success:** Few drivers liked the steep banking at Avus, but Tony Brooks mastered it for Ferrari in 1959. *Below* **How not to finish the first lap:** Cars scatter in all directions at Silverstone in 1973 after Jody Scheckter spun in front of them at the end of the opening lap.

ITALY LEADS THE WAY

As a result of being among the founding group of countries that held grands prix in the World Championship's inaugural year (1950) and having hosted two grands prix per year (the Italian and San Marino) for

several decades, Italy has hosted more grands prix than any other nation. It leads the way (at the end of 2013) with 91, Germany is second with 74 (its tally boosted by hosting the additional European GP for many years), Great Britain is third on 67 and France fourth on 59.

WORTH A GAMBLE

Two F1 former circuits have horse racing connections – Aintree, and Adelaide's street circuit which wrapped around the Victoria Park Racecourse. The Las Vegas, Montreal and Monaco circuits all passed a casino.

HOW NOT TO FINISH THE FIRST LAP

Jody Scheckter was looking to impress when he made his fourth grand prix appearance for McLaren at the 1973 British GP. Starting sixth, he was up to fourth when he ran wide out of Woodcote at the end of the first lap, went on to the grass, then took out a third of the field as he scattered the cars behind. Only 19 of 28 starters were able to take the restart 90 minutes later.

COVERING THE GLOBE

The World Championship is a much more accurate term in the 21st century than it was in the 1950s. Back then, almost all grands prix were held in Europe. Now, with the addition of races in the Middle East, South Korea and India, with Russia debuting in 2014 and Mexico City returning in 2015, European races have recently become the exception rather than the rule.

DOES ANYONE WANT TO FINISH?

A heavy burst of rain that hit the far side of the circuit led to carnage in the 1975 British GP, when car after car aquaplaned off into the catch fencing at Stowe and Club to bring the race to a premature halt. Race leader Emerson Fittipaldi managed to pussyfoot his McLaren through the corners, but Carlos Pace and Jody Scheckter, who were classified second and third, did not, along with 10 others.

SPREADING THE JOY

The global expansion of the World Championship with the introduction of new grands prix has led to the outcome of the championship being decided on new ground. When Sebastian Vettel wrapped up his fourth drivers' title in 2013, he did so at the Indian GP, making India the 20th country to have hosted a title decider and the 10th outside F1's traditional European heartland.

A CHANGE OF TACK

Several circuits that hosted grands prix have disappeared under urban sprawl. Riverside, in California – home to the 1960 US GP – is now under a housing development. The upper reaches of Kyalami (South Africa) are now a part of an industrial estate, while the far end of the Zandvoort circuit in the Netherlands is a complex of holiday chalets in the sand dunes.

EUROPE LEADS THE WAY

Europe has hosted grands prix at 38 circuits. They are: A1-Ring, Aintree, Anderstorp, Avus, Brands Hatch, Bremgarten, Catalunya, Clermont-Ferrand, Dijon-Prenois, Donington Park, Estoril, Hockenheim, Hungaroring, Imola, Jarama, Jerez, Le Mans Bugatti, Magny-Cours, Monaco, Monsanto, Montjuich Park, Monza, Nivelles, Nürburgring, Österreichring, Paul Ricard, Pedralbes, Pescara, Porto, Red Bull Ring, Reims, Rouen-les Essarts, Silverstone, Spa-Francorchamps, Valencia, Zandvoort, Zeltweg and Zolder.

NUMBER OF F1 CIRCUITS BY CONTINENT

1	Europe	37
2	North/Central America	14
3	Asia	12
4	Africa	3
=	South America	3
6	Australasia	2

ASIA MAKES IT A DOZEN

It took until 1976 for Asia to host a grand prix, when F1 visited Fuji. Suzuka was Asia's next venue, in 1987, and races have followed in Malaysia, Bahrain, China, Turkey, Singapore, Abu Dhabi, Korea and India. The 2014 Russian GP at Sochi brought the continent's tally up to 12, third behind Europe and North America.

HOTSPOT LOCATIONS

Three F1 circuits have volcanic connections: Fuji Speedway in Japan is situated on the side slopes of Mount Fuji; France's Clermont-Ferrand is built among volcanic outcrops; and the Mexico City circuit is actually located in a volcanic basin, along with the rest of the city.

Above **Covering the globe:** The Sochi Autodrom on Russia's Black Sea coast hosted its fist formula One GP in 2014. *Below* **Suzuka:** The Casio Triangle.

SUZUKA

Grand prix years: 1987-2006, 2009 onwards

No. of grands prix held: 27

Lap length: From 3.641 miles to 3.644 miles to current 3.609 miles

Fastest qualifying lap: 1 min 29.599 secs, Felipe Massa (Ferrari), 2006

Fastest race lap: 1 min 31.540 secs, Kimi Raikkonen (McLaren), 2005

Driver with most wins: Michael Schumacher – six (1995, 1997, 2000, 2001, 2002, 2004)

LAP RECORDS

RED-HOT RUBENS

||||||||||||||||||||||||||||||||||

Qualifying inevitably produces the fastest laps of a grand prix meeting. These laps are often set with special rubber or next to no fuel on board, and the fastest ever of these was set at Monza by the Brazilian Rubens Barrichello in his Ferrari as he secured pole for the 2004 Italian GP in front of the *Tifosi*. His pole time was 1 min 20.089 secs, equating to 161.802mph.

FAST, FASTER, FASTEST

Monza and Spa-Francorchamps used to vie for the fastest average race-winning speed – a mind-boggling 150mph. Then chicanes were inserted. But the cars kept getting faster and faster and the winning average speed for Michael Schumacher's Ferrari in the 2003 Italian GP at Monza was 153.842mph. The fastest Spa average dates back to 1970 on the old circuit, when Pedro Rodriguez lapped his BRM in a race-winning average of 149.942mph.

MONZA, THE FASTEST OF THEM ALL

The home of the Italian GP, Monza, remains the circuit with the highest race lap speed recorded – 159.909mph set in 2004. Those circuits ranked behind Monza in terms of lap speed are: Silverstone, Spa-Francorchamps, the Österreichring, Hockenheim, Avus, Suzuka, A1-Ring, Reims and Melbourne. Of these, only Monza, Suzuka and Melbourne have a similar track configuration to when these fastest laps were set.

GET A MOVE ON

Not all circuits produce average lap speeds that are double what you'd normally travel at in the fast lane of a motorway. The tight confines of Monaco limit drivers to average speeds in double rather than treble figures, as do many of the other street circuits used, notably in the USA. However, the slowest fastest lap in a grand prix was set by Juan Manuel Fangio at Monaco in 1950, at 64.085mph. Detroit's track is second on this list.

A DOUBLE DISASTER

The 1960 Belgian GP at Spa-Francorchamps had already bared its teeth before the race; Stirling Moss broke his legs in practice and Mike Taylor received considerable injuries in another crash. Worse was to follow in the race as first Chris Bristow crashed to his death while dicing with Willy Mairesse at Burnenville, then five laps later Alan Stacey was hit in the face by a bird and was killed by the resulting crash.

Below **Get a move on:** A narrow track littered with hairpins slows drivers at Monaco, as shown by Juan Manuel Fangio in 1950 as he recorded the slowest ever fastest lap. *Bottom* **Red-hot Rubens:** Barrichello has the pedal to the metal as he streaks around Monza for a record lap of 161.802mph.

A MEDAL FOR BRAVERY

Gilles Villeneuve famously spun at almost every corner in practice at his first grand prix, at Silverstone in 1977. This was his way of finding the maximum. Always wanting to run right on the ragged edge, he put on a masterclass of driving in the wet in practice at the 1979 US GP when he went out and lapped all but 10 secs faster than anyone else. As it was only practice it counted for nothing, but it certainly laid down a marker.

MIND THE WALLS

Street circuits are almost invariably a bit "point-and-squirt", with tight turns surrounded by walls or barriers rather than fast, open sweeps. However, the Valencia circuit, which has hosted the European GP since 2008, breaks the mould with a more open layout and has an appreciable straight. This resulted in a lap record of 122.837mph, set by Toyota racer Timo Glock in 2009.

ALMOST ALL STRAIGHTS

The Avus circuit in Berlin had a remarkably simple layout. It was an up-and-down dual carriageway, with a corner at its southern end that made its shape look like a hairclip and at the northern end there was a high, banked corner. These were its only features. As a result, lap speeds were high, with Tony Brooks's winning average speed for Ferrari being 143.342mph all the way back in 1959.

LOOKING FOR SPEED

When the Silverstone circuit was reshaped for 2010 and beyond, as part of its modernization project, there was talk that its average lap speed would soar. However, such headlines had to be forgotten when the new Arena infield section failed to boost average lap speeds. Indeed, Fernando Alonso's fastest race lap equated to 145.011mph, falling short of the 146.059mph lap average that Michael Schumacher set on the previous layout in his Ferrari F2004 back in 2004.

Official fastest laps are recorded during the race only and are exceeded almost always by single, flying laps in qualifying, when the tyres are fresh and the fuel load often optimum. For 19 years, the fastest ever lap in qualifying was set by Keke Rosberg when he lapped Silverstone in his Williams at 160.925mph in 1985. Rubens Barrichello driving a Ferrari at Monza in 2004 beat it by just under 1mph.

Above **Fastest of the fast:** Keke Rosberg took his Williams to a new level when he took pole for the 1985 British GP with a lap at 160.925mph. *Below* **Barcelona:** The downhill run past the pits.

TOP 10 CIRCUITS WITH FASTEST LAP RECORDS

	Circuit	Avg. speed
1	Monza	159.909mph
2	Silverstone	153.053mph
3	Spa-Francorchamps	152.049mph
4	Österreichring	150.509mph
5	Hockenheim	150.059mph
6	Avus	149.129mph
7	Suzuka	141.904mph
8	A1-Ring	141.606mph
9	Reims	141.424mph
10	Melbourne	141.009mph

BARCELONA

Grand prix years: 1991 onwards

No. of grands prix held: 25
2.875 miles to current 2.892 miles

Fastest qualifying lap: 1 min 19.995 secs, Mark Webber (Red Bull), 2010

Fastest race lap: 1 min 21.670 secs, Kimi Raikkonen (Ferrari), 2008

Driver with most wins: Michael Schumacher – six (1995, 1996, 2001, 2002, 2003, 2004)

VICTORY ROLLS

HOME SWEET HOME

If you are going to set the record for the most wins in a particular country's grand prix by drivers from a particular nation, then you may as well do it at home. This is what British drivers have managed, winning the British GP 21 times, first with Stirling Moss at Aintree for Mercedes in 1955 and most recently with Lewis Hamilton for McLaren in 2008.

ALL BUT A FEW

British teams have won more races than teams based in other countries, in every country that the World Championship has visited since 1950 bar one. This is Switzerland, where Alfa Romeo and Ferrari both won two of the five grands prix held at Bremgarten and Mercedes-Benz the other.

Below **Buenos Aires:** Coulthard and Hakkinen lead the field in F1's last visit to Argentina. *Right* **Ferrari's Monza magic:** The *Tifosi* celebrates a Ferrari one-two at Monza in 2004.

THAT SPECIAL RELATIONSHIP

British drivers grew to love their forays across the Atlantic to the US GP not only because they spoke the same language and the largest winner's cheque of the year was up for grabs, but because they enjoyed remarkable success. There was a run of nine straight US wins for British drivers between Stirling Moss's triumph in 1960 and Jackie Stewart's in 1968.

STREETS AHEAD

British teams experienced significant success in Monaco in the 1950s, 60s and 70s. Sure, there was extra work for the mechanics as they repaired the damage from brushes with the barriers and worn gearboxes had to be changed, but the drivers tended to come up trumps, winning there 16 times in a row from Maurice Trintignant's win in Rob Walker's Cooper in 1958 to Ronnie Peterson's victory for Lotus in 1974.

GIMME FIVE

Ferrari and McLaren have claimed five wins in succession in a particular grand prix. The British team achieved this first, winning the Belgian GP at Spa-Francorchamps each year from 1987 to 1991, with a win for Alain Prost followed by four for Ayrton Senna. Ferrari took its sequence in the Japanese GP at Suzuka between 2000 and 2004, with four going to Michael Schumacher, and one to Rubens Barrichello in 2003.

FERRARI'S MONZA MAGIC

The Italian GP is one of the originals and it is here above all other venues that Ferrari wants to win, right in front of its fans (the *Tifosi*). The team, whose scarlet cars bear the famous prancing horse emblem, has done just that on 18 occasions, from Alberto Ascari's victory in 1951 to Fernando Alonso's in 2010.

HIGH FIVE

Ayrton Senna rose to the challenge of the Monte Carlo street circuit like no other driver and won there five times in a row for McLaren from 1989 to 1993. He also won there for Lotus in 1987. He led the first 66 laps in 1988 before crashing out with 12 laps to go, and if things had turned out differently that day his run at Monaco would have been a predominant seven. Jim Clark (twice), Juan Manuel Fangio and Michael Schumacher (twice) have all won a particular grand prix four times in a row.

BUENOS AIRES

Grand prix years: 1953-1958, 1960, 1972-1975, 1995-1998

No. of grands prix held: 20

Lap length: From 2.431 miles to 3.708 miles to 2.646 miles

Fastest qualifying lap: 1 min 24.473 secs, Jacques Villeneuve (Williams), 1997

Fastest race lap: 1 min 27.981 secs, Gerhard Berger (Benetton), 1997

Driver with most wins: Juan Manuel Fangio – four (1954, 1955, 1967, 1957)

TOP 10 TEAMS WITH MOST WINS AT ONE CIRCUIT

1	18	Ferrari	Monza
2	15	McLaren	Monaco
3	14	Ferrari	Nürburgring
4	13	Ferrari	Silverstone
5	12	Ferrari	Spa-Francorchamps
=	12	McLaren	Silverstone
7	11	Ferrari	Hockenheim
=	11	McLaren	Hungaroring
9	10	Ferrari	Montreal
10	9	Williams	Hockenheim

⫸ FOUR STARTS, THREE WINS

Alfa Romeo all but swept the board in the first two years of Formula 1 before it quit and Ferrari came on strong in 1952. As a result of this, it was Ferrari that collected records through the 1950s and Ferrari that became the first team to win three times at any circuit, doing so at Silverstone in 1954.

Above **The most dangerous place to race:** Niki Lauda was lucky to survive this fiery crash in 1976. *Right* **Achieving across the board:** Michael Schumacher celebrates his first win, at Spa in 1992. *Below* **Rolling the dice:** Ayrton Senna races to his sixth and final win around the streets of Monaco in 1993. This was his fifth in succession there for McLaren.

THE MOST DANGEROUS PLACE TO RACE

The Nürburgring Nordschleife had the reputation as the sport's most deadly circuit, as it claimed the lives of seven F1 drivers: Onofre Marimon in practice in 1954, Erwin Bauer in a sports car race in 1958, Peter Collins in the 1958 grand prix, Carel Godin de Beaufort in practice in 1964, John Taylor in 1966, Georges Berger in an endurance race in 1967 and Gerhard Mitter in practice in 1969. Niki Lauda was almost added to that list in 1976.

⫸ ACHIEVING ACROSS THE BOARD

Michael Schumacher, the setter of so many records, proved his versatility by winning at 22 circuits. They were, in the order he conquered them: Spa-Francorchamps, Estoril, Interlagos, TI Circuit, Imola, Monaco, Montreal, Magny-Cours, the Hungaroring, Jerez, Barcelona, Hockenheim, the Nürburgring, Suzuka, Monza, Buenos Aires, Silverstone, Melbourne, Indianapolis, Sepang, the A1-Ring and Bahrain.

ROLLING THE DICE

Monaco is famed both for its grand prix and its casino, as well as the all-enclosing barriers which mean that there's more than a little luck involved in winning there. However, McLaren, a team that is too organized to factor in luck, has clearly found the winning formula as it holds the record for the most consecutive wins at a circuit, six, and did so at Monaco of all places thanks to Alain Prost in 1988 then Ayrton Senna each year through to 1993.

NUMBER OF RACES HELD

BEFORE FANS HAD PROTECTION

F1 spectators sometimes complain that they are kept back from the action, but there is a very good reason for this – their safety. In 1961 there was little protection for them and certainly no chain-link fencing. Had there been, then 14 fans at Monza probably wouldn't have died after Jim Clark and Wolfgang von Trips touched and von Trips's Ferrari was sent cart-wheeling into the crowd, killing the German aristocrat as well.

MORE AND EVER MORE

The trend for the number of grands prix in each World Championship is on the up, as 2012 had the most grands prix, 20, and the 2016 calendar contained 21 grands prix. The average number of grand prix in the 1950s (excluding the Indianapolis 500 that was part of the World Championship) was 7.4, it was 9.9 in the 1960s, 14.4 in the 1970s, 15.6 in the 1980s, 16.2 in the 1990s and 17.4 in the 2000s.

BUSY, BUSY

The 2012 World Championship was the first season to have 20 grands prix. It ran for 36 weeks, from mid-March to mid-November. This total was passed in 2016, as the German GP at Hockenheim returned and there was a new European GP at Baku, Azerbaijan. This 21-race campaign spanned 37 weeks from 20 March to 27 November. Fortunately for team personnel, the FIA leaves a month's gap in August so that they can have a holiday.

HONOUR OF OPENING THE SEASON

Australia holds record for hosting the most opening grands prix of the season, having done so on 17 occasions at Melbourne's Albert Park. Second is Buenos Aires in Argentina, which has hosted 15 openers. South Africa's Kyalami circuit is the third most popular place to kick off the action, having held the opening race eight times.

SOMETHING ON THE SIDE

The World Championship was augmented by non-championship races in the early years, with the six championship grands prix in 1950 supported by 16 non-championship events in which the drivers raced for prize money. Juan Manuel Fangio won four of them.

VARIETY APLENTY

The Long Beach street circuit in California has been used just eight times as a second US GP, but its tricky, bumpy course is one that no individual driver conquered as pole position went to a different driver each time, from Clay Regazzoni in 1976 to Patrick Tambay in 1983, both driving for Ferrari.

TOP 10 MOST-USED CIRCUITS

1	Monza	65
2	Monaco	62
3	Silverstone	49
4	Spa-Francorchamps	48
5	Nürburgring	40
6	Montreal	36
7	Hockenheim	34
8	Interlagos	33
9	Hungaroring	30
=	Zandvoort	30

Above **Busy, busy:** Nico Hulkenberg kept his best for last in 2012, shining in the season-ending Brazilian GP. *Below* **Doubling up:** Michael Schumacher is greeted by a fan after winning the 2006 San Marino GP at Imola.

DOUBLING UP

Italy is the country that has hosted the most grands prix since the World Championship began in 1950. It has outstripped Great Britain, Monaco and Belgium, all of which hosted races in 1950 and are still doing so in 2013, because it held a second race each year at Imola from 1981 to 2006 under the nominal title of the San Marino GP. By the end of 2013, Italy had hosted 90 grands prix, 16 ahead of Germany, which has hosted the European GP 12 times and the Luxembourg GP twice to boost its tally to 74.

A CLASH WITH TRAGIC CONSEQUENCES

|||||||||||||||||||||||||||||||

Ronnie Peterson was a driver admired around the world for his spectacular style. Sadly, he was not to survive the 1978 Italian GP as his Lotus was caught up in a shunt as the cars accelerated away from the start, with 10 cars left battered and Peterson's on fire. Vittorio Brambilla was knocked out and Peterson had to be taken to hospital with leg injuries. He died during the night.

⟫⟫⟫ AND SO TO BED

Countries fight over who will hold the final grand prix of the year as this more often than not has the added drama of being the title battle decider. Brazil and Abu Dhabi have hosted it most of late, but the USA edges Australia overall, 12 to 11, with Sebring, Riverside, Watkins Glen and the Caesar's Palace circuit in Las Vegas all having brought the curtain down on the season. Australia's closers were all held on the Adelaide street circuit.

Below **Kyalami:** The drop then climb from the start to Sunset bend. *Bottom* **A clash with tragic consequences:** The aftermath of the first-lap accident at Monza in 1978, with Ronnie Peterson's Lotus (6) on the left.

KYALAMI

Grand prix years: 1967-1980, 1982-1985, 1992-1993

No. of grands prix held: 20

Lap length: From 2.544 miles to 2.550 miles to 2.648 miles

Fastest qualifying lap: 1 min 15.486 secs, Nigel Mansell (Williams), 1992

Fastest race lap: 1 min 17.578 secs, Nigel Mansell (Williams), 1992

Driver with most wins: Niki Lauda – three (1976, 1977, 1984)

HIGHEST AND LOWEST SPEEDS

CIRCUIT BOUND

David Coulthard was something of an expert at getting cars to fly in a low downforce setting when he raced for McLaren, as he proved when he recorded F1's fastest speed-trap figure of 224.8mph at Monza in 1999. This exceeded the previous record of 221.5mph that he'd set just a year earlier in practice for the German GP at Hockenheim. (This was when the Hockenheim layout had a long loop through the forest before it was cut back.)

TAKING IT TO EXTREMES

Honda Racing decided to show what its F1 car could do if it was given every opportunity to go for the max, not constrained by the limits of circuits. In 2006, test driver Alan van der Merwe drove its RA106 on the Bonneville salt flats and clocked a top speed of 246.908mph on an early morning run over the flying mile, making it the fastest F1 car ever, but falling just short of its 248.5mph (400kph) target.

SURPRISE, SURPRISE

One glance at the tight layout of the Monte Carlo street circuit and it comes as no surprise that it's the slowest circuit used by F1. Its first World Championship grand prix in 1950 was won by Juan Manuel Fangio in his

Alfa Romeo, doing an average speed of just 61.331mph. There have been circuit modifications since, but not appreciable ones, yet the highest winning average rose to 96.655mph when Fernando Alonso won for McLaren in 2007.

Below **Taking it to extremes:** Alan van der Merwe took a 2006 Honda to the Bonneville Salt Flats and hit 246mph. *Bottom* **Circuit bound:** With wings angled as far back as possible on his McLaren, David Coulthard goes for broke at Monza in 1999.

STOP AT THE RED LIGHT

The highest speed recorded on a street circuit by an F1 car was in 2012 during the fifth race on the Valencia circuit around the Spanish city's dock. Seven-time World Champion Michael Schumacher clocked 199.149mph at the end of the back straight just before the sharp righthander at Turn 12 in his Mercedes F1 W03.

IT NEVER HAPPENED

Having spent his childhood in his family home overlooking Interlagos, Rubens Barrichello always dreamt that one day he would stand on top of the podium there as winner of the Brazilian GP. However, he seemed to be "cursed" at his home race and, by the end of 2009, had a best result of only third, despite having led the race in 1999, 2000, 2002, 2003, 2004 and 2009.

TOP 10 HIGHEST SPEEDS IN 2015

1	Mexico City	226.365mph
2	Monza	220.337mph
3	Montreal	211.576mph
4	Interlagos	211.328mph
5	Yas Marina	210.085mph
6	Sakhir	208.656mph
7	Shanghai	207.910mph
8	Sochi	207.786mph
9	Barcelona	207.724mph
10	Melbourne	204.431mph

All figures recorded at speed trap.

FASTER IN THE WET

So slow were the grands prix around the streets of Monaco in the 1950s that the average speeds were never faster than 70mph, and thus lower even than the average speed for race winner Ayrton Senna in the rain-hit 1991 Australian GP at Adelaide. However, the washed-out and interrupted 2011 Canadian GP set a new record, with Jenson Button setting an average of 46.518mph.

MIKEY LIKES IT

Interlagos is a circuit that provides more than its share of race incidents, which is why it isn't one of those circuits where one driver has managed to produce a string of wins. Ayrton Senna managed to win only twice here, but Michael Schumacher kept out of trouble at the tricky first corner enough to win four times, in 1994, 1995, 2000 and 2002.

FOR THE FANS

Interlagos has a proud boast of being a good track for Brazil's F1 stars, as both Emerson Fittipaldi and Carlos Pace won there during the circuit's first spell of hosting the Brazilian GP in the 1970s, sending the partisan crowd home happy. Ayrton Senna and Felipe Massa have won there since it took over the race again from Rio de Janeiro's Jacarepagua circuit in 1990, but Rubens Barrichello was never able to manage a victory.

Above **Still waiting:** Rubens Barrichello has done everything but win at his home circuit, Interlagos, even after starting from pole position in 2009. *Below* **Melbourne:** Aerial shot of Albert Park with its attractive lakeside setting. *Right* **Show us the numbers:** The spectacular Yas Marina, Abu Dhabi, circuit might see drivers exceed 200mph on its long straight. Here, in 2009, Lewis Hamilton leads Sebastian Vettel.

SHOW US THE NUMBERS

Arab petrolheads love performance cars and F1 too, but enticing them to watch it in the flesh has proved a problem, with Bahrain failing to draw in large crowds for its grand prix. Perhaps with this in mind, Abu Dhabi's incredible Yas Marina circuit was built with a straight that could produce speeds of almost 200mph, the sort of figure that really impresses car nuts and hopefully encourages them to turn up rather than watch it on TV.

MELBOURNE

Grand prix years: 1996 onwards

No. of grands prix held: 20

Lap length: 3.295 miles

Fastest qualifying lap: 1 min 23.919 secs, Sebastian Vettel (Red Bull), 2010

Fastest race lap: 1 min 24.125 secs, Michael Schumacher (Ferrari), 2004

Driver with most wins: Michael Schumacher – four (2000, 2001, 2002, 2004)

PART 2

LEGENDARY DRIVERS

To top the all-time tables in Formula One a driver has to race for the right team at the right time. However, to appreciate the merits of the greatest drivers from the early decades of the World Championship, one has to consider that they contested fewer than half the number of races each year and, sadly, often failed to live long enough to gather as many scalps as today's best drivers. Dig a little deeper and it is clear that the brilliance of early champions Alberto Ascari, Juan Manuel Fangio and Jim Clark easily stands comparison with multiple-winners Ayrton Senna, Alain Prost, Michael Schumacher or Sebastian Vettel.

Below **Championship contenders:** *Fernando Alonso, Sebastian Vettel and Lewis Hamilton have enjoyed a healthy share of podium visits, having secured eight F1 drivers' titles between them by the end of the 2014 season.*

MICHAEL SCHUMACHER

Michael Schumacher had been in F1 for a year before his first grand prix win. Then the victories kept rolling in. Over the next decade, he won seven world titles - two for Benetton, five for Ferrari - so it's no surprise that he is at the top of almost every list of statistics, but sadly his retirement has been ruined by a head injury suffered when skiing in 2013.

Below **Winning for Ferrari:** *When Michael Schumacher won the Japanese GP at Suzuka for Ferrari in 2000 his normal podium delight was taken to a new level as it gave him the first of his five world titles with Ferrari.*

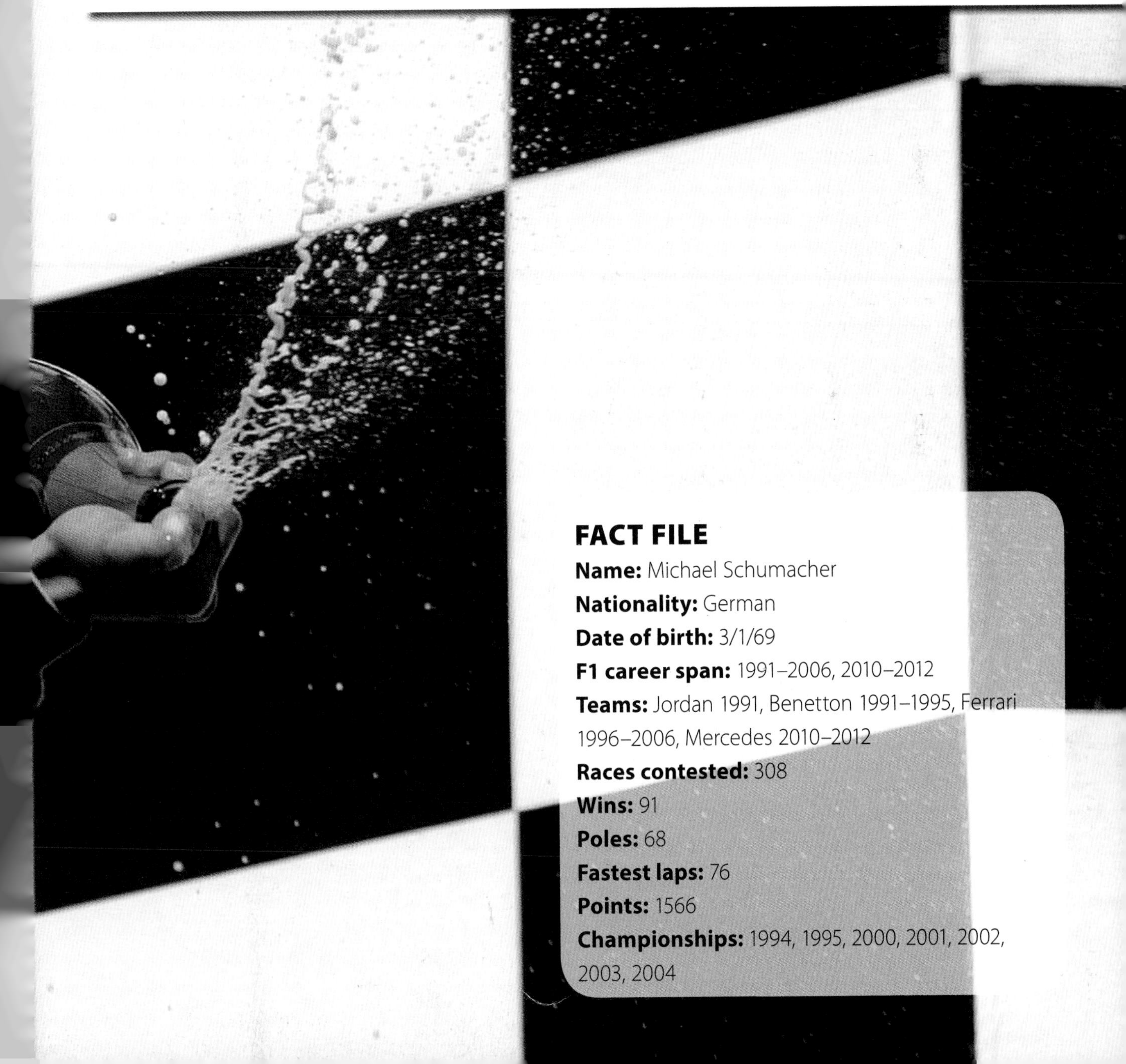

FACT FILE

Name: Michael Schumacher
Nationality: German
Date of birth: 3/1/69
F1 career span: 1991–2006, 2010–2012
Teams: Jordan 1991, Benetton 1991–1995, Ferrari 1996–2006, Mercedes 2010–2012
Races contested: 308
Wins: 91
Poles: 68
Fastest laps: 76
Points: 1566
Championships: 1994, 1995, 2000, 2001, 2002, 2003, 2004

A HAPPY ANNIVERARY

|||||||||||||||||||||||||||||||||||||

Michael's first win came at his 18th start, on the anniversary of his debut, at the 1992 Belgian GP. After qualifying his Benetton third behind Nigel Mansell and Ayrton Senna, he enjoyed three slices of luck. Senna's gamble to start on slicks on a damp track backfired. Mansell's engine lost power. Finally, he slid off the circuit and rejoined behind team-mate Martin Brundle, noticed his tyres were blistering and changed his own at the optimum moment.

CAREER STATS

Year	Team	Races	Wins	Points	Ranking
1991	Jordan & Benetton	6	0	4	12th
1992	Benetton	16	1	53	3rd
1993	Benetton	16	1	52	4th
1994	Benetton	14	8	92	1st
1995	Benetton	17	9	102	1st
1996	Ferrari	16	3	59	3rd
1997	Ferrari	17	5	78	Not placed*
1998	Ferrari	16	6	86	2nd
1999	Ferrari	10	2	44	5th
2000	Ferrari	17	9	108	1st
2001	Ferrari	17	9	123	1st
2002	Ferrari	17	11	144	1st
2003	Ferrari	16	6	93	1st
2004	Ferrari	18	13	148	1st
2005	Ferrari	19	1	62	3rd
2006	Ferrari	18	7	121	2nd
2010	Mercedes	19	0	72	9th
2011	Mercedes	19	0	76	8th
2012	Mercedes	20	0	49	13th

* Removed from championship ranking for driving into Jacques Villeneuve in the final round at Jerez

MAKING AN IMPRESSION

Michael gained his F1 break during 1991 when Jordan driver Bertrand Gachot was jailed for assaulting a taxi driver. He outpaced team-mate Andrea de Cesaris to qualify seventh for the Belgian GP, but burnt out his clutch at the start. By the next race, he had been snapped up by Benetton.

Right **Making an Impression:** Michael was on the pace on his F1 debut for Jordan in Belgium, but his race was a short one.
Below **A Happy Anniverary:** One year on from his debut at Spa-Francorchamps, now driving for Benetton, Michael raced to his first victory there in 1992.

A YEAR OF CONTROVERSY

With wins in the first three races of 1994, and the death of chief rival Ayrton Senna, it was clear that Michael was heading for his first F1 title. Damon Hill stepped up for Williams and challenged him, but the matter was settled at the final round in Adelaide when Michael swerved his damaged car into Hill's Williams, after a year that had already seen Schumacher's disqualification from the British and Belgian GPs and a subsequent two-race suspension.

KART BLANCHE

Michael was given the flying start of which other aspiring racers can only dream. His father Rolf ran a kart circuit, so Michael spent all his spare time during his childhood in Kerpen behind the wheel.

WHO NEEDS FULL POWER?

Perhaps Michael's greatest race performance came at the 1996 Spanish GP. This was in his first year with Ferrari, coming off the back of two consecutive title-winning seasons with Benetton, and the team was at a low ebb. However, Michael produced an extraordinary drive at a very wet Circuit de Catalunya. His Ferrari dropped onto only nine of its 10 cylinders at mid-distance, but he was still able to press on at scarcely abated speed for his first win for Ferrari.

13 IS UNLUCKY FOR OTHERS

Michael's illustrious career was never better than when taking the most recent of his seven world titles. This was in 2004 when he claimed his fifth title in succession for Ferrari with the remarkable tally of 13 wins from the season's 18 grands prix. No other driver has ever matched such an impressive tally. Having won the first five races and then clashed with Juan Pablo Montoya at Monaco, he duly won the next seven.

MAKE IT TWO SCHUMACHERS

Racing alongside one's brother is a rare thing, but Michael and Ralf Schumacher were pitched together in F1 from 1997 to 2006. In this time, they established the most joint podium finishes for a pair of brothers, managing it 16 times. In that time, Ralf finished ahead of Michael just three times, in Canada in 2001, Malaysia in 2002 and France in 2003.

IN FRONT AT LAST

It was only the pace of the Williams drivers that kept Michael Schumacher from pole position in 1992 and 1993, but he finally claimed his first pole position in the 1994 Monaco GP, the fourth race of the season and the one after which that arch pole qualifier Ayrton Senna had died at the San Marino GP. Michael would go on to score 67 more before he took his sabbatical from F1 at the end of 2006, but none since his return in 2010.

Right **Seven in Succession:** Michael celebrates scoring seven grand prix victories in a row to put him on the cusp of landing his seventh world title. *Above* **In Front at Last:** Monaco yielded the first pole position of Michael's F1 career, for Benetton in 1994, and the 2006 French GP for Ferrari the last.

SEVEN IN SUCCESSION

Michael and Ferrari were simply dominant in 2004 in a manner seldom seen in F1, save for Alberto Ascari in 1952/53, Jim Clark in 1963 and 1965 plus Nigel Mansell in 1992. If 2002 was a great season for Michael, then 2004 was even better and in it he achieved his greatest winning sequence, being first to the chequered flag at the European, Canadian, US, French, British, German and Hungarian GPs. He then wrapped up his seventh title next time out.

ALAIN PROST

Alain Prost was extremely fast but seldom looked it as he wasn't flamboyant. It was the way that he used his head to drive supremely tactical races that earned him the sobriquet "Le Professeur". This cerebral driving style guided him to his four world drivers' titles for McLaren and then Williams.

Below **Finishing off with Williams:** Alain rounded out his illustrious career in 1993 by claiming his fourth title with Williams thanks to wins like this one at the German GP at Hockenheim which proved to be his last.

FACT FILE

Name: Alain Prost

Nationality: French

Date of birth: 24/2/55

F1 career span: 1980–1991 & 1993

Teams: McLaren 1980, Renault 1981–83, McLaren 1984–89, Ferrari 1990–91, Williams 1993

Races contested: 200

Wins: 51

Poles: 33

Fastest laps: 41

Points: 798.5

Championships: 1985, 1986, 1989, 1993

SOCCER GETS THE BOOT

Alain had other sporting pretensions before he settled on a racing. He was a handy football player, good enough to be given trials, but after trying karting when he was on holiday aged 14 he made up his mind on the matter.

FIRST PAST 50

Alain now has only marginally more than half of Michael Schumacher's career tally of 91 wins, but he was once clear at the top of the list of winners. His victory in the 1993 British GP made him the first driver to score 50. Alain added one more to that tally at the next race at Hockenheim, but this proved to be his last as his Williams team-mate Damon Hill came on strong and won three of the remaining six grands prix.

CAREER STATS

Year	Team	Races	Wins	Points	Ranking
1980	McLaren	11	0	5	15th
1981	Renault	15	3	43	5th
1982	Renault	16	2	34	4th
1983	Renault	15	4	57	2nd
1984	McLaren	16	7	71.5	2nd
1985	McLaren	16	5	76	1st
1986	McLaren	16	4	74	1st
1987	McLaren	16	3	46	4th
1988	McLaren	16	7	95	2nd
1989	McLaren	16	4	81	1st
1990	Ferrari	16	5	73	2nd
1991	Ferrari	15	0	31	5th
1993	Williams	16	7	99	1st

STEPPING UP IN STYLE

Back in the days when outstanding Formula 3 drivers could leap direct to F1, Alain Prost demonstrated that the skills that landed him the 1979 European F3 crown were more than good enough for F1. On his debut in the 1980 Argentinian GP, Alain qualified his McLaren midgrid and advanced from there to sixth place. When he finished fifth next time out, Prost emphasised the talents that would land him four world titles.

FALLING AT THE LAST

Renault was so confident that Alain would clinch the title in 1983 that the manufacturer flew out plane loads of journalists to South Africa to cover the occasion. Alain held a two-point lead over Nelson Piquet but wasn't confident as he felt Brabham was still pushing on with its development. Piquet vaulted from second into the lead at the start and Alain could run only fourth, which wasn't going to be enough. When he felt his turbo start to fail, Alain quit the race.

Below **First Past 50:** Alain's victory for Williams at Silverstone in 1993 made him the first to top 50 grand prix wins.

Above **Fresh start:** Alain's win for Williams at Hockenheim in 1993 helped him to claim a fourth world title. *Left* **Alain's arrival:** The first of Alain's 51 grand prix wins came in 1981, at his home grand prix.

THE CLOSEST MISS

After quitting Renault at the end of 1983, Alain had a fruitful year with McLaren in 1984, starting with victory first time out at the Brazilian GP (above). After adding wins at Imola, Hockenheim, Zandvoort and the Nürburgring, Alain went to the final round at Estoril just 3.5 points down on team-mate Niki Lauda. Alain did all he could, passing Nelson Piquet for the lead. However, Lauda gained second place when Nigel Mansell spun out and that was enough to clinch the title by half a point.

SCORING TO THE VERY END

When Alain Prost came home second behind Ayrton Senna in his final race, the 1993 Australian GP at Adelaide, he cemented his position as the scorer of the highest tally of points, reaching 798.5 points, a total that Michael Schumacher passed in the final round of 2001. Michael went on to score 1,369 points before boosting that to 1,566 after his return with Mercedes. This has since been exceeded by Fernando Alonso (1,767) and Sebastian Vettel (1,618).

FINISHING THE JOB

Having been runner-up in 1983 and 1984, Alain was desperate to go one better in 1985, his second year with McLaren. And so he did, thanks to a good mid-season run of results. By the time he reached Brands Hatch for the European GP, Alain was in touching distance. An evasive move at the start of the race dropped him to 14th and it took a solid run to fourth to end the title bid of closest challenger Michele Alboreto whose Ferrari's turbo failed.

FRESH FROM A YEAR OUT

After quitting F1 in 1991 after two years with Ferrari, Alain came back from his year's sabbatical to prove his ability yet again, this time with Williams. The car was very much the class of the field in 1993. Alain claimed seven wins (equalling his record haul for a season as recorded in 1984 and 1988) to land his fourth title, wrapping it up with second place at the Portuguese GP at Estoril.

ALAIN'S ARRIVAL

Impressed by his maiden season with McLaren, Renault snapped Alain up for 1981. He was soon proving that he was the best French driver of his generation by claiming his first podium, coming third in the third round in Argentina. Alain went better still at his home grand prix at Dijon-Prenois (right) by not only setting his first fastest lap but going on to secure his first win, heading home John Watson in a race interrupted by a downpour.

AYRTON SENNA

The late Ayrton Senna was a driver who polarized opinions. He was supremely fast but spoiled that, for some, by his 'win at all costs' approach. No-one, though, could deny his presence and unswerving focus. His career with McLaren was synonymous with winning but shortly after a move to Williams his life came to a sudden end at Imola.

Below **Natural winner:** *Ayrton celebrates his final win for McLaren after being first to the chequered flag at Adelaide in 1993.*

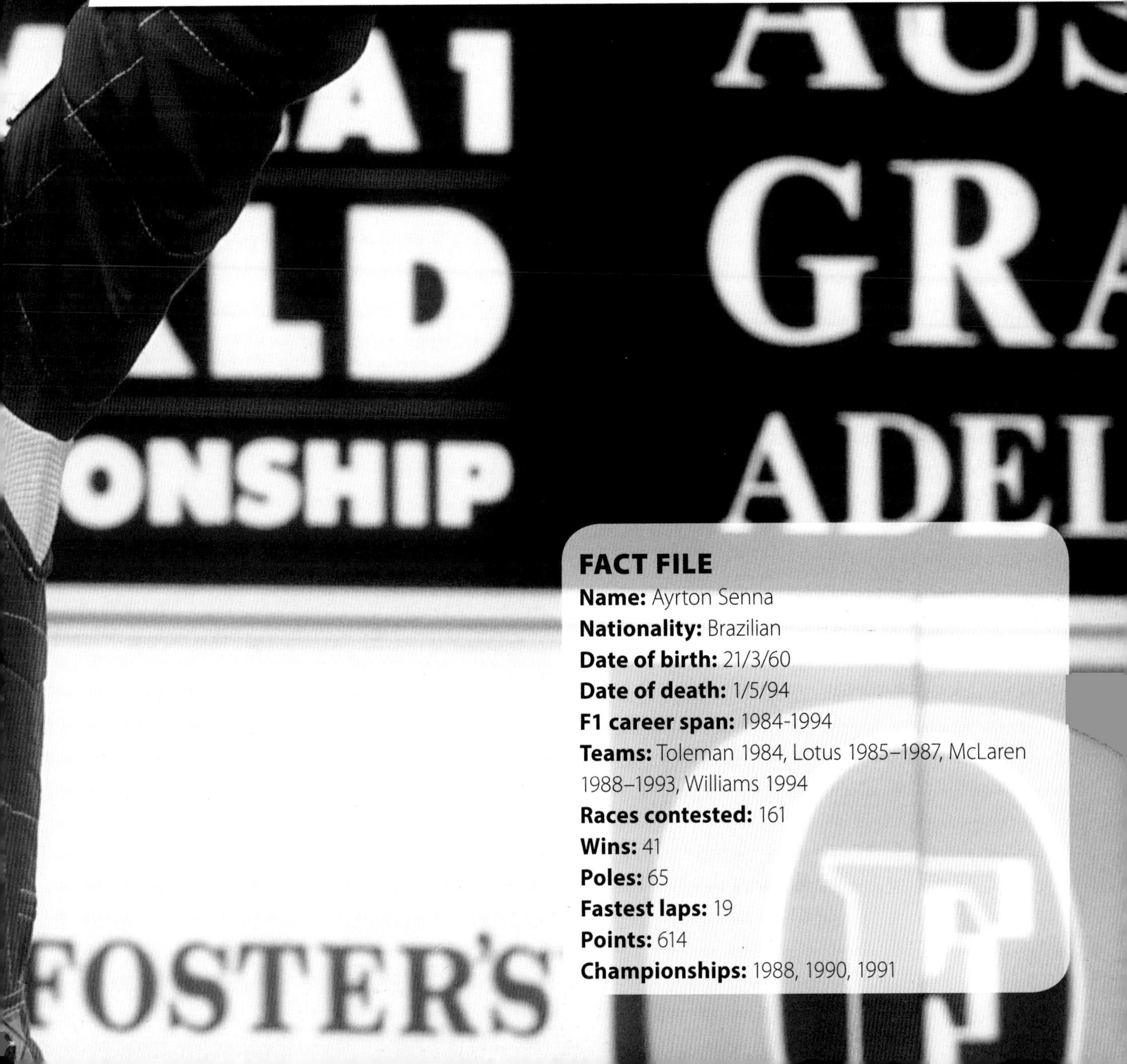

FACT FILE

Name: Ayrton Senna
Nationality: Brazilian
Date of birth: 21/3/60
Date of death: 1/5/94
F1 career span: 1984-1994
Teams: Toleman 1984, Lotus 1985–1987, McLaren 1988–1993, Williams 1994
Races contested: 161
Wins: 41
Poles: 65
Fastest laps: 19
Points: 614
Championships: 1988, 1990, 1991

IN A CLASS OF HIS OWN

Ayrton could be untouchable in qualifying, as you would imagine from someone who claimed 65 poles. His day of days in qualifying came at the 1989 Japanese GP, when he was fastest by 1.730s. His speed advantage was greatest at Monaco and he qualified on pole there by more than 1s in 1988 and 1989, also enjoying that massive margin at Detroit in 1985, Phoenix in 1989 and the Hungaroring in 1991.

Above **In a class of his own:** Ayrton dominated qualifying at Suzuka in 1989, but team-mate Alain Prost got a grippier start and led. *Below* **Wet weather masterpiece:** Ayrton was untouchable in the wet at Donington Park in 1993 and was soon lapping his rivals, including Riccardo Patrese and Fabrizio Barbazza.

A FALSE START

Anyone who had watched Ayrton Senna trounce his rivals in the junior single-seater formulae knew that he was special. However, when he made his break into F1 with Toleman in 1984, not much was expected as the team was midfield at best. Having qualified 17th out of 27 starters for his first grand prix, at home in Brazil, he climbed three places in the opening few laps before retiring with turbo failure.

THWARTED BY A RED FLAG

Having scored points on his second and third grand prix outings, Ayrton produced a stunning drive at his sixth attempt, at the 1984 Monaco GP. Conditions were extremely wet and very treacherous, but the Brazilian rookie was still able to reel in experienced race leader Alain Prost's McLaren. But, just as Ayrton latched onto Prost's tail, the race was red-flagged and brought to a premature conclusion by Clerk of the Course, Jacky Ickx.

WET WEATHER MASTERPIECE

Ayrton produced some mesmerising performances among his 41 runs to grand prix victories, but his greatest race of all was the 1993 European GP at Donington Park. Conditions were wet and he lost a place at the start, falling to fifth. However, with a singular focus and outstanding car control, Ayrton picked off each and every one of the drivers ahead to take the lead before lap 1 was complete and then raced ever further clear.

AYRTON'S TREBLE BREAKTHROUGH

Joining Lotus for his second year in F1, after his rookie season with the Toleman team, was a great move for Ayrton Senna. He claimed his first pole position on his second outing at the 1985 Portuguese GP. Better than that, he was then able to set the fastest lap in the race around a very wet Estoril circuit and lead every lap through the deluge to record his first grand prix win.

Above **Ayrton's treble breakthrough:** The Estoril circuit was streaming with water at the 1985 Portuguese GP, but Ayrton was in control from start to finish. *Below* **A proud Brazilian:** Ayrton waves the flag for Brazil after victory at the 1988 Japanese GP was enough for him to become world champion.

CAREER STATS

Year	Team	Races	Wins	Points	Ranking
1984	Toleman	15	0	13	9th
1985	Lotus	16	2	38	4th
1986	Lotus	16	2	55	4th
1987	Lotus	16	2	57	3rd
1988	McLaren	16	8	94	1st
1989	McLaren	16	5	60	2nd
1990	McLaren	16	6	78	1st
1991	McLaren	16	6	96	1st
1992	McLaren	16	3	50	4th
1993	McLaren	16	5	73	2nd
1994	Williams	3	0	0	-

A NATION MOURNED

Such was the impact of Ayrton's death in the 1994 San Marino GP that Brazil declared three days of national mourning. It was estimated that a million people lined the streets of São Paulo for his funeral.

PICKING OFF THE POLES

Acknowledged as the supreme qualifier, Ayrton Senna notched up 65 pole positions, at an average that the more long-serving Michael Schumacher has never been able to match. Ayrton achieved the remarkable tally of 13 pole positions in a season twice. Once in 1988 and again in 1989 when he guided his McLaren to 13 poles, starting 1988 with six straight poles and rounding out 1989 with the same sequence.

TWO SETS OF FOUR

Ayrton Senna was far more than the king of the qualifying lap, as his world titles in 1988, 1989 and 1991 attest. Indeed, he claimed 41 wins to put him second in the rankings behind Alain Prost (later third when Michael Schumacher moved past both). His best winning sequence was four in a row, which he managed twice by winning the British, German, Hungarian and Belgian GPs in 1998 then the US, Brazilian, San Marino and Monaco GPs in 1991.

MIND OVER MATTER

Winning in a competitive car is one thing, but doing so in one that is not the pick of the pack deserves even more respect. In 1993, his final season with McLaren, Ayrton drove some of his greatest races. And, in the final race of the campaign, at Adelaide, he managed to manhandle his Ford-powered MP4/8 around faster than the dominant Williams-Renaults for his only pole of the year. He then outraced Prost for what proved to be the last of his 41 wins.

NIGEL MANSELL

Nigel Mansell never had a quiet race. They were all packed with drama, malady or performances of dogged brilliance. When all was right, he would wring every last drop of speed out of the car and out of himself in a flamboyant, entertaining style. Then, when his chance came in 1992, he grabbed it.

*Below **A British bulldog:** The passion that Nigel always put into his racing is shown on his face as he celebrates victory at Silverstone for Williams in his title-winning year: 1992.*

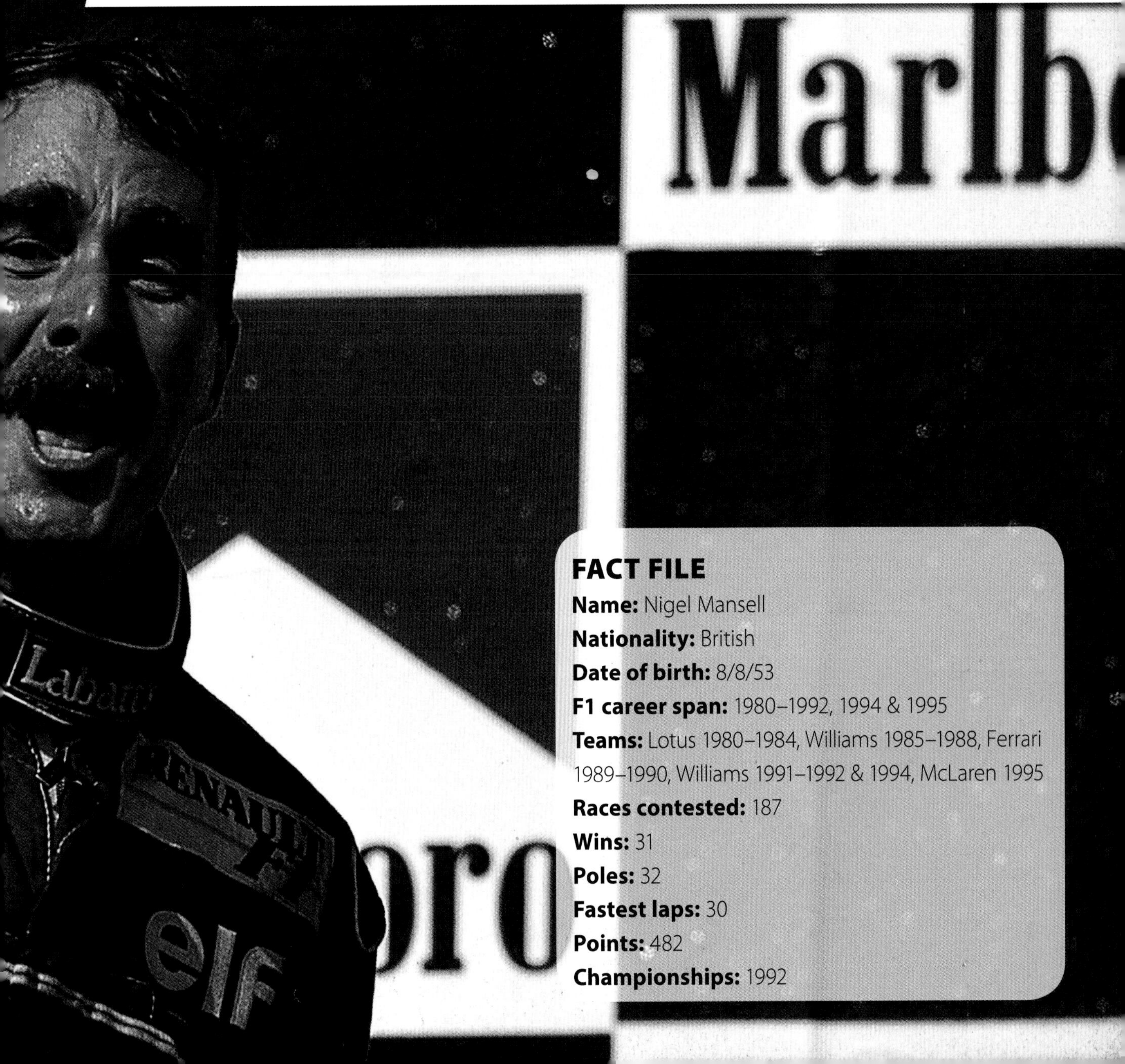

FACT FILE

Name: Nigel Mansell

Nationality: British

Date of birth: 8/8/53

F1 career span: 1980–1992, 1994 & 1995

Teams: Lotus 1980–1984, Williams 1985–1988, Ferrari 1989–1990, Williams 1991–1992 & 1994, McLaren 1995

Races contested: 187

Wins: 31

Poles: 32

Fastest laps: 30

Points: 482

Championships: 1992

CAREER STATS

Year	Team	Races	Wins	Points	Ranking
1980	Lotus	3	0	0	-
1981	Lotus	14	0	8	14th
1982	Lotus	13	0	7	14th
1983	Lotus	15	0	10	13th
1984	Lotus	16	0	13	9th
1985	Williams	16	2	31	6th
1986	Williams	16	5	72	2nd
1987	Williams	15	6	61	2nd
1988	Williams	14	0	12	9th
1989	Ferrari	15	2	38	4th
1990	Ferrari	16	1	37	5th
1991	Williams	16	5	72	2nd
1992	Williams	16	9	108	1st
1994	Williams	4	1	13	9th
1995	McLaren	2	0	0	-

LOOKING DOWN ON OTHERS

All aspiring racing drivers conjure images of themselves smiling down from the podium. Obviously, mounting the top step as a winner would be best, but Nigel would have been happy enough to claim his first podium finish. This came in the 1981 Belgian GP at Zolder when he brought his Lotus home behind Carlos Reutemann's Williams and Jacques Laffite's Ligier. For his first win, he'd have to wait another four years and more.

MOVING TO THE FRONT

To top timesheets or win grands prix, a driver needs a really competitive car. Nigel Mansell never really had that in his first few years of F1. However, by 1984, with Renault turbo power, he was on the pace and duly delivered his first pole position halfway through the season on the World Championship's one and only visit to the Dallas street circuit. This didn't result in his first win, though, as Nigel could finish no higher than sixth.

PLEASING THE HOME CROWD

There can be no better place to secure your first win than on home ground and Nigel did just that in the 1985 European GP at Brands Hatch. He qualified his Williams behind Ayrton Senna and Nelson Piquet but lost a place to Keke Rosberg at the start. Nigel moved into second when Rosberg spun while attacking Senna and Piquet hit him. Three laps later, Nigel took a lead he was never to lose when he passed Senna. With the monkey off his back, he won the following race at Kyalami.

Left **Looking down on others:** Nigel savours his first grand prix podium after finishing third in the 1981 Belgian GP. *Below* **Dogged determination:** Nigel was soaked with fuel, burning his back, but he kept going on his F1 debut for Lotus in the 1980 Austrian GP until his car's engine failed.

DOGGED DETERMINATION

Nigel Mansell had had to fight more than almost any of his rivals to get his break in F1 and, because of this, he was not going to give up when the going got tough. This it did on his F1 debut at the 1980 Austrian GP. Petrol leaked into the cockpit of Nigel's Lotus, causing him extreme pain. He soldiered on until the car's engine failed, earning Nigel increased respect from team boss, Colin Chapman, and first degree burns to his back.

MAKING THE MOST OF IT

||||||||||||||||||||||||||||||||||

Having been so close to landing the world title in 1986, only to be robbed by a blow-out, Nigel must have felt that he deserved the crown, and his 1992 campaign finally produced it. That year's Williams FW14B was the pick of the pack and Nigel made the most of it, starting with a run of five straight wins, in the South African, Mexican, Brazilian, Spanish and San Marino GPs. This provided the largest part of his tally of nine wins that landed him the title with five rounds to spare.

CROSSING THE ATLANTIC

After not being kept on by Williams for 1993, Nigel headed instead to the USA where he became the only driver to win the F1 and Indycar titles in successive years.

INSTANT AFFECTION

The Tifosi don't immediately warm to Ferrari's new signings, but Nigel Mansell gave them every reason to love him when he joined in 1989. How? By winning on his first outing. He did this at the Brazilian GP at Jacarepagua when he qualified sixth alongside team-mate Gerhard Berger. Nigel was up to third on the opening lap before working his way past Thierry Boutsen's failing Williams and then Alain Prost's McLaren. He would win just once more in 1989.

A SEASON TO FORGET

The loss of the Honda engine cost Williams dear in 1988 when it had to replace them with Judd engines. Nigel Mansell dropped from second in the 1987 title race to ninth in 1988 – his worst ever year in terms of retirements, failing to finish in 12 of the 14 rounds, albeit four of these were due to driver error. Showing the thwarted promise, he came home second in each of the races he finished.

NO RESPECT FOR YOUTH

The best way to augment one's reputation after retiring is to pop back for a cameo performance and stick it to the young guns. Nigel Mansell achieved this in 1994 when the fourth of his stand-in outings for Williams resulted in victory. This happened at the Australian GP when third place turned into first place after Michael Schumacher collided with Damon Hill while fighting over the lead. It was Nigel's final F1 win.

Left **Instant affection:** Nigel showed how to win friends with the tifosi by winning on his first outing, in Brazil. *Below* **Making the most of it:** Supplied with a pace-setting car by Williams in 1992, Nigel did the rest to record nine wins and land the title.

JACKIE STEWART

The immaculate Jackie Stewart was a driver who raced by the principle of wanting to win grands prix by the lowest speed possible. He had all the pace in the world but, in an age when cars were fragile and drivers died if they slipped up, he calculated his victories and earned himself three world titles.

Below **Emotions under control:** *Jackie is held aloft after beating his teammate Francois Cevert to win the 1973 Dutch GP at Zandvoort, the 16th of his 17 grand prix victories for the Tyrrell team.*

FACT FILE

Name: Jackie Stewart

Nationality: British

Date of birth: 11/6/39

F1 career span: 1965–1973

Teams: BRM 1965–1967, Matra 1968–1969, Tyrrell 1970–1973

Races contested: 99

Wins: 27

Poles: 17

Fastest laps: 15

Points: 360

Championships: 1969, 1971 & 1973

Below **Keeping busy:** Jackie savours Stewart GP's first podium with son Paul after Rubens Barrichello finished second at Monaco in 1997.

A PAIR OF THREES

Jackie Stewart twice enjoyed a hat-trick of wins, taking three wins in a row at the Dutch, French and British GPs in his Ken Tyrrell-run Matra in 1969, his first title-winning year. In 1971 he achieved the feat again at the French, British and German GPs in his Elf-sponsored Tyrrell to claim the second of his three F1 titles.

STARTING IN THE POINTS

Jackie Stewart made his F1 debut in 1965 after strong seasons in F3 then F2. Driving for BRM, after turning down the chance to join fellow Scot Jim Clark at Lotus, Jackie qualified 11th out of 25 on his debut in the South African GP at East London. Jackie advanced to sixth place and claimed points first time out. This feat remains something of a rarity, even with points extended first to the top eight then the top 10 finishers.

A FAMILY ENTERPRISE

Jackie retired from F1 in 1973, but he returned full-time in 1997 when he and his eldest son Paul established Stewart GP after running teams in Formula Ford, F3 and F3000. The team took one win, at the Nurburgring, before being sold to Jaguar in 2000.

Below **Leaving his mark:** Jackie jumps his Tyrrell 006 over one of the Nurburgring's many brows en route to his 27th and last grand prix win.

LEAVING HIS MARK

Victory in the 1973 Dutch GP put Jackie clear as the driver with the most grand prix wins, exceeding the record held by fellow Scot Jim Clark. Then, at the Nürburgring, not only did Jackie head home Tyrrell team-mate Francois Cevert for his 27th win, but this final win would leave him at the top of the list until Alain Prost passed this mark in 1987. The Frenchman would go on to win 51 times, a record bettered only by Michael Schumacher with 91.

IN FRONT AT THE FINISH

Having been in the points on his debut in the South African GP and scored his first podium finish next time out at Monaco, it seemed likely that Jackie Stewart would take his first win in his maiden season. And so he did at the 1965 Italian GP. Jackie started the race third on the grid and worked his way up to enjoy a typical Monza slipstreaming battle with BRM team-mate Richie Ginther before taking the lead with two laps to go.

Left **On the podium:** Jackie races through Monaco's narrow streets in his BRM in 1965, heading for third place for his first podium finish.
Below **In front at the finish:** Having scored points on his F1 debut in South Africa, Jackie would claim his first victory in just his eighth race, at Monza in the 1965 Italian Grand Prix.

NO DRIP IN THE WET

The Nürburgring Nordschleife sorted the men from the boys. Add rain to that mix and the potential gap in performance was even greater. For the 1968 German GP, there was low cloud too and Jackie Stewart produced his greatest ever drive to jump from sixth on the grid to lead before the end of the first 14-mile lap. His Matra was then never headed again and he won by four minutes from Graham Hill's Lotus.

A DOUBLE VICTORY

To win an F1 drivers' title is a feather in any driver's cap, but to do so with a victory adds immeasurably, and this is what Jackie Stewart managed when he claimed the first of

his three titles in 1969. He lined up his Matra third on the grid for the Italian GP behind Jochen Rindt's Lotus and Denny Hulme's McLaren, then jumped both and raced clear before holding off a slipstreaming pack to land his sixth win of the year and the title.

Above **No drip in the wet:** Jackie splashes his Matra around the Nurburgring to score a famous win in 1968, crossing the finish line just over four minutes of Graham Hill's second-placed Lotus.

MISSING OUT ON A CENTURY

Jackie Stewart was a driver of immense precision and he would have liked the fact that the last race before he quit driving would have been his 100th. However, the death of his Tyrrell team-mate Francois Cevert in practice for the 1973 United States GP at Watkins Glen led to the team withdrawing, and so Jackie remains eternally with 99 not 100 grands prix starts to his name.

CAREER STATS

Year	Team	Races	Wins	Points	Ranking
1965	BRM	10	1	34	3rd
1966	BRM	8	1	14	7th
1967	BRM	11	0	10	9th
1968	Matra	10	3	36	2nd
1969	Matra	11	6	63	1st
1970	Tyrrell	13	1	25	5th
1971	Tyrrell	11	6	62	1st
1972	Tyrrell	11	4	45	2nd
1973	Tyrrell	14	5	71	1st

JIM CLARK

Jim Clark was a driver who was so effortlessly quick in whatever type of car he drove that he appeared to be in a different class to even his closest rivals. In the years when his flying Lotus was strong enough for the job, he was crowned World Champion, but then a freak accident in an F2 race claimed his life.

Below **The first flying Scot:** *Jim and Lotus boss Colin Chapman made a remarkable pair, their combined genius dominating the early and mid-1960s before the Scot's fatal accident at Hockenheim in 1968.*

FACT FILE

Name: Jim Clark

Nationality: British

Date of birth: 4/3/36

Date of death: 7/4/68

F1 career span: 1960–1968

Teams: Lotus 1960–1968

Races contested: 72

Wins: 25

Poles: 33

Fastest laps: 28

Points: 274

Championships: 1963 & 1965

Above **Conquering his fear:** Jim loathed Spa-Francorchamps, but still managed to win there on four occasions, including this run in 1964.

CONQUERING HIS FEAR

Spa-Francorchamps in the 1960s was a circuit to be feared. This wasn't surprising as it was ultra-fast with little to stop cars from flying off into the trees. Jim Clark loathed it after his first visit in 1958 saw Archie Scott-Brown killed, followed by team-mate Alan Stacey and Chris Bristow in 1960. However, he managed to put the fear aside and win there each year from 1962 to 1965, with his 1962 victory the first of his 25 grand prix wins.

A FALSE START

Jim Clark didn't take long to reach F1. When Aston Martin scrapped its F1 project for 1960, Clark bounced back to sign for Lotus to race in F2. His pace was such that he was granted his F1 debut in the season's third round, the Dutch GP. The Scot qualified 11th out of 21, but his Lotus 18 retired from fifth when the transmission failed. He scored his first points next time out, at Spa-Francorchamps.

STARTING FROM THE FRONT

The predominance of Jim Clark and the Lotus 25 in 1963 led to his best seasonal tally of pole positions when he claimed the top spot in qualifying seven times in 10 rounds. He took pole position at Monaco, Zandvoort, Reims, Silverstone, the Nürburgring, Mexico City and East London. They didn't all result in wins, but he still managed seven of those that year.

Right **Overtaking no problem:** Jim powers through the field to regain the lead at the 1967 Italian GP at Monza.
Below **The beginning of the end:** Winning at the 1968 South African GP.

ARISE PRINCE JIM THE FIRST

Jim Clark was always going to be World Champion and an improvement in Lotus' reliability in 1963 allowed him the tools to do the job.

Such was his form, winning four of the first six races, that the Scot was able to clinch his first title at the Italian GP with three rounds still to run. To become champion, he raced to his fifth win by 35s over Richie Ginther's BRM.

THE BEGINNING OF THE END

Going into 1968 the second campaign in which Lotus was powered by Ford's pace-setting Cosworth DFV engine, Jim Clark laid down his marker by dominating the season-opening South African GP at Kyalami. Such was Clark's advantage that he started from pole, demoted Jackie Stewart's fast-starting Matra on the second lap and led every remaining lap to beat team-mate Graham Hill by 25.3s. Tragically, he died in an F2 race before the second round.

OVERTAKING NO PROBLEM

One of Jim Clark's most remarkable drives came at the 1967 Italian GP at Monza. He started from pole position and was leading before his Lotus had to pit to have a flat tyre replaced on the 13th of 70 laps, dropping him to 15th of the 16 remaining runners. Clark then tore through the field, making up an entire lap to retake the lead with seven laps to go, only to suffer fuel pump problems on the final lap and fall to third.

AN AIR OF INVINCIBILITY

When Jim Clark was in his pomp, his rivals might have felt that second place behind his Lotus was the best that they could hope for. This would certainly have been the case in 1965 when Jim achieved his best winning sequence, following victory in the opening round in South Africa with five more wins in the next five races in Belgium, France, Britain, Holland and Germany.

CAREER STATS

Year	Team	Races	Wins	Points	Ranking
1960	Lotus	6	0	8	8th
1961	Lotus	8	0	11	7th
1962	Lotus	9	3	30	2nd
1963	Lotus	10	7	73	1st
1964	Lotus	10	3	32	3rd
1965	Lotus	9	6	54	1st
1966	Lotus	9	0	16	6th
1967	Lotus	11	4	41	3rd
1968	Lotus	1	1	9	11th

⟫IT COULD HAVE BEEN FOUR STRAIGHT

Jim Clark's death in 1968 scuppered any hopes of a third F1 title but, had his luck been better, he could have had four titles to his name by the end of 1965.

All set to land the title in 1962, Jim's Lotus was sidelined by oil line failure in the final round. Although champion in 1963 and 1965, Clark came within an ace of taking the 1964 crown too, but suffered another oil line failure in Mexico City.

⟫A TOURING CAR STAR

All F1 drivers in Jim's day would race everything they could for money, often on the same weekend as a grand prix. Jim was so good at this that he was also British Touring Car Champion in 1964.

Below **An air of invincibility:** Jim shows his smooth style as he guides his Lotus 25 to victory at Silverstone in 1965, as the fourth of six wins in a row.

JUAN MANUEL FANGIO

Although approaching 39 when the World Championship kicked-off in 1950, Juan Manuel Fangio showed that skill counted more than age as he rattled off five F1 titles between 1951 and 1957 (and he didn't even compete in 1952 after a life-threatening accident before the opening round).

Below **His greatest drive:** *Juan Manuel looks drawn on the podium after a remarkable drive to victory in his Maserati in the 1957 German GP.*

FACT FILE

Name: Juan Manuel Fangio

Nationality: Argentinian

Date of birth: 24/6/11

Date of death: 17/7/95

F1 career span: 1950–1951 & 1953–1958

Teams: Alfa Romeo 1950–1951, Maserati 1953–1954, Mercedes-Benz 1954–1955, Ferrari 1956, Maserati 1957, Scuderia Sud Americana 1958, own team 1958

Races contested: 51

Wins: 24

Poles: 29

Fastest laps: 23

Points: 277.14

Championships: 1951, 1954, 1955, 1956 & 1957

THE GREATEST CHASE

||||||||||||||||||||||||||||||||||||

Juan Manuel Fangio's final win was his most dramatic. It came in 1957 at the German GP around the 14-mile Nürburgring Nordschleife. Despite qualifying his Maserati on pole, he completed the opening tour in third behind the Ferraris of Mike Hawthorn and Peter Collins. Two laps later, he was leading, but his gamble to stop for fresh tyres did not pay off when a slow pitstop dropped him to third. He then had to claw back 48s before passing both Ferraris on the penultimate lap to take victory and claim his fifth world title.

CAREER STATS

Year	Team	Races	Wins	Points	Ranking
1950	Alfa Romeo	6	3	27	2nd
1951	Alfa Romeo	7	3	37	1st
1953	Maserati	8	1	29	2nd
1954	Maserati & Mercedes	8	6	57.14	1st
1955	Mercedes	6	4	41	1st
1956	Ferrari	7	2	33	1st
1957	Maserati	7	4	46	1st
1958	Scuderia Sud Americana & Fangio	2	0	7	14th

⟫ GOVERNMENT ASSISTANCE

Considered his country's greatest racing talent after dominating its long-distance road races, Juan Manuel was propelled into single-seaters with support from the government as President Peron was keen to build Argentina's reputation abroad. After taking on Europe's best in races in Buenos Aires, he and compatriot Oscar Galvez headed to Europe and he did so well then and in 1949 that Alfa Romeo signed him for the first year of F1.

⟫ FALLING AT THE FIRST

Juan Manuel had already tried his hand racing in Europe in 1948 and was back from his native Argentina to contest the inaugural World Championship in 1950. Racing for Alfa Romeo, he was part of an all-Alfa Romeo front row for the British GP at Silverstone. After running third in the opening stages behind Giuseppe Farina and Luigi Fagioli, he was up to second with seven laps to go when an oil pipe burst.

⟫ SHOPPING AROUND

Juan Manuel didn't sit still in his quest for F1 titles. Indeed, his five crowns were won with four different teams. His first, in 1951, was with Alfa Romeo who then quit the sport. Back from injury for 1953, he started the year with Maserati but transferred to Mercedes-Benz when the German team's cars were ready. He won with Mercedes again in 1955 before winning for Ferrari in 1956 then rounding it off with Maserati in 1957.

Below **The greatest chase:** The German crowd hails Juan Manuel after he'd hunted down and passed the Ferraris in 1957.

Above **The face of experience:** Juan Manuel won in France in 1954 after his 43rd birthday. *Left* **Shopping around:** After starting with Alfa Romeo, Juan Manuel kept changing teams. *Below* **Bouncing right back:** Juan Manuel's wins flowed from Monaco in 1950.

THE FACE OF EXPERIENCE

Racing drivers tended to be older in the early days and Juan Manuel was no exception, being 38 when the World Championship started in 1950. Armed with the experience of making cars last in the rough, long-distance races held on open roads in Argentina, he allied speed with mechanical sympathy and landed his first world title at the age of 40 in 1951. His final title, in 1957, came when he was 46.

FAST TO THE VERY END

With Maserati closing its operation after his 1957 title, Juan Manuel raced on with independently-entered Maseratis. He raced in only two World Championship events in 1958 and in the second of these, the French GP at Reims he finished fourth after completing the entire race without the benefit of a clutch. Showing great respect, winner Mike Hawthorn backed off on the final lap rather than lap the great ace.

STUCK ON THE SIDELINES

Fangio wasn't able to defend his first world title, as he didn't contest a single World Championship round in 1952 after being thrown from his own Maserati in the non-championship Monza GP.

BOUNCING RIGHT BACK

After the disappointment of Silverstone, Juan Manuel Fangio bounced back to win at the second attempt in 1950. This was at Monaco, where he placed his Alfa Romeo 158 on pole position, set the race's fastest lap and led all the way for his first win. Fortune had smiled on him as there had been a nine-car pile-up behind him on the opening lap but he managed to thread his way through the wreckage on lap 2.

NELSON PIQUET

Nelson Piquet was renowned for his speed and his irreverent humour. It was the speed that won out, though, for this pacy Brazilian won world titles with Brabham in 1981 and 1983, then outscored his Williams team-mate Nigel Mansell to be crowned World Champion for a third time in 1987.

Below **Winning with a smile:** Nelson gave the impression of seldom being serious out of the car, but his career tally of 23 wins proved that he was deadly serious when behind the wheel.

FACT FILE

Name: Nelson Piquet

Nationality: Brazilian

Date of birth: 17/8/52

F1 career span: 1978-1991

Teams: Ensign 1978, BS Fabrications 1978, Brabham 1978–1985, Williams 1986–1987, Lotus 1988–1989, Benetton 1990–1991

Races contested: 203

Wins: 23

Poles: 24

Fastest laps: 23

Points: 485.5

Championships: 1981, 1983 & 1987

THE DAY IT ALL CAME GOOD

After increasingly impressive performances through 1979, his first full season of F1, Nelson stamped his mark at Long Beach in 1980. He not only qualified his Brabham on pole (his first), but held off a challenge by Renault's René Arnoux into the first corner before setting the fastest lap (his first) around the Californian street circuit on the way to his first grand prix win.

ONE YEAR, THREE CARS

Nelson Piquet didn't only win the British F3 title in 1978 but he also made his F1 debut midway through the season. This was with Ensign at the German GP. However, he moved on to drive a McLaren for the BS Fabrications team for the next three grands prix. Then, making it a trio of F1 teams in his first year, he was entered in a third Brabham alongside Niki Lauda and John Watson for the Canadian GP.

OLD FRIENDS' REUNION

It really was a case of it being a small world on the podium at the 1990 Japanese GP. Nelson Piquet shared the stage with childhood friend and karting buddy Roberto Moreno who had just joined his compatriot in the Benetton team after Alessandro Nannini had been severely injured in a helicopter crash. Amazingly, Moreno duly finished second behind Piquet and so their mutual congratulation truly was heartfelt.

MAINLY A BRABHAM MAN

When people think of Nelson's F1 career, they usually think of Brabham, and that's not surprising as he drove for the team for seven of his 13 and a bit years in F1, from the end of 1978 until 1985. However, he also managed two-year stints with Williams, Lotus and then Benetton between leaving Bernie Ecclestone's team and his final race in 1991.

Above **The day it all came good:** Nelson (middle) rounded up a collection of firsts at the 1980 US GP West. *Below* **Never a hat-trick:** Nelson takes victory at the Hungaroring in 1987, but he had to settle for second in the next race and thus missed a hat-trick.

NEVER A HAT-TRICK

For a driver who claimed three F1 titles, Nelson achieved very few dominant runs. Indeed, he never scored more than two wins in a row across his 203 grands prix. These were at: the 1980 Dutch and Italian GPs; the 1981 Argentinian and San Marino GPs; the 1983 Italian and European GPs; the 1984 Canadian and US (Detroit) GPs; the 1986 German and Hungarian GPs; and the 1987 German and Hungarian GPs.

Right **Title rival can't compete:** Nelson was able to relax at Suzuka in 1987 and free to land the title, after Nigel Mansell's accident in qualifying left him unable to race.

TITLE RIVAL CAN'T COMPETE

The third and final time that Nelson won the F1 title came in 1987 when his greatest rival was his Williams team-mate, Nigel Mansell. Heading to the penultimate race, at Suzuka, the Brazilian held a 12-point advantage (with nine points for a win), but his job was made a whole lot easier when Mansell crashed in qualifying and suffered heavy bruising which kept him from racing, making Nelson champion.

SMEARING THE FAMILY NAME

Numerous F1 drivers are followed into racing by their offspring. Unfortunately, Nelson Jr's F1 career with Renault ended in disgrace after he agreed to crash in the 2008 Singapore GP to help team-mate Fernando Alonso.

BEATING THE FAVOURITE

Nelson didn't head to Caesar's Palace for the final round of 1981 as championship favourite. That fell to Williams racer Carlos Reutemann, who arrived in Las Vegas with a one-point advantage. However, Reutemann faded, perhaps overcome by nerves, while an exhausted Nelson did just enough on the last lap to hold off challengers to take the fifth place required to claim the first of his three titles.

Above **Beating the favourite:** Nelson was one of the few to enjoy F1's first visit to Las Vegas, as he won his first world title there. *Right* **Career stats:** Seven years with Brabham gave Nelson 13 wins, but he also won for Williams and Benetton, as shown on the right, as he celebrates his victory in the 1991 Canadian GP.

CAREER STATS

Year	Team	Races	Wins	Points	Ranking
1978	Ensign & BS Fabrications	5	0	0	-
1979	Brabham	15	0	3	15th
1980	Brabham	14	3	54	2nd
1981	Brabham	15	3	50	1st
1982	Brabham	15	1	20	11th
1983	Brabham	15	3	59	1st
1984	Brabham	16	2	29	5th
1985	Brabham	16	1	21	8th
1986	Williams	16	4	69	3rd
1987	Williams	16	3	76	1st
1988	Lotus	16	0	22	6th
1989	Lotus	15	0	12	8th
1990	Benetton	16	2	44	3rd
1991	Benetton	16	1	26.5	6th

FERNANDO ALONSO

Fernando Alonso took little time advancing from karts to Formula One, then made an instant impact as soon as he was given a competitive car. Wins were followed by world titles for Renault in 2005 and 2006. A near miss with McLaren was followed by a strong spell at Ferrari before rejoining McLaren.

*Below **Fernando's coronation:** Fernando Alonso celebrates with the Renault team at Interlagos in 2005 after clinching the world title with two rounds to spare. He would follow this up with another title in 2006.*

FACT FILE

Name: Fernando Alonso
Nationality: Spanish
Date of birth: 29/7/81
F1 career span: 2001 then from 2003
Teams: Minardi 2001, Renault 2003–2006, McLaren 2007, Renault 2008–2009, Ferrari 2010–2014, McLaren 2015 onwards
Races contested: 254
Wins: 32
Poles: 22
Fastest laps: 21
Points: 1,778
Championships: 2005, 2006

KARTING GLORY

Almost all F1 drivers have won karting championship titles along the way, but few have been crowned World Kart Champion. Fernando claimed kart racing's most prestigious title in 1996. Then, for good measure, he also won the Spanish junior title, the Spanish senior one, twice, plus the Italian senior title, all by the age of 16.

A YEAR TO LEARN F1

Placed with Minardi for 2001 to learn the circuits, practices and techniques needed to shine in F1, Fernando did a solid job. He was never going to win for this backmarking team, but he impressed, peaking with 10th place in the German GP at Hockenheim. This was worth no points, as they were only awarded to sixth back then.

ROCKETING UP THE LADDER

As soon as Fernando turned 17, he turned his mind to car racing. Former Spanish F1 driver Adrian Campos signed him up to race for his team in Euro Open by Nissan in 1999 after seeing him equal the lap times of more experienced compatriot Marc Gene in testing. Fernando duly won six of the 15 rounds to become champion. It was then straight up to Formula 3000 in 2000. Racing for Astromega, Fernando got faster and faster through the season to rank fourth. His one win came at Spa-Francorchamps. Benetton team principal Flavio Briatore swiftly got him under contract, paying for his maiden F1 season.

LOSING OUT BY A POINT

Even before he'd secured the second of his consecutive F1 titles with Renault, Fernando had decided to move on to McLaren. This was for 2007 and he would be partnered by rookie Lewis Hamilton. A win in the second round, in Malaysia, suggested great things would follow, but Hamilton began to push. Fernando thought the team was supporting his number two, no him, and the atmosphere soured. Then, at the final round in Brazil, they were overhauled by Ferrari's Kimi Raikkonen, both losing out by a point.

Above **A year to learn F1:** Fernando made his F1 debut with Minardi in Melbourne in 2001. *Below* **Losing out by a point:** It was all smiles as Lewis Hamilton helped Fernando celebrate his first McLaren win at Sepang in 2007, but it all turned sour.

ENDING SCHUEY'S FIVE-YEAR RUN

There were times during Michael Schumacher's five-year reign as World Champion that it seemed as though he would never be toppled. When he was, in 2005, the driver to move ahead was Fernando who bounced back from a winless 2004 season to secure seven wins and the title for Renault, beating Ferrari's Rubens Barrichello by 34 points. This made Fernando the then-youngest World Champion, at 24 years and 59 days, breaking Lotus driver Emerson Fittipaldi's record from 1972. He then added the 2006 title for emphasis.

CAREER STATS

Year	Team	Races	Wins	Points	Ranking
2001	Minardi	17	0	0	23rd
2003	Renault	16	1	55	6th
2004	Renault	18	0	59	4th
2005	Renault	19	7	133	1st
2006	Renault	18	7	134	1st
2007	McLaren	17	4	109	3rd
2008	Renault	18	2	61	5th
2009	Renault	17	0	26	9th
2010	Ferrari	19	5	252	2nd
2011	Ferrari	19	1	257	4th
2012	Ferrari	20	3	278	2nd
2013	Ferrari	19	2	242	2nd
2014	Ferrari	19	0	161	6th
2015	McLaren	18	0	11	17th

FLYING FOR FERRARI

Fernando won race after race with Ferrari between 2010 and 2015, but no drivers' titles. Had his time with Ferrari not corresponded with the ascendancy of Red Bull Racing, he certainly would have added to his two titles. In 2010, he ended up just four points behind Sebastian Vettel, stymied in the final round by Vitaly Petrov. Then in 2012, Fernando's displays were better still as he ended up just three points behind Vettel after perhaps the best performances of his career. He was second again in 2013, but only sixth in 2014 as Mercedes and Lewis Hamilton dominated.

⫸ GOING BACK HOME, TWICE

It was never Fernando's plan to stay for just one year with McLaren, but his relationship with Ron Dennis crumbled, leading him to seek the another drive. This was with Renault, so he returned to his old team in 2008, but the car was nowhere near as competitive as the McLaren and it got worse in 2009, but benefitted from Kimi Raikkonen's departure to rallying to join Ferrari. In 2015, though, he returned to McLaren, just as the team changed to Honda engines and lost form.

Left **Flying for Ferrari:** Fernando didn't win the drivers' title in 2012, but he pushed Red Bull's Sebastian Vettel all the way with wins like this one at Valencia.
Below **The youngest F1 winner:** The Spanish flag flies as Fernando flashes across the finish line at the Hungaroring in his Renault in 2003 for his first F1 victory.

THE YOUNGEST F1 WINNER

Fernando spent 2002 as a test driver for Renault, supporting Jarno Trulli and Jenson Button. When Button moved to BAR in 2003, Fernando was promoted to a race seat and didn't waste the opportunity as he won the Hungarian GP to become the then-youngest grand prix winner, at 22 years and 26 days, breaking Bruce McLaren's record set in 1959. Earlier in the year, at the Malaysian GP, Fernando had become F1's youngest polesitter, at just 21 years and 236 days.

SEBASTIAN VETTEL

Sebastian Vettel burst into Formula One in 2007 as a 19-year-old and immediately made himself at home by scoring a point on his debut. A win for Scuderia Toro Rosso in 2008 earned him a ride with Red Bull Racing and he hasn't looked back, landing the 2010, 2011, 2012 and 2013 titles in a manner that proves that he can now be called one of the all-time greats.

Below **Punch the air:** Sebastian's unbridled delight is clear for all to see after wrapping up the first of his Formula One titles with victory for Red Bull Racing in the 2010 shoot-out at Abu Dhabi's Yas Marina circuit.

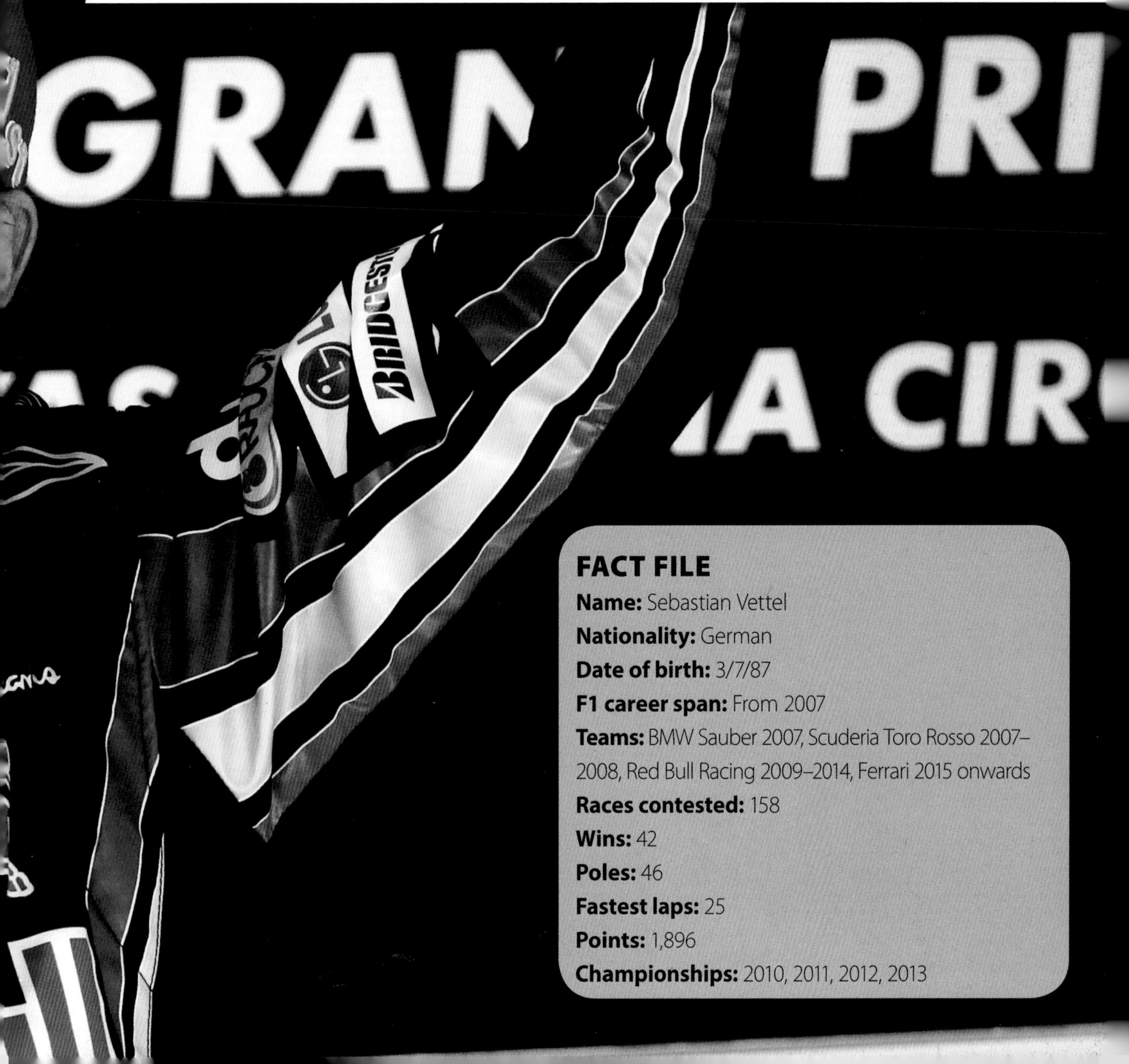

FACT FILE

Name: Sebastian Vettel

Nationality: German

Date of birth: 3/7/87

F1 career span: From 2007

Teams: BMW Sauber 2007, Scuderia Toro Rosso 2007–2008, Red Bull Racing 2009–2014, Ferrari 2015 onwards

Races contested: 158

Wins: 42

Poles: 46

Fastest laps: 25

Points: 1,896

Championships: 2010, 2011, 2012, 2013

STRAIGHT INTO THE POINTS

It took injury to Robert Kubica in an accident in the 2007 Canadian GP for Sebastian to get his Formula One break a week later at Indianapolis. Taking the Pole's place at BMW Sauber, Sebastian made an immediate impact by qualifying seventh and recovering from falling to 11th in a first lap melée to finish eighth and so record a point first time out. He went on to race for Scuderia Toro Rosso later in the year, taking Scott Speed's place. Sebastian became the youngest driver to lead a race later that season, in the Japanese GP.

››› LEAVING IT TO THE LAST

The first of Sebastian's four drivers' titles came at the final round of the 2010 World Championship in Abu Dhabi. He arrived third on points behind Ferrari's Fernando Alonso and Red Bull team-mate Mark Webber. Sebastian started from pole and led throughout, except for when Jenson Button moved ahead by making his one pit stop later. With Alonso finishing only seventh and Webber eighth, the title was his. In 2012, he also clinched the title at the final round despite being spun on the first lap.

››› MAKING IT FOUR IN A ROW

When Sebastian wrapped up his second F1 crown at the 2011 Japanese GP, he became the ninth driver to achieve back-to-back titles, following the example of Alberto Ascari, Juan Manuel Fangio, Jack Brabham, Alain Prost, Ayrton Senna, Mika Hakkinen, Michael Schumacher and Fernando Alonso. At 24 years and 98 days, Sebastian was the youngest, taking almost a year off Alonso's record, set in 2006. In 2013, he became the second driver to win four in a row, at 26 years and 116 days.

››› THE MOST POINTS IN A YEAR

The 2013 World Championship marked not just Sebastian Vettel's fourth F1 title, but also a record points tally. The points for a win had been boosted from 10 to 25 for 2010, and so all World Champions since then have far higher totals than those who went before them. In 2013, though, Sebastian dwarfed his own tally of 256 from 2010 and edged ahead of his 2011 score of 392 by five points. The driver who has the third greatest seasonal tally is Lewis Hamilton, who collected 384 with Mercedes in 2014.

››› TOTAL CONTROL RACING

Great races are often marked out by a driver experiencing a problem and then working his way back to the front, but this scenario hasn't occurred yet in Sebastian's career. So his greatest performances can only be picked from races where he has controlled proceedings from the front, and there are many of these. His first win for Red Bull, at the 2009 Chinese GP, stands out because although Sebastian had the advantage of starting from pole on a wet circuit and thus had clear vision, he still needed the maturity to ensure that he crossed the line first to score Red Bull's maiden win.

Above **Straight into the points:** Sebastian powers past Indianapolis's grandstands en route to a point on his 2007 debut.
Below **Unexpected victory:** Sebastian's breakthrough win for Toro Rosso came at Monza in 2008, after mastering a wet race.

UNEXPECTED VICTORY

Sebastian had been marked out as a star for the future when he went increasingly well in races through 2008, his first full season with Scuderia Toro Rosso. However, this was always seen as a way of earning a seat with the senior team, Red Bull Racing, for 2009. However, Sebastian didn't wait that long to secure his first Formula One win, as he proved the master of wet conditions to qualify on pole at Monza then was unsurpassed in a wet race to win unchallenged. It was a massive advance as his previous best finishes had been fifth places at Monaco and Spa.

KING OF THE FLYING LAP

Sebastian's ability to set the fastest flying lap in qualifying resulted in 45 pole positions between the 2008 Italian GP and the end of the 2013 season. However, as he honed his skills and Red Bull's Adrian Newey-designed cars became ever more competitive, Sebastian started to record runs of pole positions. His best to date is five in a row from the 2010 season finale in Abu Dhabi to the 2011 Turkish GP, and then again in 2011 from the Hungarian to Japanese GPs.

Above **King of the flying lap:** The most recent of Sebastian's 46 pole positions came with Ferrari in Singapore in 2015.
Below **Leading the way:** Sebastian congratulates teammate Mark Webber after the Australian won the 2011 Brazilian GP.

CAREER STATS

Year	Team	Races	Wins	Points	Ranking
2007	BMW Sauber/Toro Rosso	8	0	6	14th
2008	Toro Rosso	18	1	35	8th
2009	Red Bull	17	4	84	2nd
2010	Red Bull	19	5	256	1st
2011	Red Bull	19	11	392	1st
2012	Red Bull	20	5	281	1st
2013	Red Bull	19	13	397	1st
2014	Red Bull	19	0	167	5th
2015	Ferrari	19	3	278	3rd

THE BEST OF THE REST

Sebastian marked his first season with Red Bull in 2009 by finishing runner-up, beating his more experienced teammate, Mark Webber (who finished fourth), by two places. Not only did Sebastian give Red Bull its first GP win, in the third round, but he then added three more, which made only Jenson Button the more successful driver that season. Button's Brawn GP car won six of the first seven rounds to build a 32-point lead that Sebastian cut to 11 points by the season's end.

LEWIS HAMILTON

Great British hope Lewis Hamilton landed McLaren support when he was still in karts and the team financed his rise all the way to F1 in 2007. Not fazed by being paired with double champion Fernando Alonso, he missed out on the title by a point. Bouncing back in 2008, Lewis became World Champion, but it took a move to Mercedes for him to add another, which he did in 2014, then added a third in 2015.

*Below **Make mine a double:** Lewis Hamilton sprays the champagne after his victory in the 2015 US GP made him Britain's first ever back-to-back World Champion and alongside Sir Jackie Stewart as three-time British winners.*

FACT FILE

Name: Lewis Hamilton
Nationality: British
Date of birth: 7/1/85
F1 career span: From 2007
Teams: McLaren 2007–2012, Mercedes 2013 onwards
Races contested: 167
Wins: 43
Poles: 49
Fastest laps: 28
Points: 1,867
Championships: 2008, 2014, 2015

BECOMING A FORMULA 1 WINNER

From the charge to the first corner at the opening grand prix of his F1 career - the Australia GP in Melbourne in 2007 - it was clear Lewis had no fear of anyone. He threatened not just his McLaren team-mate Fernando Alonso, but everyone. Third place in Australia was followed by second in the next four grands prix. Most would have been happy with this, but Lewis felt he was held back in Monaco. Next time out, in Canada, it all came good and so Lewis became F1's second youngest winner, at 22 years and 154 days.

⫸⫸ SUPPORT FROM HIGH PLACES

Lewis was a hot ticket in karting, from the time that he won the British Cadet Karting title in 1995 at the age of 10. What marked him out as he gathered increasingly senior titles up to the European Formula A title in 2000, was that he'd already landed the financial input of what was then one of the top F1 teams: McLaren. This came after a after a cheeky request at an awards dinner bore fruit a while later and gave Lewis's father Anthony a welcome rest from chasing finance.

⫸⫸ SECOND TIME AROUND

The pain of being beaten in 2007 gave way as Lewis won four races in the first half of 2008. With Felipe Massa flying for Ferrari, a win at the penultimate race left Lewis with a seven-point lead going to Brazil. The outcome was extremely dramatic as Lewis was slow to change to rain tyres and fell to sixth, one place too low as Massa swept to victory. Luckily, Toyota's Timo Glock had stayed on slicks and Lewis got by him coming out of the final corner of the last lap to win the title by a point.

⫸⫸ FOUR YEARS, NO PRIZES

World Champion at just 23, Lewis must have thought that he had years of success ahead, but his run was stopped when Brawn GP found a technical advantage in 2009 and Lewis won but twice to rank fifth. Any hope that matters would improve for Lewis in 2010 were knocked when Red Bull Racing came on strong and Sebastian Vettel started a run of four titles on the trot. Lewis kept winning races, but never rose above fourth in the championship before he elected to quit McLaren at the end of 2012.

⫸⫸ GAMBLING ON SUCCESS

There were two reasons for Lewis joining Mercedes for 2013. Some considered the move extraordinary, as McLaren had nurtured his career from karting to F1, but he had felt increasingly stifled by the mentoring of McLaren boss Ron Dennis and was frustrated by not being able to set the pace in any of the seasons after 2008, with a best ranking of fourth as Sebastian Vettel cleaned up for Red Bull Racing. Mercedes wasn't yet competitive after three years since it took over Brawn GP, but the move proved a good one when he won the title at his second attempt in 2014.

Above **Becoming a Formula 1 winner:** After four near misses, Lewis won his first Grand Prix at the sixth attempt in the 2007 Canadian GP. *Below* **Almost at the First Attempt:** David Coulthard (right) consoles Lewis Hamilton after a seventh-place finish at the 2007 season-finale in Brazil left him one point behind Kimi Raikkonen in the Drivers' World Championship table.

ALMOST AT THE FIRST ATTEMPT

When Lewis slid into the pit entry gravel trap at the 2007 Chinese GP, scuppering his chances of victory, he put a positive spin on the fact that there was still a race to go, so he could still become F1's first rookie champion. Then, despite running off the circuit early in the final round In Brazil, he was still set for the title, only to have his McLaren slow with a gear-changing problem. Following advice over the radio, he fixed it, but he'd lost 30s and had fallen to 18th. Yet, he kept advancing to finish seventh, which was one place down on where he needed to be to prevent Ferrari's race winner Kimi Raikkonen taking the title.

DOUBLE POINTS AT THE FINALE

The points allocation was given a twist for 2014. To keep interest going all the way to the conclusion, a double allocation of points was to be handed out at the final round, thus the winner collecting 50 points. Arriving in Abu Dhabi, headed Mercedes team-mate Nico Rosberg by 17 points, so second place would give him his second title, even if Rosberg won, but Lewis powered into the lead and the title was his when Rosberg's car lost 160bhp when its ERS failed.

Above **Double points at the finale:** Lewis took 50 points by winning at Abu Dhabi in 2014; Alain Prost's 50 points in 1981 gave him the title. *Below* **Two turns into three:** Lewis takes the 2015 US GP chequered flag to win his third Championship, to the delight of his team.

CAREER STATS

Year	Team	Races	Wins	Points	Ranking
2007	McLaren	17	4	109	2nd
2008	McLaren	18	5	98	1st
2009	McLaren	17	2	49	5th
2010	McLaren	19	3	240	4th
2011	McLaren	19	3	227	5th
2012	McLaren	20	4	190	4th
2013	Mercedes	19	1	189	4th
2014	Mercedes	19	11	384	1st
2015	Mercedes	19	10	381	1st

TWO TURNS INTO THREE

Lewis's third title followed directly on from his second as he beat Mercedes team-mate Nico Rosberg again in 2015. This time around, he was able to relax long before the end of the season, securing the title with three of the 19 grands prix still to run. Lewis got himself into this position by winning five wins in the first half of the season before adding five more. Then, with the title in the bag, he appeared to lose focus a little and Rosberg beat him in all three of Mercedes' end-of-year one-two finishes.

It takes more than a big budget to win in Formula 1, although it certainly helps. The teams that have succeeded and endured are those that are led from the top, with strong leadership helping Ferrari, McLaren, Williams and Red Bull Racing cement their place at the top of almost all team records listings. Some teams, such as Mercedes, are on the rise, while others have had their time in the limelight and are now consigned to history, remembered by only the most fanatical fans.

Below **Cream rises to the top:** McLaren's Lewis Hamilton and Jenson Button at the start of the Bahrain GP in 2012. McLaren are one of the top teams but Ferrari still has more wins, titles and points than any other outfit.

FERRARI

The most famous marque in motor racing, Ferrari has tasted success in each decade from the 1950s on, and the allure of its road-going sportscars adds to its appeal. In the early 2000s, the team enjoyed its best spell, being all but invincible as Michael Schumacher starred, setting record after record, with Fernando Alonso adding more wins from 2010.

*Below **Red and rapid:** Ferrari is still the most famous team in Formula One but Fernando Alonso, shown here racing to second place in the 2013 Italian GP at Monza, was unable to do enough to prevent Sebastian Vettel from dominating for Red Bull Racing that year.*

FACT FILE
Founded: 1946
Years in F1: 1950 onwards
Country: Italy
HQ: Maranello, Italy
Team principal: Maurizio Arrivabene
Constructors' titles: 1961, 1964, 1975, 1976, 1977, 1979, 1982, 1983, 1999, 2000, 2001, 2002, 2003, 2004, 2007, 2008

⟫ 15 OUT OF 18

Ferrari made it six constructors' titles in succession in 2004, and did it in truly dominant style as it won 15 of the 18 rounds, almost exclusively through the efforts of World Champion Michael Schumacher who won 13. Team-mate Rubens Barrichello won twice to be runner-up and this helped Ferrari finish with more than double the score of its closest rival, BAR. It's amazing therefore that it wasn't able to win again in 2005.

⟫ TWO IN ONE GO

It took until the fourth round of the second World Championship for Ferrari to start a grand prix from pole position for the first time. This was thanks to the efforts of chunky Argentinian Jose Froilan Gonzalez for the 1951 British GP and that wasn't the end of his glory at Silverstone as he then raced to Ferrari's first victory after swapping the lead with compatriot Juan Manuel Fangio before pulling clear to win by 51s.

⟫ TITLE NUMBER ONE

Alberto Ascari clinched the first of his two world titles in 1952 and this was the first of the 15 drivers' championship titles earned by nine Ferrari drivers through to Kimi Raikkonen's title in 2007. He wrapped up the championship after just five of the seven rounds, at the German GP at the Nurburgring, when he scored his fourth win in a row and then backed that up by winning the final two rounds.

⟫ STARTING WITH A BANG

Ferrari didn't contest the first round of the inaugural World Championship in 1950, but it was at Monaco for the second one. Not only that, the Italian team came away with its first podium finish and first points as Alberto Ascari worked his way forward from seventh on the grid to finish second behind Juan Manuel Fangio's Alfa Romeo. The fact that he was a lap behind showed that Ferrari wasn't ready for that first win.

Left **Career stats:** Gilles Villeneuve was a star for Ferrari between 1977 and 1982.

CAREER STATS

Year	Races	Wins	Points	Ranking	Year	Races	Wins	Points	Ranking
1950	5	0	N/A	N/A	1983	15	4	89	1st
1951	7	3	N/A	N/A	1984	16	1	57.5	2nd
1952	7	7	N/A	N/A	1985	16	2	82	2nd
1953	8	7	N/A	N/A	1986	16	0	37	4th
1954	8	2	N/A	N/A	1987	16	2	53	4th
1955	6	1	N/A	N/A	1988	16	1	65	2nd
1956	7	5	N/A	N/A	1989	16	3	59	3rd
1957	7	0	N/A	N/A	1990	16	6	110	2nd
1958	10	2	40	2nd	1991	16	0	55.5	3rd
1959	7	2	32	2nd	1992	16	0	21	4th
1960	8	1	26	3rd	1993	16	0	28	4th
1961	7	5	40	1st	1994	16	1	71	3rd
1962	5	0	18	5th	1995	17	1	73	3rd
1963	10	1	26	4th	1996	16	3	70	2nd
1964	10	3	45	1st	1997	17	5	102	2nd
1965	10	0	26	4th	1998	16	6	133	2nd
1966	7	2	31	2nd	1999	16	6	128	1st
1967	10	0	20	4th	2000	17	10	170	1st
1968	11	1	32	4th	2001	17	9	179	1st
1969	10	0	7	5th	2002	17	15	221	1st
1970	13	4	52	2nd	2003	16	8	158	1st
1971	11	2	33	4th	2004	18	15	262	1st
1972	12	1	33	4th	2005	19	1	100	3rd
1973	13	0	12	6th	2006	18	9	201	2nd
1974	15	3	65	2nd	2007	17	9	204	1st
1975	14	6	72.5	1st	2008	18	8	172	1st
1976	15	6	83	1st	2009	17	1	70	4th
1977	17	4	95	1st	2010	19	5	396	3rd
1978	16	5	58	2nd	2011	19	1	375	3rd
1979	15	6	113	1st	2012	20	3	400	2nd
1980	14	0	8	10th	2013	19	2	354	3rd
1981	15	2	34	5th	2014	19	0	216	4th
1982	16	3	74	1st	2015	19	3	428	2nd

SUCCESS ON A SAD DAY

The 1961 Italian GP at Monza will always be remembered as the race that claimed the life of popular German Ferrari driver Wolfgang von Trips. However, Ferrari also remembers it for another reason, as this was the race at which it landed its first constructors' title. This came through Phil Hill giving the team a home win. As his only rival for the title at the final round at Watkins Glen was von Trips, he too was crowned.

Above **Success on a Sad Day:** Phil Hill runs his Sharknose Ferrari high around the Monza banking in 1961, to win the race and the title, but team-mate Wolfgang von Trips had died earlier in the race. *Below* **Ferrari's Greatest Run:** Alberto Ascari was the main man in Ferrari's 14-race winning run across 1952 and 1953, winning 11 times, including here at Bremgarten in 1953.

⟫ TEAM WINS, DRIVER LOSES

Although Kimi Raikkonen won the drivers' crown in 2007, Ferrari's most recent constructors' title came in 2008 when the combined talents of Felipe Massa and Kimi Raikkonen were enough to help Ferrari outscore the team that fielded champion Lewis Hamilton, McLaren, as Heikki Kovalainen didn't score much in the second McLaren car. Ferrari clinched the crown at the dramatic final race at Interlagos. Although Massa won the race, it was Hamilton who grabbed the drivers' prize.

⟫ UNLUCKY THIRTEEN

Ferrari is associated with success in F1, but 2014 was a rude awakening when neither Fernando Alonso nor Kimi Raikkonen could score a win. This was the team's first winless campaign since 1993 and its 13th in all.

FERRARI'S GREATEST RUN

Although Michael Schumacher gave Ferrari a huge number of wins in the 2000s, scoring eight in a row from 2003 into 2004, it was more than half a century before that Ferrari scored its best winning sequence. This was 14 races in a row, from Piero Taruffi's victory in the 1952 season-opener at Bremgarten to Alberto Ascari at the same Swiss circuit in 1953, with Ascari winning 11 of these and bagging two drivers' titles.

McLAREN

Founded by racer and engineer Bruce McLaren, this team started winning races in the late 1960s, took titles in the 1970s, was reinvented by Ron Dennis in the 1980s and went on to dominate F1 before the decade was out. Now the most professional team of all, it continues to chase Ferrari's records as Dennis returns to take control.

Below **On the Button:** *Jenson Button has been a revelation since joining McLaren in 2010, stepping up a gear to beat teammate Lewis Hamilton. This is the Englishman racing to third behind the Red Bulls in Brazil in 2011.*

FACT FILE

Founded: 1963
Years in F1: 1966 onwards
Country: England
HQ: Woking, England
Racing Director: Eric Boullier
Constructors' titles: 1974, 1984, 1985, 1988, 1989, 1990, 1991, 1998

CAREER STATS

Year	Races	Wins	Points	Ranking	Year	Races	Wins	Points	Ranking
1966	6	0	3	9th	1991	16	8	139	1st
1967	6	0	3	10th	1992	16	5	99	2nd
1968	12	3	59	2nd	1993	16	5	84	2nd
1969	11	1	49	4th	1994	16	0	42	4th
1970	12	0	36	4th	1995	17	0	30	4th
1971	11	0	13	6th	1996	16	0	49	4th
1972	12	1	66	3rd	1997	17	3	63	4th
1973	15	3	68	3rd	1998	16	9	156	1st
1974	15	4	87	1st	1999	16	7	124	2nd
1975	14	3	65	3rd	2000	17	7	152	2nd
1976	16	6	88	2nd	2001	17	4	102	2nd
1977	17	3	65	3rd	2002	17	1	65	3rd
1978	16	0	16	8th	2003	16	2	142	3rd
1979	15	0	15	7th	2004	18	1	69	5th
1980	14	0	11	7th	2005	19	10	182	2nd
1981	15	1	28	6th	2006	18	0	110	3rd
1982	16	4	69	2nd	2007	17	8	0*	-
1983	15	1	34	5th	2008	18	6	151	2nd
1984	16	12	143.5	1st	2009	17	2	71	3rd
1985	16	6	90	1st	2010	19	5	454	2nd
1986	16	4	96	2nd	2011	19	6	497	2nd
1987	16	3	76	2nd	2012	20	7	378	3rd
1988	16	15	199	1st	2013	19	0	122	5th
1989	16	10	141	1st	2014	19	0	181	5th
1990	16	6	121	1st	2015	19	0	27	9th

* All points annulled for alleged spying infringement

›› TAKING TO THE STREETS

Bruce McLaren gave his team its first grand prix outing at Monaco in 1966 and qualified 10th out of 16. Sadly, its US-sourced Ford V8 was not only down on power but was the cause of his early retirement after an oil pipe came loose. A different engine was sought for the next race, at Spa, and this was the start of a team that would be a winning outfit within two years.

Above **Career Stats:** Mika Hakkinen in his 1998 championship-winning MP4/13. *Below* **McLaren's First Eleven:** Another masterclass from Ayrton Senna during his triumphant 1988 grand prix season.

MCLAREN'S FIRST ELEVEN

Beating your rivals is always gratifying, but asserting dominance throughout a season is extra satisfying. McLaren had a remarkable campaign in 1988 as its MP4/4 was the pick of the crop and with Ayrton Senna and Alain Prost the team had the best drivers. So, perhaps it shouldn't come as a shock that the team won 11 on the trot, from the season-opening Brazilian GP at the start of April all the way through to the Belgian GP at the end of August.

THE BOSS TAKES THE FIRST WIN

Two years after McLaren's World Championship debut, having had Denny Hulme finish second at the 1968 Spanish GP, the team landed its first win at the next race, the Belgian GP at Spa-Francorchamps. Fittingly, this came at the hands of Bruce McLaren, who started that race from sixth on the grid, fell to 11th on the opening lap but then guided his M7A to victory when Jackie Stewart's Matra ran out of fuel on the final lap.

WINS FIRST, POLES SECOND

Despite taking its first win at the start of its third year in F1, McLaren didn't claim its first pole until the end of its seventh year. This breakthrough came at the 1972 Canadian GP at Mosport Park when Peter Revson scored the fastest lap and team-mate Denny Hulme helped the team take its first one-two on a grid. Sadly, Jackie Stewart soon propelled his Tyrrell to the front and the McLaren's had to settle for second and third.

THEY WEREN'T ALWAYS GREY

Younger fans will be surprised that McLarens have ever raced in any livery other than a predominantly silver-grey one. However, red and white were McLaren's colours for an incredible 23 years, thanks to backing from cigarette manufacturer Philip Morris's Marlboro brand. Red and white first adorned the flanks of a McLaren in 1974 and continued until 1996 when the West tobacco brand took over for 1997.

TRAGEDY AT GOODWOOD

McLaren was dealt a mighty blow in June 1970 when its founder Bruce McLaren was killed when testing at Goodwood. He was driving one of the Can-Am sportscars that helped finance the team's F1 programme.

FIXTURES AND FITTINGS

David Coulthard and Mika Hakkinen raced at McLaren for so long that they became part of the furniture. Hakkinen arrived in 1993 and was joined by Coulthard in 1996. By 2000, they'd become F1's longest serving driver pairing, racing as team-mates 99 times until the end of a sixth season in 2001, when Hakkinen took what he thought would be a sabbatical but turned into retirement from F1.

Left **Fixtures and fittings:** Mika Hakkinen and David Coulthard raced together 99 times. *Above* **Tragedy at Goodwood:** Just six weeks after Bruce McLaren raced to second place at Jarama in 1970, he was killed when testing at Goodwood.

TWO TITLES IN ONE YEAR

Grand Prix wins were flowing for McLaren in the 1970s and Emerson Fittipaldi helped the team advance to a new level in 1974 after arriving from Lotus. Not only did he win three times that year to become the team's first World Champion, but his team-mate Denny Hulme's tally of points was enough to help the team outscore Ferrari to claim the first of its eight constructors' championship titles to date.

Below **Two titles in one year:** Emerson Fittipaldi guided McLaren to the 1974 Drivers' and Constructors' titles.

RED BULL RACING

Energy drinks manufacturer Red Bull entered Formula One when it sponsored the Sauber team in 1995, but its involvement grew when it purchased underachieving Jaguar Racing in 2005. Red Bull's title-winning aspirations, made possible by large financial backing, meant they were able to assemble one of the top teams on the grid. This team was winning races within three years and then titles too, with Sebastian Vettel in 2010, 2011, 2012 and 2013.

*Below **Leading the way:** Sebastian Vettel and Mark Webber turned Red Bull Racing into a force to be reckoned with from 2009. In 2014, though, Daniel Ricciardo arrived and started showing Vettel the way, like here in Canada.*

FACT FILE

Founded: 1961

Years in F1: 1997*

Country: England

HQ: Milton Keynes, England

Team principal: Christian Horner

Constructors' titles: 2010, 2011, 2012, 2013

* Raced as Stewart Grand Prix before becoming Jaguar Racing in 2000 then Red Bull Racing in 2005

FIRST RACE, FIRST POINTS

|||||||||||||||||||||||||||||||||||||

Red Bull Racing's first grand prix after being rebranded from Jaguar Racing was the 2005 opener in Melbourne. David Coulthard and team-mate Christian Klien qualified fifth and sixth and raced to fourth and seventh to score seven points, which amounted to 70 per cent of Jaguar Racing's 2004 total points tally in one race. By the year's end, they had scored 34 points, to rank seventh, as Fernando Alonso and Renault combined to lift both titles.

››› FROM BACKING TO OWNING

Dietrich Mateschitz has made a considerable fortune from marketing the Red Bull energy drink around the world and his desire to promote it as a brand associated with adrenaline sports drew him to Formula One. At first he sponsored Sauber, but as he wanted to increase control over his involvement, he expanded his operations and took over the team that had been Jaguar Racing for 2005. Having started life as Stewart Grand Prix in 1997, this was the team's second change of identity and the one that would move it from the midfield to the front.

››› BEATEN BY JUNIOR

It was always assumed that Red Bull Racing would lead the way and that its junior team, Scuderia Toro Rosso, would follow. However, after Sebastian Vettel's shock win for Toro Rosso at Monza in 2008, Red Bull Racing had to wait until the third round of the following season before it claimed its first victory. This came at Shanghai, with Vettel the driver to do it, again demonstrating his considerable prowess in very wet conditions. For good measure, teammate Mark Webber made it a Red Bull Racing one-two.

››› STARTING TO DOMINATE

Before 2013, Red Bull Racing's best run of wins was the quartet of first places from the last two races of the 2010 season and the first two of 2011. This was nothing, though, as Sebastian Vettel hit a purple patch of form in the second half of 2013, following up his win in the Belgian GP with eight more in a row. The team's success in qualifying has been even greater, securing 16 pole positions in succession, starting with the final race of 2010 and lasting until Lewis Hamilton took pole for McLaren at the 2011 Korean GP.

Above **First race, first points:** David Coulthard raced to fourth place on the team's debut in the 2005 Australian GP. *Below* **Strength in depth:** Mark Webber, shown leading into Ste Devote at Monaco, added two of the team's wins in 2012.

STRENGTH IN DEPTH

Red Bull Racing's brilliant success in the three World Championship campaigns from 2009 to 2013, with 48 wins, 58 pole positions and 41 fastest laps, is underpinned by the fact that it can run two strong cars, not just one. Over the four campaigns, Mark Webber has pushed teammate Sebastian Vettel hard, not only claiming nine of those wins but being part of 12 one-two finishes for the team from Milton Keynes, in which he was the first driver home on three occasions.

CAREER STATS

Year	Races	Wins	Points	Ranking
2005	19	0	34	7th
2006	18	0	16	7th
2007	17	0	24	5th
2008	18	0	29	7th
2009	17	6	153.5	2nd
2010	19	9	498	1st
2011	19	12	650	1st
2012	20	7	460	1st
2013	19	13	596	1st
2014	19	3	405	2nd
2015	19	0	187	4th

NEWEY BOOSTS THE TEAM

If Red Bull Racing took a few years to get into its stride after morphing from Jaguar Racing, its success rate since its first Adrian Newey-designed car - the RB3 - appeared in 2007 has been markedly greater. Race wins started flowing from early 2009, his success rate had improved to 50 per cent by the end of the 2013 season, matching McLaren precisely from 2009 to 2012, but then pulling ahead in 2013 and really improving his average as Vettel scored 13 more wins that year.

⟫⟫ TAKING THE REINS

When Daniel Ricciardo was promoted from Scuderia Toro Rosso to Red Bull Racing for 2014, it was expected that the Australian would be dominated by Sebastian Vettel who had won four consecutive drivers' titles with the team. However, Ricciardo outperformed Vettel in the opening round in Australia, albeit being disqualified from second place. It became clear that Vettel didn't like the car and he failed to win a race all year, ranking fifth at season's end, two positions behind Ricciardo who won at Montreal, the Hungaroring and Spa-Francorchamps.

Left **Newey boosts the team:** Adrian Newey (right) has given Christian Horner (left) and Dietrich Mateschitz plenty of reason to smile since joining the team. *Below* **Training ground:** Toro Rosso graduate Sebastian Vettel celebrates giving Red Bull Racing its first victory, in China in 2009.

TRAINING GROUND

||||||||||||||||||||||||||||||||||||||||

Scuderia Toro Rosso, the team that spent its first two decades as Minardi, was taken over for 2006 with a brief to act as a training ground for Red Bull Racing's drivers of the future. Sebastian Vettel was the first to graduate to the senior team, as he inevitably would after winning the 2008 Italian GP in the wet, and has gone on to collect 38 wins, four drivers' titles and four constructors' titles for Red Bull Racing. Dietrich Mateschitz is hoping that 2014 signing Daniel Ricciardo will make a similarly successful leap from Toro Rosso to become world champion.

WILLIAMS

When Frank Williams first ran a team in F1, money was short and it looked as though he'd never field a grand prix winner. Teaming up with engineer Patrick Head changed all that and the team hit the front in the 1980s before enjoying another spell of domination in the 1990s, which it's hoping to replicate today after a one-off win in 2012.

Below **Back on track:** *Pastor Maldonado got everything right to hold off Fernando Alonso's Ferrari to win the 2012 Spanish GP for the team's first win since 2004, suggesting that more wins may be coming the team's way at last.*

FACT FILE

Founded: 1968

Years in F1: 1972 onwards

Country: England

HQ: Grove, England

Team principal: Sir Frank Williams

Constructors' titles: 1980, 1981, 1986, 1987, 1992, 1993, 1994, 1996, 1997

FRANK'S BAD BREAK

Frank Williams' life took an unwanted turn in 1986 when he was involved in a car crash on the way back from testing at Paul Ricard that broke his neck, leaving him wheelchair-bound.

HANGING ON TO HIS DRIVE

Williams is a team that likes to keep its drivers on their toes – it famously let both Nigel Mansell and Damon Hill know during their title-winning campaigns (1992 and 1996) that they would not be needed for the following year. So Riccardo Patrese, Williams' longest-serving driver, did well to stay for five full seasons. The Italian clocked-up 80 grand prix starts between 1988 and 1992 before being replaced by Hill.

THE TEAM'S ROTTEN RUN

Many thought that when Juan Pablo Montoya won the Brazilian GP in 2004, scoring Williams' first win for more than a year, that the team was back on form. However, he left to join McLaren and the team entered its worst-ever winless streak. This ran all the way through to the fifth round of 2012 when Pastor Maldonado finally put a smile back on Sir Frank Williams' face by taking victory in Barcelona. In 2014, the team ranked third.

Above **The team's bad run:** Juan Pablo Montoya won at Interlagos in 2004 but it wasn't until 2012 that the team won again. *Below* **Hanging on to his drive:** Riccardo Patrese (trailing team-mate Nigel Mansell) enjoyed two victories in 1991.

A TROUBLED BEGINNING

Defining when Williams started in F1 is slightly hazy, as Frank Williams fielded cars as long ago as 1969. However, the first time he entered a car that was unique to his team came in 1972, at the British GP at Brands Hatch, when Henri Pescarolo was slowest of the qualifiers in his Politoys FX3. Unfortunately, it was written-off on the third lap and it would be another seven years until Williams scored its breakthrough win.

MADE IN BRITAIN

Alan Jones was Williams' lead driver in 1979, but it was team-mate Clay Regazzoni who claimed the team's first grand prix victory. This came at the British GP at Silverstone. Up until lap 38 of 68 it looked as though the pole-starting Australian would be winner, but then his water pump failed and Regazzoni was free to canter home. As the team had a Saudi sponsor, Regazzoni had to decline the champagne celebration.

THE FIRST AND MOST-LOVED

Alan Jones is a driver long-departed from Williams, but his memory lives on with founders Frank Williams and Patrick Head. Not only was he the team's first title-clincher but he also provided the template of a perfect Williams driver – an uncompromising, unflinching racer who wouldn't moan. Jones wrapped up the 1980 title when he raced to victory at the penultimate race, the Canadian GP at Montreal.

Above **The first and most-loved:** Alan Jones's fourth win of 1980, in Canada, made him Williams' first world champion.
Below **Career stats:** Nigel Mansell has scored most victories for Williams, with 28 spread across three spells with the team.

PROVING IT WAS NO FLUKE

The best way for Alan Jones to expunge any disappointment at not having been the driver to give Williams its first win was to win the next race, the 1979 German GP at Hockenheim. Having got the jump on Jean-Pierre Jabouille's pole-sitting Renault, Jones then led every lap to take victory. Clay Regazzoni completed Williams' first one-two finish, advancing when Jabouille spun and then passing Jacques Laffite's Ligier.

IT CAME TO A SUDDEN STOP

When Williams secured the 1997 constructors' championship title at the European GP at Jerez, it was the team's fifth title in six years, so more were sure to follow. Amazingly, as McLaren came back to form, Williams' form faded and the 1997 success, shaped by champion Jacques Villeneuve and team-mate Heinz-Harald Frentzen, remains the most recent time that Williams reached the top of the pile.

CAREER STATS

Year	Races	Wins	Points	Ranking	Year	Races	Wins	Points	Ranking
1972	1	0	0	-	1995	17	5	118	2nd
1973	15	0	2	10th	1996	16	12	175	1st
1974	15	0	4	10th	1997	17	8	123	1st
1975	12	0	6	9th	1998	16	0	38	3rd
1976	13	0	0	-	1999	16	0	35	5th
1978	16	0	11	9th	2000	17	0	36	3rd
1979	15	5	75	2nd	2001	17	4	80	3rd
1980	14	6	120	1st	2002	17	1	92	2nd
1981	15	4	95	1st	2003	16	3	144	2nd
1982	15	1	58	4th	2004	18	1	88	4th
1983	15	1	38	4th	2005	19	0	66	5th
1984	16	1	25.5	6th	2006	18	0	11	8th
1985	16	4	71	3rd	2007	17	0	33	4th
1986	16	9	141	1st	2008	18	0	26	8th
1987	16	9	137	1st	2009	17	0	34.5	7th
1988	16	0	20	7th	2010	19	0	69	6th
1989	16	2	77	2nd	2011	19	0	5	9th
1990	16	2	57	4th	2012	20	1	76	8th
1991	16	7	125	2nd	2013	19	0	5	9th
1992	16	10	164	1st	2014	19	0	320	3rd
1993	16	10	168	1st	2015	19	0	257	3rd
1994	16	7	118	1st					

LOTUS

This team was the one to watch through the 1960s and 1970s. Team founder Colin Chapman's ideas revolutionized F1, leading to periods of domination with Jim Clark and then, in the late 1970s, with Mario Andretti. However, Chapman died and the team fell away after a late flurry with Ayrton Senna. Its name has been revived twice, but these teams have no link to original Lotus and the Lotus name dropped out of F1 again at the end of the 2015 season.

Below **Streets paved with gold:** Graham Hill helped Lotus recover from Jim Clark's death by racing to victory in Monaco in 1968 around the streets where Stirling Moss was the first person to win a grand prix in a Lotus in 1960.

FACT FILE

Founded: 1952

Years in F1: 1958–1994*

Country: England

HQ: Wymondham, England

Team principal: Colin Chapman

Constructors' titles: 1963, 1965, 1968, 1970, 1972, 1973, 1978

* The Lotus name reappeared in F1 in 2010 but this and a subsequent revival with another team in 2012 are not related to the original team.

STARTING WITH A WHIMPER

When Cliff Allison and Graham Hill turned up at Monaco for the second grand prix of 1958, qualifying their Lotus 12s 13th and 15th, they were both roughly 5s off the pace. Allison ultimately finished 13 laps down on Maurice Trintignant's winning Cooper and Hill not at all, revealing few signs that this new marque was going to be the lead team of the following decade, but history relates that this is what Lotus would become.

A HOLLOW VICTORY

Lotus was left reeling when Jim Clark was killed in an F2 race early in 1968, but Graham Hill galvanized the team around him and helped it to that year's title double. Cruelly, in 1970, Lotus' soaring hopes were sent crashing when championship leader Jochen Rindt was killed at Monza. Yet, Rindt was to end the year as F1's only posthumous champion, as second-placed Jacky Ickx failed to beat his points score.

THE END OF THE LINE

When a team is at the top of its game, it's hard to imagine its winning ability coming to an end. Jim Clark's death in 1968 knocked Lotus back, but Ayrton Senna's departure to McLaren for 1988 sealed the teams' fate, with the final Lotus win coming at the 1987 Detroit GP when Senna made his tyres last to outwit Williams' Nigel Mansell. His best results in the remaining 11 rounds were a pair of second places.

BLAZING A TRAIL

It was always a question of when, not if, Lotus was going to land a constructors' title. Having finished second three years in a row, it all came right in 1963. And how! Almost entirely through the efforts of Jim Clark, who won seven of the 10 rounds, and with the advances wrought by Lotus introducing F1's first monocoque, both team and driver wrapped up their titles with victory at Monza with three rounds still to run.

Top **A hollow victory:** Jochen Rindt guides his Lotus 72 to victory in the 1970 French GP. He was later killed at Monza.
Above **Blazing a trail:** Both Jim Clark and team boss Colin Chapman (on car) had reason to celebrate at Monza in 1963.
Below **Elio hangs around:** de Angelis took his final win for Lotus in the 1985 San Marino GP after Alain Prost was disqualified.

BEATING THE WORKS TEAM

Statisticians can be confused by Lotus's very early days in F1 as the most successful Lotus entry wasn't fielded by the works team, but by privateer Rob Walker instead. He had Stirling Moss as his driver and Moss scored not only the first pole position (Monaco 1960) and first win at the same race, but the marque's first fastest lap as well at the following race at Zandvoort. Then the works Lotus team got up to speed.

ELIO HANGS AROUND

In terms of years, Jim Clark was the longest-serving Lotus driver, racing with the team from 1960 to the start of 1968. That encompassed 72 grands prix up to his death. Mario Andretti was at Lotus for five years in the 1970s and managed three more, 75. Then along came Elio de Angelis in 1980 and he raced for Lotus on a record 90 occasions before moving on to Brabham in 1986.

CAREER STATS

Year	Races	Wins	Points	Ranking	Year	Races	Wins	Points	Ranking
1958	9	0	3	6th	1977	17	5	62	2nd
1959	8	0	5	4th	1978	16	8	86	1st
1960	8	0	34	2nd	1979	15	0	39	4th
1961	8	3	32	2nd	1980	14	0	14	5th
1962	9	3	37	2nd	1981	15	0	22	7th
1963	10	7	58	1st	1982	16	1	30	5th
1964	10	3	40	3rd	1983	15	0	11	7th
1965	10	6	56	1st	1984	16	0	47	3rd
1966	9	1	21	5th	1985	16	3	71	3rd
1967	11	4	50	2nd	1986	16	2	58	3rd
1968	12	5	62	1st	1987	16	2	64	3rd
1969	11	2	47	3rd	1988	16	0	23	4th
1970	12	6	59	1st	1989	16	0	15	6th
1971	11	0	21	5th	1990	16	0	3	7th
1972	12	5	61	1st	1991	16	0	3	9th
1973	15	7	92	1st	1992	16	0	13	5th
1974	15	3	42	4th	1993	16	0	12	6th
1975	14	0	9	7th	1994	16	0	0	-
1976	16	1	29	4th					

⟫ HATS OFF TO THE WINNER

Team founder Colin Chapman had a trademark celebration for any win in the 1970s – he would climb over the pitwall, onto the track and hurl his black corduroy cap into the air.

Right **Career Stat:** Emerson Fittipaldi took nine wins and the 1972 world title for Lotus. *Below* **Triumph and tragedy:** Ronnie Peterson raced to a dominant win in Austria in 1978, but he died two races later.

TRIUMPH AND TRAGEDY

Lotus's most recent title came off the back of one of Colin Chapman's many technical innovations. Having introduced ground effects in 1977, Mario Andretti and Ronnie Peterson took control in 1978. With win following win, the team landed the title by the 12th of the 16 rounds. Sadly, Peterson would die two races later.

MERCEDES GP

Mercedes-Benz entered a team in 1954 and 1955. This, however, has no bloodline connection, as it's one of several F1 teams that has raced under several identities before its current one. Since Mercedes money led to its fourth incarnation in 2010, the foundations have been firmed up and Lewis Hamilton has guided the team to a couple of titles.

Below **Championship class:** *Nico Robserg fleetingly resists team-mate Lewis Hamilton in the 2014 Abu Dhabi GP, the year in which Mercedes GP claimed the first of two consecutive title doubles.*

FACT FILE

Founded: 1999
Years in F1: 1999 onwards
Country: England
HQ: Brackley, England
Team principal: Toto Wolff
Constructors' titles: 2009, 2014, 2015

MUCH FANFARE, BUT NO POINTS

Launched with the motto "a tradition of excellence", BAR failed to score a point in its debut season. However, changes were made, most notably the improvement of the Honda engines it used from 2000 and then the arrival of Jenson Button in 2003. Together, they made great strides and the Geoff Willis-designed chassis was good enough for Button to press Ferrari's Michael Schumacher in 2004 when BAR finished as runners-up to the Italian team, with Button third overall.

NEW NAME, NEW FORTUNE

Honda involvement in the team continued to increase to the point that BAR became Honda Racing for 2006. Honda got its reward, too, when Button mastered changing conditions to win a rain-hit Hungarian GP, giving him his first win after 113 races without victory.

SHOWING ITS BRAWN

Honda Racing dwindled as fast it soared and the onset of a global recession forced it to close its doors at the end of 2008. Amazingly, not only

did an eleventh-hour revival and renaming after technical director Ross Brawn put it back on the grid for 2009, but Button and Rubens Barrichello were given a performance advantage as the car exploited a loophole to run a double-decker diffuser and so Brawn GP took eight wins and romped to both titles.

MERCEDES TAKES OVER

Having supplied engines to McLaren for years, Mercedes decided that it wanted to try and win with cars bearing its name, so Brawn GP was bought and the name changed to Mercedes GP for 2010. Michael Schumacher was coaxed out of retirement, but the seven-time World Champion could do nothing as Red Bull, McLaren and Ferrari fought over the title. By 2012, though, Mercedes GP had its first win when Nico Rosberg triumphed in China.

CAREER STATS

Year	Races	Wins	Points	Ranking
1999	16	0	0	N/A
2000	17	0	20	=4th
2001	17	0	17	5th
2002	17	0	7	8th
2003	16	0	26	5th
2004	18	0	119	2nd
2005	19	0	38	6th
2006	18	1	86	4th
2007	17	0	6	8th
2008	18	0	14	9th
2009	17	8	172	1st
2010	19	0	214	4th
2011	19	0	165	4th
2012	20	1	142	5th
2013	19	3	360	2nd
2014	19	16	701	1st
2015	19	16	703	1st

* As BAR 1999–2005, Honda Racing 2006–2008, BAR 2009

Below **New Name, New Fortune:** BAR morphed into Honda Racing in 2006 and Jenson Button gave the team its first win, at the Hungarian GP.

Bottom **An All-New Team for 1999:** Craig Pollock and Jacques Villeneuve thought that they could storm F1 with BAR, but scored no points.

AN ALL-NEW TEAM FOR 1999

The Tyrrell team had been in decline through the 1990s and, after it scored only two points to rank 10th in 1997, team owner Ken Tyrrell was only too happy to sell up. Jacques Villeneuve's manager Craig Pollock had coaxed British American Tobacco into buying the team's entry and it metamorphosed into British American Racing in 1999, with Villeneuve as its lead driver, supported by 1997 Formula 3000 champion Ricardo Zonta.

SILVER STAR TAKES GOLD MEDAL

The 2014 season heralded the arrival of a major set of technical changes, with smaller, turbocharged engines introduced, along with reduced fuel flow and increased power harvesting. To say that Mercedes GP came out ahead is an understatement as Hamilton won 11 grands prix and Rosberg five to give the team both the drivers' title for Hamilton and the constructors' titles for the first time as Mercedes GP. Previous champions Red Bull Racing ended up second overall, almost 300 points adrift.

Above **Silver Star Takes Gold Medal:** It's all smiles at Sepang in 2014 as Hamilton and Rosberg celebrate a dominant one-two.
Below **Keeping the Winning Habit:** Hamilton got past Rosberg on lap 1 and victory in the 2015 US GP gave him his third F1 title.

HAMILTON JOINS THE LINE-UP

Having decided that Michael Schumacher had been given a fair go, Lewis Hamilton took his place for 2013 and so resumed a rivalry with his former karting team-mate, Nico Rosberg. In their first year together, they had to fight for the scraps left by dominant Red Bull Racing, but they pipped Ferrari to rank second thanks to three mid-season wins, with Hamilton taking only one to Rosberg's two, but ranking higher, in fourth place overall.

KEEPING THE WINNING HABIT

Such was Mercedes GP's margin of advantage in 2014 that it was always considered unlikely that any of their rivals would close the gap enough to challenge them. And so it proved as Mercedes GP topped 700 points again as Hamilton made it two drivers' titles in succession with 10 wins and Rosberg added six of his own, leaving just the remaining three for Ferrari's Sebastian Vettel. They emphasized this as these included 12 one-two finishes.

RENAULT

Renault won the first ever grand prix, the French GP of 1906, and made its first World Championship appearance in 1977 when it introduced turbocharged engines. Renault became a winning team in 1979 but bowed out after 1985. It returned in 2002 when it took over the Benetton team, running as Renault until rebadging as Lotus for 2012, then being changed back again to Renault for the 2016 season.

Below **Yellow car on a golden day:** *Winning at home was always important for Renault, so Rene Arnoux delighted the bosses when he led home Alain Prost in a Renault one-two at Paul Ricard in 1982.*

FACT FILE

Founded: 1977
Years in F1: 1977–1985, 2002–2011, 2012-2015 as Lotus
Country: France
HQ: Enstone, England
Team principal: Gerard Lopez
Constructors' titles: 2005, 2006

A REALLY LONG WAIT

Although the French hosted the first grand prix, back in 1906 (won by a Renault incidentally) the nation really took its time to get going in Formula 1. Indeed, although Bugatti, Gordini and Talbot tried to win for the glory of France in the 1950s, it took until 1979 for that first race win and a further 26 years for the first title to be won by a French team. Mind you, by this point, it was a French team operating out of Britain.

FIRST POINTS, BUT ONLY JUST

The almost ceaseless mechanical failures that blighted Renault's debut season in 1977 were reduced for its second campaign and Jean-Pierre Jabouille claimed the team's first points at the 1978 US GP at Watkins Glen. He qualified ninth but advanced as others fell off and was fourth at flagfall. It could have been third but his engine spluttered with eight laps to go. He let Jody Scheckter's Wolf by, then just limped home.

CAREER STATS

Year	Races	Wins	Points	Ranking
1977	5	0	0	-
1978	14	0	3	12th
1979	15	1	26	6th
1980	14	3	38	4th
1981	15	3	54	3rd
1982	16	4	62	3rd
1983	15	4	79	2nd
1984	16	0	34	5th
1985	16	0	16	7th
2002	17	0	23	4th
2003	16	1	88	4th
2004	18	1	105	3rd
2005	19	7	191	1st
2006	18	8	206	1st
2007	17	0	51	3rd
2008	18	2	80	4th
2009	17	0	26	8th
2010	19	0	163	5th
2011	19	0	73	5th
2012	20	1	303	4th
2013	19	1	315	4th
2014	19	0	19	8th
2015	19	0	78	6th

Above **Career stats:** Fernando Alonso took the drivers' titles in 2005 and 2006.
Below **Now that's something new:** Jean-Pierre Jabouille at Silverstone in 1977.

AT HOME AND AWAY

Renault's two spells in F1 are distinct as the first, from 1977 to 1985, was based in France and the second spell, from 2002, based in Britain, taking over the Benetton team premises and personnel.

NOW THAT'S SOMETHING NEW

There was considerable interest when Renault made its F1 debut midway through 1977. This wasn't just because an all-new team arrived for the British GP at Silverstone with an all-new car, but also because the yellow racer was powered by the first turbocharged engine in F1. Jean-Pierre Jabouille qualified 21st and was making progress when the car pulled off with, you've guessed it, turbo-charger failure…

Above **Topping the ton:** Fernando Alonso waves to the fans at Interlagos in 2006. He raced more than 100 times for Renault.
Below **Landmark flying laps:** Rene Arnoux lost out to Gilles Villeneuve in the 1979 Franch GP, but he did set the fastest lap.

 ## DOING IT IN STYLE

When Renault scored its breakthrough victory, it did so in style. This wasn't simply because it did so on home ground when Jean-Pierre Jabouille was first to the chequered flag in the 1979 French GP at Dijon-Prenois, but because the battle over second place was all but explosive in the closing laps, with team-mate Rene Arnoux and Ferrari's Gilles Villeneuve changing places at almost every bend and entertaining royally.

 ## BEING DOUBLY HONOURED

Despite Renault's successes in the late 1970s and early 1980s in the days when the team was wholly French, it took until 2005 for the now British-run team representing the French marque to take its first constructors' championship. Then, like buses, a second title came along straight after it, with Fernando Alonso's second place behind Ferrari's Felipe Massa in the 2006 Brazilian GP at Interlagos sealing the deal.

TOPPING THE TON

Even before he returned for his second spell with the team in 2008, Fernando Alonso had become Renault's longest-serving driver. Before he left for his troubled year with McLaren in 2007, the Spaniard had raced 71 times for the team, more than long-term Renault racers Rene Arnoux, Jean-Pierre Jabouille and Alain Prost. Alonso's two-year second stint in 2008 and 2009 then boosted that total to 106 grands prix.

LANDMARK FLYING LAPS

Renault brought turbocharged engines into F1 in 1977 and their power soon made them almost untouchable around a lap. For races, the boost had to be turned down, not just to increase fuel consumption, but to ensure they didn't blow. So, although Renault's first pole came at the 1979 South African GP, it took another five races before it took its first fastest lap, through Rene Arnoux in the French GP, a race won by team-mate Jean-Pierre Jabouille.

BENETTON

The team was born out of the Toleman team after it ran into financial difficulties in 1985 and was bailed out by the Benetton knitwear company. Racing as Benetton from 1986, they took Michael Schumacher to titles in 1994 and 1995 but disappeared when taken over by Renault for 2002. In 2012, it changed its name again, to Lotus.

Below **Life after Michael:** *Benetton was never as successful after Michael Schumacher left for Ferrari in 1996, with only one more win. Giancarlo Fisichella was one of its best drivers, finishing third in the 2001 Belgian GP.*

FACT FILE

Founded: 1986
Years in F1: 1986–2001
Country: England
HQ: Enstone, England
Team principal: N/A, as team defunct
Constructors' titles: 1995

END OF YEAR, END OF NAME

The record books show that Benetton's last grand prix was at the final round of the 2001 World Championship, the Japanese GP, as Renault's buy-in meant that the Enstone-based team would be known as Renault from 2002 onwards. It hadn't been a good season for either Giancarlo Fisichella or Jenson Button, and although they qualified sixth and ninth at Suzuka, neither scored, with Button seventh and Fisichella on the sidelines.

Left **End of year, end of name:** Jenson Button was the last driver to finish a race in a Benetton car, finishing seventh at Suzuka in the 2001 season finale.

STRAIGHT INTO THE POINTS

Benetton wasn't a brand new team when it made its debut at the 1986 season-opener in Brazil, rather a re-badged version of the team that had finished 1985 as Toleman. However, the investment that poured in over the close-season resulted in a superior car and Gerhard Berger qualified 16th before racing through the field to score a point for sixth, four places up on team-mate, Teo Fabi. More points would follow.

LIGHT THE TOUCHPAPER

Very few teams show pace-setting speed in their first season, but Benetton did. Propelled by turbocharged BMW engines, the green cars with multi-coloured flashes on their engine covers certainly had ample power, most especially with the boost turned up for qualifying. This resulted in the team's first pole position at the 1986 Austrian GP when Teo Fabi and Gerhard Berger shared an all-Benetton front row.

FIRST YEAR WINNERS

It took until the penultimate grand prix of its first season racing as Benetton (after its development years racing as Toleman) for the team to secure its first win. This came at the Mexican GP in 1986 when Gerhard Berger qualified fourth, gained a place at Nigel Mansell's expense on the opening lap, then kept his cool to run non-stop to victory on his Pirelli tyres while his Goodyear-shod rivals had to pit for fresh rubber.

Above **First year winners:** Gerhard Berger used his tyres sensibly in the Mexican heat in 1986 to give Benetton its first victory one race before the end of its maiden campaign. *Right* **The first and the last:** Berger surprised everyone when he came back from missing three races in 1997 to win the German GP for what would be Benetton's final grand prix success.

THE FIRST AND THE LAST

Not only did Gerhard Berger score Benetton's first win in 1986, but he returned to the team after nine years away racing for Ferrari (twice) and McLaren to be the driver who gave Benetton its last. This came in 1997 at the German GP at Hockenheim. Early-season form hadn't suggested such an outcome would be possible, and he missed three races with a sinus problem, before bouncing back with this popular win from pole.

CAREER STATS

Year	Races	Wins	Points	Ranking
1986	16	1	19	6th
1987	16	0	28	5th
1988	16	0	39	3rd
1989	16	1	39	4th
1990	16	2	71	3rd
1991	16	1	38.5	4th
1992	16	1	91	3rd
1993	16	1	72	3rd
1994	16	8	103	2nd
1995	17	11	137	1st
1996	16	0	68	3rd
1997	17	1	67	3rd
1998	16	0	33	5th
1999	16	0	16	6th
2000	17	0	20	4th
2001	17	0	10	7th

FIRST DRIVER THEN TEAM

|||||||||||||||||||||||||||||||||||||||||||||

Michael Schumacher won the drivers' championship for Benetton in a controversial 1994 season, but the team had to wait until he secured the championship again in 1995 before it could celebrate its own crown. This constructors' championship was wrapped up at the Japanese GP when Schumacher qualified on pole and then led every lap (apart from when pitting). He had already claimed the drivers' title two races earlier.

Above **Career Stats:** Nelson Piquet claimed both of Benetton's wins in 1990 then added another in 1991.
Below **First driver then team:** Michael Schumacher's victory in Germany in 1995 was an important ingredient in his second title and the team's first.

TOP OF ALL THE LISTS

Not only was Michael Schumacher Benetton's longest-serving driver, with 68 starts between his transfer from Jordan towards the end of the 1991 season and the end of 1995, but he was the team's most successful driver by some margin. His tally, before he left to race for Ferrari in 1996, was two drivers' titles, 19 wins, 10 pole positions, 24 fastest laps and 313 points.

GIFTED A VICTORY

Benetton's second win came at Suzuka in 1989, but Alessandro Nannini was only able to celebrate after McLaren's Ayrton Senna was disqualified for rejoining incorrectly after a clash with Alain Prost.

TYRRELL

Once a racer, then a team manager, Ken Tyrrell helped Matra to succeed in F1 before founding his own marque in 1970. Jackie Stewart grabbed two drivers' and one constructors' title to establish the team, but it was never as competitive again and was bought by British American Racing in 1998.

Below **Alpine star:** Jackie Stewart was the driver on whom Tyrrell's successes were built and his strong form in 1973, such as his charge to the podium in Austria, helped him to his second drivers' title with the team.

FACT FILE

Founded: 1960

Years in F1: 1970–1998

Country: England

HQ: Ockham, England

Team principal: N/A as team defunct

Constructors' titles: 1971

Below **Career stats:** Jackie Stewart helped Tyrrell to its only constructors' championship in 1971 by winning six of the 11 rounds, in Spain, Monaco, France, Britain, Germany and Canada.

CAREER STATS

Year	Races	Wins	Points	Ranking
1970	3	0	0	-
1971	11	7	73	1st
1972	12	4	51	2nd
1973	14	5	82	2nd
1974	15	2	52	3rd
1975	14	1	25	5th
1976	16	1	71	3rd
1977	17	0	27	5th
1978	16	1	38	4th
1979	15	0	28	5th
1980	14	0	12	6th
1981	15	0	10	8th
1982	16	1	25	6th
1983	15	1	12	7th
1984	12	0	0*	-
1985	16	0	7	9th
1986	16	0	11	7th
1987	16	0	11	6th
1988	15	0	5	8th
1989	16	0	16	5th
1990	16	0	16	5th
1991	16	0	12	6th
1992	16	0	8	6th
1993	16	0	0	-
1994	16	0	13	6th
1995	17	0	5	8th
1996	16	0	5	8th
1997	17	0	2	10th
1998	16	0	0	-

* All results were stripped from the team in 1984 as illegal fuel was found in its cars at the Detroit GP

VICTORY RUN THWARTED

Although Tyrrell started 1970 running a March chassis for Jackie Stewart, it wasn't until the Canadian GP, the 11th of 13 races, that the Scot was sent out to race in the team's first chassis, the Tyrrell 001. Stewart delighted the team by qualifying on pole, something he'd managed three times in the March with which they'd started the year. Then, heading to victory, his stub-axle failed just before half distance.

MAKING YOUR OWN LUCK

Jackie Stewart raced to five wins and a second in the first seven rounds of 1971. So great was his advantage that he secured the drivers' title and Tyrrell wrapped up the constructors' title at the eighth round of 11. Ironically, the team's first title was claimed at the Austrian GP, in which Stewart retired, albeit because he lost a wheel just a few laps after his closest rival, Ferrari's Jacky Ickx, had dropped out, leaving BRM's Jo Siffert to win.

IMPRESSING THE BOSSES

If you're powered by Ford, winning the Detroit GP isn't a bad way to impress the right people on the streets of the world's automotive capital. This is what happened to Tyrrell in 1983 when Michele Alboreto worked his way forward from sixth to third then gained a place when Rene Arnoux retired his Ferrari from the lead. When new leader Nelson Piquet's Brabham picked up a puncture Alboreto secured the team's 23rd and final win.

Above **Impressing the bosses:** Michele Alboreto keeps his Tyrrell away from the walls in Detroit in 1983 as he motors on towards what would be the team's final victory.

Left **Six wheels for victory:** Patrick Depailler stayed with Tyrrell from 1974 to 1978. This is the French ace in the team's P34 six-wheeler in 1976.

ENDING WITH A WHIMPER

Tyrrell's time in F1 came to an end at the 1998 Japanese GP at Suzuka after 29 years. Sadly, this once proud team, whose World Championship entry was taken over by BAR, went out with a whimper when Ricardo Rosset failed to qualify and Toranosuke Takagi crashed out just after mid-distance in a collision with Minardi's Esteban Tuero. That they were scrapping over last place emphasised how far the team had fallen.

STAYING CLOSE TO HOME

F1 standards have changed greatly, but even in its day it came as a shock to learn that Ken Tyrrell ran his successful team from sheds alongside his family's timber yard business.

WITHDRAWAL HITS TITLE HOPE

Tyrrell was on course for its second constructors' title in 1973 after a year-long battle with Lotus. However, Francois Cevert's death in qualifying for the final round, the United States GP, led Ken Tyrrell to withdraw the team. This left the way clear for Ronnie Peterson to win for Lotus to gift them the crown, meaning that Tyrrell's final title was the drivers' one that Jackie Stewart claimed three races earlier at the Austrian GP.

SIX WHEELS FOR VICTORY

With its typically sensible and somewhat workmanlike cars, Tyrrell wasn't considered to be a team that pursued revolution in design until it launched the P34 in 1976. It had four small wheels at the front to give the car a lower frontal area in order to reduce its drag co-efficient, and it worked well enough for Jody Scheckter to lead Patrick Depailler home in a one-two in the Swedish GP at Anderstorp. But no other team saw fit to copy it.

GETTING BACK ON TRACK

||||||||||||||||||||||||||||||||||||||

With Jackie Stewart's retirement at the end of 1973, and Francois Cevert's tragic death, it was left to Tyrrell's new guard of Patrick Depailler and Jody Scheckter to keep the team at the front. It all came together for the pair in the seventh round, the Swedish GP at Anderstorp, when they claimed the team's first one-two in qualifying before the South African got the jump on the Frenchman and led all the way.

Below **Getting back on track:** After giving Tyrrell its first win of 1974 in Sweden, Jody Scheckter was a winner again three races later in the British GP at Brands Hatch.

COOPER

This was the team that bucked traditional thinking when it entered cars with an engine behind the driver rather than in front and proved that big wasn't best. However, after title glory in 1959 and 1960, its form rather dropped away and instead made its money from selling chassis for others to drive.

*Below **Black Jack:** Jack Brabham had a great run to help himself to the drivers' title and Cooper to the constructors' crown in 1960, although a mechanical problem slowed his progress in the final round, the US GP at Riverside.*

FACT FILE

Founded: 1946
Years in F1: 1953–1968
Country: England
HQ: Surbiton, England
Team principal: N/A as team defunct
Constructors' titles: 1959, 1960

A FOOT IN THE DOOR

Harry Schell's family team entered a Cooper in the 1950 Monaco GP and assorted privateers ran Coopers in 1952. However, it was in 1953 that the Cooper Car Co finally entered a works team, starting by running a car for Adolfo Schwelm-Cruz in the season-opening race in Buenos Aires. He was the first to retire, when his car shed a wheel, and team-mates John Barber and Alan Brown finished a distant eighth and ninth.

COOPER'S HIGH FIVE

Cooper's best winning sequence came in the second year in which it won the constructors' championship, 1960. Much of the momentum required to vanquish Lotus came from this five-race winning streak that started when Jack Brabham won the Dutch GP, then added the next four in Belgium, France, Britain and Portugal.

BEATEN BY A CUSTOMER

Imagine the mixed feelings you'd experience if your marque defeated the big guns to score its maiden victory, yet the car wasn't run by your works team but a private entry. This was what happened to Cooper in 1958 when Rob Walker Racing's Stirling Moss went to the season-opener in Argentina in a Cooper and came away victorious. It would take just over a year for Jack Brabham to win for Cooper Car Co, at Monaco.

OVER AND ALMOST OUT

The last grand prix entered by Cooper Car Co was the 1968 Mexican GP. Vic Elford and Lucien Bianchi qualified 17th and 21st, but only Elford was able to finish, in eighth place. With money tight, that was the end of the works team. A Cooper made one last visit to a World Championship round in the Monaco GP the following year when Elford finished seventh for Colin Crabbe's Antique Automobiles Ltd team.

A SOARAWAY SALES SUCCESS

Cooper did more than run a successful team, as the sale of its F1 chassis enabled many privateers to enter the World Championship. The greatest number fielded was 16 at the 1959 British GP.

Above **Beaten by a customer:** Stirling Moss gave Cooper its first win, for Rob Walker Racing in Argentina in 1958. *Below left* **Career stats:** Jack Brabham won two races on his way to the 1959 title with Cooper. *Below* **One, two, nothing:** Brabham had good reason to smile in both 1959 and 1960.

CAREER STATS

Year	Races	Wins	Points	Ranking
1953	3	0	N/A*	N/A*
1955	1	0	N/A*	N/A*
1957	5	0	N/A*	N/A*
1958	9	2	31	3rd**
1959	8	5	40	1st**
1960	8	6	48	1st
1961	8	0	14	4th
1962	9	1	29	3rd
1963	10	0	25	5th
1964	10	0	16	5th
1965	10	0	14	5th
1966	9	1	30	3rd
1967	11	1	28	3rd
1968	12	0	14	6th

* There was no constructors' championship until 1958
** Including the results of privateer Cooper-fielding team Rob Walker Racing as the constructors' series points were awarded according to the make of car rather than the team running it.

ONE, TWO, NOTHING

Cooper won two constructors' titles, in 1959 and 1960. Jack Brabham led the team's attack, winning the drivers' championship in both those years, ably supported by Bruce McLaren. However, the Australian left Cooper and Kiwi McLaren soldiered on. The rise of Lotus and resurgence of Ferrari left it fighting for the minor point-scoring places through until Cooper's demise at the end of 1968.

FOLLOWING THE LEADER

You might have thought that Jack Brabham would hold the record as Cooper's longest-serving driver. However, it is Bruce McLaren, his team-mate when Jack won the drivers' titles in 1959 and 1960 who comes out far ahead, 64 to 39. The Kiwi joined Cooper at the tail end of 1958 and stayed on until the close of the 1965 season before he, like Brabham before him, headed off to found his own marque.

Above **Following the leader:** Bruce McLaren steers his Cooper T60 Climax to first place at Monaco in 1962. McLaren was Cooper's longest-serving driver. *Below* **A win/win situation:** A privately-entered Cooper driven by John Love was heading for victory in the 1967 South African GP until it had to pit for fuel and Pedro Rodriguez came through to win for the works team.

A WIN/WIN SITUATION

||||||||||||||||||||||||||||||||

The season-opening 1967 South African GP is a race remembered for a 'what if' performance as it was the most famous upset in F1 history. John Love, a driver from neighbouring Rhodesia (now Zimbabwe) was heading for victory in a privately-entered Cooper when he had to pit for fuel with seven laps to go. Love's hiccough left the way clear for one of the works cars, driven by Pedro Rodriguez, to come through to victory.

PART 4

GREAT TRACKS

There are great drivers, great teams and undoubtedly great circuits where the race action has been staged over the decades. The newer circuits outside Europe may possess the latest facilities, but the likes of Monza, Monaco, Silverstone, Spa-Francorchamps and the Nürburgring are steeped in history, packed with the memories of legendary races they have hosted. Some of these are wide open and flat-out, producing mind-boggling average speeds, others narrow and waiting to bite at every tight corner.

Below Room with a view: A privileged few with balcony space in Monaco are blessed with this astonishing view of the exit from the tunnel on the left, the run from the Nouvelle Chicane to Tabac then past the yachts to Piscine.

MONZA

This historic parkland circuit has always been blessed with superlatives, from the fastest race average speed, fastest straightline speed, the closest group finish and even the greatest number of lead changes during a grand prix. And, being in Italy, every second of Ferrari action at Monza is cheered on by the fanatical *tifosi*.

ALFA COMPLETES DOMINATION

The pattern was set when the World Championship came to Monza for the first time in 1950 to round out its inaugural season: Alfa Romeo would win as it had in the previous five races. Indeed, Giuseppe Farina controlled proceedings, but Ferrari challenged for the first time, with Alberto Ascari running second until his engine overheated. After taking over team-mate Dorino Serafini's car, Ascari recovered to bag second place.

A ROYAL APPOINTMENT

Motor racing circuits tend to be built on greenfield sites,
but Monza is a little different, as it was built in 1922 on the parkland surrounding Monza royal palace, which explains the mature trees that surround it, adding to its appeal.

USING THE FAMOUS BANKING

Monza is still considered fearsome, but it was far more so in 1955, 1956, 1960 and 1961 when the Italian GP was held on a layout that included an extra loop with massive banked corners at either end, bringing its lap length up to 6.214 miles. After 1961, when 14 spectators were killed when Wolfgang von Trips crashed into the crowd, the World Championship reverted to Monza's 3.573-mile layout, cutting out the banking.

FANGIO'S HAT-TRICK

Juan Manuel Fangio is the only driver to have achieved three wins in a row at Monza, the great Argentinian achieving this hat-trick between 1953 and 1955. He took the first of these for Maserati, hitting the front out of the final corner when race-leader Giuseppe Farina crashed out. Fangio then added the next two while leading the Mercedes-Benz attack, albeit with a fortunate win in 1954 when others retired and a clear run in 1955.

Right **Fangio's hat trick:** Juan Manuel Fangio races his works Maserati towards victory at Monza in 1953.

Above **Track Facts:** Monza is located in a royal park to the north-west of Milan and its lay-out can be made out, as well as that of the oval circuit cutting the through the trees.

TRACK FACTS

Opened: 1922

Country: Italy

Location: 10 miles north-west of Milan

Active years in F1: 1950–1979, 1981 onwards

Most wins/driver: Michael Schumacher, 5 (1996, 1998, 2000, 2003, 2006)

Most wins/team: Ferrari, 18 (1951, 1952, 1960, 1961, 1964, 1966, 1970, 1975, 1979, 1988, 1996, 1998, 2000, 2002, 2003, 2004, 2006, 2010)

Lap length: 3.600 miles

Number of turns: 11

Lap record: 1m21.046s, 159.909mph, Rubens Barrichello (Ferrari), 2004

Right **Slowing down the cars:** Chris Amon's Matra heads a slipstreaming pack in 1971. *Below* **Exit of Parabolica::** Jenson Button guides his McLaren through this final corner of Monza's lap in 2010 en route to second place.

EXIT OF PARABOLICA

The final corner of Monza's lap, the Parabolica, is a long, long corner. Approached at 210mph, this is a fourth gear bend, with drivers still travelling at 130mph as they turn through this right-hander. Exit speed is critical, and drivers should be changing up to fifth gear and hitting 150mph by the exit, as they need to carry as much speed as possible onto the start/finish straight past the grandstand and on down to the first chicane.

THREE FOR TWO

Lotus and Ferrari share the bragging rights for the longest victory sequence, with the British team having won at Monza three years running from 1972 to 1974, all with its increasingly venerable Lotus 72. Emerson Fittipaldi claimed the first of these, then Ronnie Peterson added the next two. Ferrari's run came 30 years later, as Rubens Barrichello won in 2002 and 2004, with Michael Schumacher taking the flag in 2003.

DELIGHTING THE TIFOSI

Fangio, Moss, Peterson, Piquet, Prost and Vettel have all won three grands prix at Monza. Rubens Barrichello has claimed four victories, but the driver who really put Ferrari back on the map from the late 1990s, Michael Schumacher, is top of the pile, with five wins. These came in 1996, 1998, 2000, 2003 and 2006. To the delight of the Tifosi, Ferrari is the team with the greatest winning record, having taken 19 wins.

SLOWING DOWN THE CARS

Packs of cars slipstreaming around the lap at Monza was a recipe for disaster and so the circuit lay-out was slowed with the insertion of three chicanes for 1972 – one on the run to Curva Grande (the original first corner), another at Roggia and a third at Vialone. As a result Emerson Fittipaldi's race-winning average in his Lotus in 1973 was fully 19.16mph slower than the previous year's mark.

GOING FASTEST AND FASTER

Monza has always been an ultra high-speed circuit. Ferrari's Phil Hill was the first to set an average speed of more than 130mph in 1960. John Surtees topped 140mph in his Honda in 1967.

Just four years later, in the closest group finish ever, Peter Gethin was first with a winning average of over 150mph. Three chicanes were inserted in 1972 and it wasn't until 2003 that Michael Schumacher's average speed topped 150mph with them in place…

MONACO

By rights, there should no longer be a grand prix at Monaco, as its streets are too narrow for contemporary F1 cars, but to discard it would strip the World Championship of the race with the strongest identity. The yachts and beautiful people add glamour, and F1 would be the poorer without it.

IN A CLASS OF HIS OWN

Juan Manuel Fangio was very much the star of the show at Monaco's first World Championship race in 1950. Not only did he put his Alfa Romeo 158 on pole position by 2.6s from team-mate Giuseppe Farina but he also shot off to win the race by a lap, setting fastest lap as he went. His advantage over the slowest of the 20 qualifiers, Johnny Claes in Ecurie Belge Talbot was 20.8s…

EVERY WHICH WAY BUT…

There has been some enthralling racing at Monaco, but Nigel Mansell's pursuit of Ayrton Senna in 1992 was debatably even more exciting than Jochen Rindt's successful chase of Jack

Brabham in 1970. Mansell had led from the start, but what made it Monaco's most memorable race was when a wheel weight came loose and Mansell had to pit for new tyres. On rejoining, with six laps to go, he was 5s down on Senna, then closed right in and was all over him but just couldn't find a way past.

MONACO'S DARKEST DAY

The 1967 Monaco GP was shaping up into an hugely exciting battle between Denny Hulme's Brabham and Lorenzo Bandini's Ferrari when the Italian began to close in. After Hulme's team-mate Jack Brabham retired with engine failure, the Kiwi driver must have been dreading the same. Then, on lap 83, Bandini crashed at the chicane, flipped and was trapped

underneath as his car caught fire. He died three days later.

SIX IN SUCCESSION

McLaren enjoyed an amazing run at Monaco when its drivers won in the principality six years running from 1988 to 1993. Alain Prost inherited victory in the first of these when team-mate Ayrton Senna crashed inexplicably out of a clear lead. Senna then made amends and won the next five races here. Incredibly, Senna's victory at Monaco in 1987 for Lotus was the only non-McLaren win in the 10 years from 1984.

McLAREN'S MONTE MAGIC

One might have thought, given its lengthy history in

F1 that Ferrari would be the team with the most wins at Monaco, but the Italian team has underachieved there by its own standards. For, while it has 18 wins on home ground at Monza, it has won only eight times at Monaco since 1950. McLaren is way clear at the top of the pile at Monaco, having recorded 15 wins up to and including the 2013 season.

THE PRINCE'S PLEASURE

Like Monza, Monaco has a royal connection. Not only was cigarette manufacturer Antony Noghes given permission to stage racing on a street circuit by Prince Louis II, but the Grimaldis' castle overlooks the circuit from on high.

GETTING CLOSE TO THE TON

The fastest ever Monaco GP took place in 2007 when Fernando Alonso won for McLaren at an average speed of 96.655mph, helped in no small part by the race taking place without interruption from the safety car. Lewis Hamilton was confident that he could have gone faster, if only he'd been allowed to attack. By way of comparison, the slowest Monaco GP, in 1950, was won by Juan Manuel Fangio at 61.331mph.

Above **Six in succession:** When Alain Prost won at Monaco in 1988, McLaren had no way of knowing that it would triumph in the next five races there as well.
Left **Getting close to the ton:** The McLarens of Fernando Alonso and Lewis Hamilton dominated in Monaco's fastest ever grand prix in 2007.

Below **Track facts:** The way in which the circuit has to thread its way between Monaco's buildings, twisting around tight corners, is clear from this view of the stretch from Mirabeau to Portier.

TRACK FACTS

Opened: 1922

Country: Monaco

Location: Monte Carlo

Active years in F1: 1950, 1955 onwards

Most wins/driver: Ayton Senna, 6 (1987, 1989, 1990, 1991, 1992, 1993)

Most wins/team: McLaren, 15 (1984-1986, 1988-1993, 1998, 2000, 2002, 2005, 2007-2008)

Lap length: 2.075 miles

Number of turns: 19

Lap record: 1m14.439s, 100.373mph, Michael Schumacher (Ferrari), 2004

WHEN CARS USED TO BREAK

People often view 'the olden days' through rose-tinted spectacles, as it tends to be forgotten that the cars were nowhere near as reliable as today. Take the 1966 Monaco GP when there were just four classified finishers from the 16 starters. Certainly, this was the first race of the new 3-litre engine regulations but this was a pathetic result. Actually, two other cars were still circulating, but they were 25 and 27 laps adrift…

Below **Casino Square:** Denny Hulme drifts his Repco-powered Brabham BT20 as he turns right across the brow onto the descent to Mirabeau in his winning drive in 1967.

CASINO SQUARE

||||||||||||||||||||||||||||||||||||||||||||

One of the most glamorous of Monaco's glamorous spots, Casino Square, passes in a flash for the drivers when the grand prix circus comes to town. The cars arrive over a brow into the preceding corner, Massenet, then feel funnelled by crash barriers and a patch of shade before bursting back into the sunlight as they enter the square.

SILVERSTONE

The site of the first ever World Championship round in 1950, Silverstone is more than the home of the British GP. It's one of the true homes of motor racing not just because of its long history but also because the majority of the teams are based in England, making this their home race.

AND THEY'RE OFF...

Silverstone had the honour of hosting the first round of the first World Championship in 1950. Watched by the royal family from a private grandstand, the race was an Alfa Romeo benefit as not only did its cars fill the first four places on the grid but Giuseppe Farina led home an Alfa one-two-three ahead of Luigi Fagioli and Reg Parnell, with team-mate Juan Manuel Fangio dropping out with a connecting rod failure.

WINNING BY MILES

The greatest winning margin for a British GP at Silverstone was an entire lap, and this has happened three times. This first occurred in 1969 when Matra racer Jackie Stewart trounced the field, with Jacky Ickx the best of the rest for Brabham. The previous biggest winning margin had been in 1956 when Juan Manuel Fangio had beaten his Ferrari team-mates Peter Collins and Alfonso de Portago by 1 min 32 secs.

SKITTLES AT SILVERSTONE

When Jody Scheckter hit F1, he was desperate to make an impression and his over exuberance at the start of the 1973 British GP led to an accident that certainly won't be forgotten. Having started sixth in his McLaren, the young South African ran wide coming out of Woodcote at the end of lap 1 scattering those behind, leaving seven cars unable to take the restart and Andrea de Adamich with leg injuries.

FEW REACH THE FINISH

The fewest finishers in a British GP at Silverstone came in 1958 when only nine cars were still circulating at the chequered flag as Peter Collins led a Ferrari one-two. There were even fewer cars still running in 1975, seven, when the race was stopped after a downpour had cars sliding off all around the circuit. However, as the race was red-flagged, the result was declared from a lap before, when 18 cars were still circulating.

Below **Track facts:** Silverstone's origins as an airfield are clear to see from an aerial shot, with the main runway running from Copse (bottom left) to Stowe (top right).

TRACK FACTS

Opened: 1948
Country: England
Location: 16 miles south-west of Northampton
Active years in F1: 1950–1954, 1956, 1958, 1960, 1963, 1965, 1967, 1969, 1971, 1973, 1975, 1977, 1979, 1981, 1983, 1985, 1987 onwards
Most wins/driver: Alain Prost, 5 (1983, 1985, 1989, 1990, 1993)
Most wins/team: Ferrari, 12 (1951–1954, 1958, 1990, 1998, 2002–2004, 2007, 2011) & McLaren, 12 (1973, 1975, 1977, 1981, 1985, 1988–1989, 1999–2001, 2005, 2008)
Lap length: 3.659 miles
Number of turns: 18
Lap record: 1m30.874s, 145.018mph, Fernando Alonso (Ferrari), 2010

Left **Few reach the finish:** Peter Collins takes the chequered flag to win the 1958 British GP for Ferrari, but only nine of the 20 starters made it to the finish.

APPROACH TO STOWE

Silverstone is an open, airy place. However, at no point does the circuit feel as broad as it does on the Hangar Straight where the drivers race down towards the grandstands and the fast right-hander at Stowe. Arriving at 190mph, the drivers have to drop down two gears to fifth and try to stop themselves from running wide as the track kinks back slightly on itself and drops into the dip known as the Vale.

WINNING FOR BRITAIN

There have been many great races at Silverstone and each generation has a favourite. What can't be denied is that the 1987 British GP was one of the most memorable. This was in a period of Williams' superiority and the battle within the team between Nigel Mansell and Nelson Piquet was as fierce as it was with rivals. With the packed crowd urging him on, Mansell's jinking move to take the lead with two laps to go was brilliant.

FLYING ROUND THE TRACK

Silverstone set something of a trend when its circuit was marked out around the perimeter roads of an airfield in 1948. The airfield had become disused in the wake of the Second World War and the race circuit gave it a new lease of life.

A YEAR OF BLOW-OUTS

Silverstone is a circuit that almost inevitably provides exciting races, but the 2013 British GP won't be remembered so much for its winner, Mercedes' Nico Rosberg, but for the fact that it was a race littered with blow-outs. Four drivers had a tyre fail suddenly, something that was fortunate not to result in an accident at this high-speed venue. Tyre supplier Pirelli had work and some explaining to do before the next race.

SEVEN SETS OF PAIRS

The best victory sequence of any driver at Silverstone is, amazingly, just two, and seven drivers have achieved this since Alberto Ascari's double in 1952 and 1953. Ferrari scored six wins in a row at Silverstone in the 1950s bookended by Gonzalez in 1951 and Peter Collins in 1958. However, the wins were not consecutive as the British GP was held at Aintree in 1955 and 1957, when Mercedes then Vanwall won.

Below **A year of blow-outs:** Ferrari's Felipe Massa was one of four drivers in for a nasty surprise in the 2013 British GP when the Pirelli tyre failures affected the day.
Bottom **Approach to Stowe:** James Hunt leads the formation lap in 1977.

SPA-FRANCORCHAMPS

A win at this Belgian circuit is a feather in any driver's cap. It's a real drivers' circuit, challenging them like few others as it follows the route of much of the circuit that opened in 1924. It has gradient change, it has fast corners and it often has changeable weather to add that extra twist.

FANGIO DRAWS FIRST BLOOD

The fourth round of the inaugural World Championship in 1950 brought the teams to Spa-Francorchamps, and Giuseppe Farina and Juan Manuel Fangio shared a lap time to be equal fastest in qualifying. It was the Argentinian who led away and records show that Raymond Sommer led in his Talbot-Lago, but this was only when Alfa Romeo's star duo pitted for fuel. Thereafter, Fangio came back to score his second win.

 VICTORY WITH TIME TO SPARE

Despite the fastest lap of the 1963 Belgian GP being covered in just under 4 mins, Jim Clark's winning margin over Cooper driver Bruce McLaren was 4 mins 54 secs. This was the largest winning margin in the history of the race and was achieved after rain hit late in the race once the Lotus driver had made his break and McLaren was just a fraction under a lap behind as they completed the circuit at a reduced pace.

ALL TOGETHER NOW...

Some accidents involve a driver throwing his car off the circuit, others one car hitting another. Then there are pile-ups, and the 1998 Belgian GP produced one of these. It happened, as most do, on the first lap and was triggered by David Coulthard after his McLaren had been tagged by a Ferrari. In all, 12 cars were involved and four were too damaged to take the restart, which also resulted in a first corner accident...

 YIELDING ONLY TO THE GREATS

Proving that Spa-Francorchamps is a circuit that is one of the ultimate tests of driving ability, the only drivers to have managed four wins apiece are three of the all-time greats, Jim Clark, Ayrton Senna and Kimi Räikkönen. The Brazilian's run of four consecutive victories followed Alain Prost's win in 1987, making McLaren the team with the longest winning run here, with five victories through until 1991.

SOMETIMES EASY, SOMETIMES HARD

As Spa-Francorchamps has a long lap, you'd expect it to have a high record number of finishers on the winning lap. It does, with 15 drivers managing this in 2013 when Sebastian Vettel led home Fernando Alonso by 17 seconds in a race in which the only change of the lead was on the first lap. The fewest was just two, and it was no freak result, as it happened in 1953, 1954, 1960, 1963, 1965, 1966 and 1987.

 SPA'S UPS AND DOWNS

Not a lot of circuits offer much in the way of gradient changes, but Spa-Francorchamps does. What made the original circuit so unusual, though, was that its 9.2-mile long lap spanned not one but two valleys, cresting the hill in between.

TRACK FACTS

Opened: 1924

Country: Belgium

Location: 20 miles south-east of Liege

Active years in F1: 1950–1956, 1958, 1960-1968, 1970, 1983, 1985–2002, 2004-2005, 2007 onwards

Most wins/driver: Michael Schumacher, 6 (1992, 1995–1997, 2001–2002)

Most wins/team: Ferrari, 12 (1952–1953, 1956, 1961, 1966, 1996–1997, 2001–2002, 2007–2009)

Lap length: 4.352 miles

Number of turns: 19

Lap record: 1m47.263s, 146.065mph, Sebastian Vettel (Red Bull), 2009

Below **Track facts:** The fearsome stretch of the original layout, between the Masta Kink and Stavelot, shows the blast back up the hill to the current circuit exiting at the top right.

EAU ROUGE

||||||||||||||||||||||||||||||||

This is a corner for which television does no justice. You really have to watch trackside at Spa-Francorchamps to appreciate how steep the drop down from La Source is then how much steeper the climb is from the start of the left-right flick as the drivers point their cars at the horizon and attempt to hit the right line over the crest to carry as much speed onto the long ascent to Les Combes.

THE BLINK OF AN EYE

The closest ever finish to a Belgian GP came in 1961 when Phil Hill pipped team-mate Wolfgang von Trips by just 0.70s as Ferrari drivers filled the top four places. The Ferraris were dominant and swapped the lead before first Olivier Gendebien then Richie Ginther dropped back, leaving von Trips and Hill to jostle for position until the American took the lead with five laps to go and stayed there, just, to the finish.

SCHUMACHER LOVES SPA

The closest grand prix circuit to Michael Schumacher's childhood home in Kerpen is actually this one in Belgium. And he loved it, not only making his F1 debut here, but scoring his first F1 win in 1992, then adding five more. Thanks to winning at Spa-Francorchamps as early as 1952, through Alberto Ascari, Ferrari is the most successful team, its 12 wins putting it one ahead of McLaren up to and including 2010.

Below **Schumacher loves Spa:** Twelve months after his F1 debut at Spa for Jordan, Michael Schumacher was able to celebrate his first win with Benetton.

Below **Eau Rouge:** Graham Hill powers through the uphill sweeper in his BRM in 1965 leading the obscured Jim Clark, who soon passed him. *Inset* **The blink of an eye:** Ferrari Dino 156s filled the first four places in 1961, with Phil Hill (4) taking the win.

NÜRBURGRING

There are two Nürburgrings. The first is a 14-mile long monster which trails through forests and was deemed too dangerous for F1 in 1976. The second, the thoroughly modern circuit used today, was built over a small area of the original and has been much modified but now at least the 'new' Nürburgring provides a challenge.

Above **Track Facts:** The opening corner underwent considerable modification for 2002, with the previous right/left Castrol S replaced by a hairpin leading into a long left, a gently sloping hairpin and then a tight right, all overlooked by the attractive grandstand (right).

TRACK FACTS

Opened: 1926
Country: Germany
Location: 35 miles north-west of Koblenz
Active years in F1: 1951–1954, 1956–1958, 1961–1969, 1971–1976, 1985, 1995–2007, 2009, 2011, 2013
Most wins/driver: Michael Schumacher, 5 (1995, 2000–2001, 2004, 2006)
Most wins/team: Ferrari, 14 (1951–53, 1956, 1963–64, 1972, 1974, 1985, 2000–02, 2004, 2006)
Lap length: 3.199 miles
Number of turns: 15
Lap record: 1m29.468s, 128.721mph, Michael Schumacher (Ferrari), 2004

ECONOMY BEATS THIRST

Germany didn't host a World Championship round in 1950, but got its first GP a year later when the Nürburgring hosted the fifth round of seven. Alberto Ascari had won an F2 race there for Ferrari 12 months earlier and used that experience to good effect to win in 1951. Juan Manuel Fangio led the early laps in his Alfa Romeo before Ascari took the lead. As his Ferrari needed only one pitstop and the Alfas needed two, Ascari won.

STEWART'S MASTERCLASS

Jackie Stewart achieved the Nürburgring's largest winning margin in 1968 when he excelled in appalling conditions. Despite qualifying sixth, the Scot took the lead in his Matra on the first lap and then extended his advantage with each of the following 13 laps of the giant Nordschleife circuit. By flagfall, he was 4 mins 3.2 secs ahead of Graham Hill who'd spun his Lotus, got out, turned it around the right way then carried on...

THE FASTEST OF THE BRAVE

The Nürburgring Nordschleife was very fast in places, with the trees lining the route making it feel all the faster. In the 22 occasions that the full circuit was used (up until it was adjudged too dangerous after the 1976 German GP) the fastest race-winning average speed was achieved in 1975 by Carlos Reutemann when he won for Brabham by more than a minute and a half from Jacques Laffite's Williams.

PROVING ITS DANGERS

There were already considerable concerns before the 1976 German GP that the Nürburging Nordschleife circuit was too dangerous for F1. Ironically, one of the main voices requesting change was Niki Lauda, who crashed on lap 2 at Bergwerk and had to be hauled from his burning Ferrari by fellow drivers, suffering major burns. The German GP only returned to the circuit once it had been shortened and made safer.

A TEST FOR CARS AND DRIVERS

The Nürburgring Nordschleife put a strain not only on the cars but the drivers too, with its undulating course containing blind brows among its 176 corners and hazards. The fewest finishers of any of the German GPs held around its 14-mile layout between 1951 and 1976 was just five and one non-classified runner in 1956. Surprisingly, the race, won by Juan Manuel Fangio for Ferrari, lost only two of the retirees to accidents.

FERRARI BEST ON THE NEW

Grands Prix held on the shorter Nürburgring used since 1984 has Michael Schumacher as the most frequent winner with six – from his 1994 victory for Benetton to the one in 2006, the last of four in a Ferrari. Adding in two more from the 16 races held on the 3.199-mile circuit, by Michele Alboreto in 1985 and Rubens Barrichello in 2002, makes Ferrari the most successful team on this track too.

Above **Ferrari best on the new:** Rubens Barrichello kept Ferrari's record on the shortened Nurburgring used since 1984 going with his victory in 2002. *Below* **NGK Schikane:** Low kerbs and an uphill entry encourage drivers to attack.

FERRARI BEST ON THE OLD

Taking only the Nürburgring Nordschleife, the best winning sequence was achieved by Juan Manuel Fangio when he won in a Mercedes in 1954, in a Ferrari in 1956 and in a Maserati in 1957 (there was no 1955 German GP). Ferrari won three in a row in its own right at the start of the decade, winning the first three German GPs from 1951 to 1953 through Alberto Ascari (twice) then Giuseppe Farina.

GOING ROUND THE BEND

The original 14.1-mile Nürburgring Norschleife circuit wasn't the longest circuit ever used in the World Championship, as Pescara was longer at 15.894 miles, but it had the most corners, at 176 per lap… If the 4.8-mile Sudschleife was added, it had more than 200.

NGK SCHIKANE

||||||||||||||||||||||||||||||||||||||

This is chicane acts as a magnet to incident. Approached up a kinked straight that drops from the Bit Kurve, reaches its lowest point at ITT Bogen, then climbs all the way to the turn-in point. If a driver carries too much speed, they will miss the racing line, clatter the kerbs and fail to get in position to accelerate through the right-hand part out of which there is just a short run to the final corner.

HOCKENHEIM

Seen at first as flat-out and boring, Hockenheim was also unloved as it claimed the life of Jim Clark. However, it hoste some classic German GPs and opinions began to change. Then, sadly, its lap was cut short in 2002 and the racing ha never been as good again.

A CLASSIC AFTER A VENUE SWAP

The Grand Prix Drivers' Association boycotted racing at the Nürburging in 1970 as it said safety improvements hadn't been made, so the German GP was held at Hockenheim instead. Jochen Rindt and Jacky Ickx were the pacesetters for Lotus and Ferrari respectively and Ickx grabbed pole, but he and Rindt swapped the lead in a five-car slipstreaming bunch before Rindt made a break with two laps remaining.

HOME ALONE

The largest winning margin for a grand prix at Hockenheim came in 1987 when Nelson Piquet inherited victory in a race of high attrition as his Williams crossed the line 99.591s ahead of Stefan Johansson's McLaren. The closest race here was the first one, in 1970, when Jochen Rindt's Lotus crossed the line just 0.7s ahead of Jacky Ickx's Ferrari, although there have been team one-twos marginally closer.

Below **Track facts:** Multi-coloured grandstand seats mark the stadium section from the Mobil 1 Kurve at the top of the photo to Nordkurve at the bottom right.

READY, STEADY, GO... STOP!

Luciano Burti was fortunate to survive an aerobatic crash on the run to the first corner in the 2001 German GP. The massed accident, the worst in the circuit's history, was triggered by Michael Schumacher's Ferrari suddenly slowing with a gear problem. Unsighted, Burti's Prost couldn't avoid it, flying over Enrique Bernoldi's Arrows. The red flag flew and those with spare cars were able to take the restart.

TRACK FACTS

Opened: 1929

Country: Germany

Location: 15 miles south of Heidelberg

Active years in F1: 1970, 1977–1984, 1986--2006, 2008, 2010, 2012, 2014

Most wins/driver: Michael Schumacher, 4 (1995, 2002, 2004, 2006)

Most wins/team: Ferrari, 10 (1977, 1982–1983, 1994, 1999–2000, 2002, 2004, 2006, 2012)

Lap length: 2.842 miles

Number of turns: 17

Lap record: 1m14.917s, 138.685mph, Kimi Raikkonen (McLaren) 2004

Left **Ready, steady, go...stop!:** The world turned upside down for Luciano Burti in 2001 when the Prost driver crashed into Michael Schumacher's stuttering Ferrari on the run to the first corner and flipped, fortunately without injury.

A TRICKY TRACK TO WIN ON

Hockenheim was a circuit that didn't yield to the same driver twice until its 11th grand prix, when Nelson Piquet scored his second win there. Ayrton Senna then scored three in a row before Michael Schumacher became the most successful visitor when he took his fourth win in 2006. Of the teams, Ferrari is out front with Fernando Alonso's win there in 2012 being its 10th, putting it two ahead of Williams.

CUTTING THE SPEED

The original Hockenheim circuit, with its 215mph straights, produced races with high average speeds. The highest came in 2001 when Ralf Schumacher achieved a winning average in his Williams of 146.176mph. The shortened circuit layout, used from 2002, has a highest average of 134.124mph, achieved by Michael Schumacher in his Ferrari in 2004 before aerodynamics were restricted and engine life extended from 2005.

A RACE OF TWISTS AND TURNS

One of Hockenheim's greatest races came in 1987 when Nelson Piquet, Ayrton Senna, Nigel Mansell and Alain Prost were fighting for honours.

Senna blasted his Lotus into the lead ahead of Mansell's Williams. Senna was soon demoted to fourth and it turned into a battle between Prost and Mansell until the Williams' engine failed. With four laps to go, Prost's McLaren had alternator failure and Piquet won the day.

THREE IN A ROW, TIMES THREE

Ayrton Senna enjoyed a period of superiority at Hockenheim at the end of the 1980s. Having just joined McLaren from Lotus, he recorded the best victory sequence by winning in 1988, 1989 and 1990. Williams also enjoyed a hat-trick of wins at Hockenheim directly after that when Nigel Mansell was triumphant in 1991 and 1992, followed by Alain Prost taking the third in his final title-winning year, 1993.

Above **A tricky track to win on:** Fernando Alonso celebrates in 2010 after giving Ferrari its 11th win at Hockenheim. *Below* **Sudkurve:** Rene Arnoux's Ferrari flashes through the final corner of the lap in 1983 chased by Andrea de Cesaris's Alfa Romeo.

ALMOST TWO MILES LOST

Until 1965, Hockenheim's lap was 4.779 miles long and ran anticlockwise. Then an autobahn was built across its old lay-out, and the area now behind the pits grandstands was lost. The next chop came for 2002, with the forest loop curtailed and the lap length cut from 4.239 miles to just 2.842.

SUDKURVE

The final corner of a lap of Hockenheim circuit is right at the foot of the giant grandstands and it's a surprisingly difficult corner. Despite being only a third-gear, 90 degree right-hander, it's awkward as it follows so closely after the previous corner, Elf Kurve, and failure to get in position to take the proper line through here hampers a driver's speed all the way past the pits to Nordkurve and on to Einfahrt Parabolika.

MONTREAL

The Circuit Gilles Villeneuve is one of the very best examples of a circuit close enough to a metropolis to attract a capacity crowd. Over the years this circuit, on an island in a river, has produced great racing, but it is better known for being a car-breaker and having a chicane that bites.

THE DREAM START

Imagine the excitement when Quebec welcomed its greatest star to its greatest city, as Montreal did for its first grand prix in 1978. Gilles Villeneuve qualified his Ferrari third behind Jean-Pierre Jarier's Lotus and Jody Scheckter's Wolf. Having slipped behind Alan Jones' Williams, he regained third when Jones had a puncture. Then he passed Scheckter. Jarier held a 30s lead but retired, leaving Villeneuve to score his first win.

Below **Final chicane:** Ayrton Senna negotiates the final chicane during the 1988 Canadian Grand Prix at the Circuit Gilles Villeneuve in Montreal, on his way to victory.

RAIN, RAIN, GO AWAY

Safety car deployments are all too common in grands prix held at the Circuit Gilles Villeneuve and Jacques Laffite's winning average in his Ligier was just 85.310mph in 1981, more than 22mph down on the previous year. Slowed by torrential rain, this was still much faster than Jenson Button's 46.518mph average in 2011 when the race was not only run on a slick and treacherous circuit but endured a two-hour stoppage too.

Below **Rain, rain, go away:** Jacques Laffite splashes his Ligier through the wet en route to victory at an average of just 85mph in 1981.

FINAL CHICANE (TURN 13)

||||||||||||||||||||||||||||||||||

All a driver can see straight ahead as they accelerate up to 200mph down the final straight from L'Epingle is the pit entry. The track disappears to the right into this very tight chicane. Getting the braking just right is very difficult, with few sighting points to judge it by. The exit is blind at this point and many drivers get the second (left-hand) part of the sequence wrong and then slam into the wall beyond.

Below **Track facts:** Looking down at the start/finish straight and the opening sequence of corners shows just how much water surrounds the circuit's island, with the Olympic rowing lake running behind the cramped paddock.

TRACK FACTS

Opened: 1978

Country: Canada

Location: Ile de Notre Dame, Montreal

Active years in F1: 1978-1986, 1988-2008, 2010 onwards

Most wins/driver:
Michael Schumacher, 7
(1994, 1997-1998, 2000, 2002-2004)

Most wins/team: Ferrari, 10 (1978, 1983, 1985, 1995, 1997, 1998, 2000, 2002-2004)

Lap length: 2.710 miles

Number of turns: 14

Lap record: 1m13.622s, 132.511mph, Rubens Barrichello (Ferrari), 2004

A VIOLENT BARREL-ROLL

Thanks to the endless efforts to make racing cars safer, drivers today unlike their predecessors stand every chance of surviving accidents. Robert Kubica had reason to thank those responsible for these advances after the 2007 Canadian GP when his BMW Sauber clipped Jarno Trulli's Toyota on the approach to the hairpin, cannoned off a wall and disintegrated as it rolled back across the track. He escaped with just bruising.

BY THE SMALLEST OF MARGINS

The closest finish to a grand prix held here came in 2000 when Michael Schumacher won by 0.174s from Ferrari team-mate Rubens Barrichello. The race was hit by rain midway and Barrichello worked his way past Giancarlo Fisichella to second but wasn't allowed to challenge for the lead. All too often, races here have been close in their first half before the circuit's car-breaking characteristics thinned the field.

ISLAND OF ADVENTURE

The Circuit Gilles Villeneuve has one of the sport's most unusual settings. Not only is it built on an island, but it runs alongside the rowing lake used at the 1976 Olympics and surrounds the futuristic pavilions built on the site of world trade show, Expo 67.

MICHAEL'S MONTREAL MAGNIFICENCE

Michael Schumacher won three Canadian GPs in succession at Montreal between 2002 and 2004 for the best winning sequence the venue has known. Had he not been beaten by brother Ralf's Williams in 2001, his winning run would have stretched for five straight years. Such was Michael's success at the Circuit Gilles Villeneuve that he was only beaten twice there from 1997 to 2004, with Mika Hakkinen winning in 1999.

FERRARI LEADS THE WAY

Seven-time World Champion Michael Schumacher won seven times – once with Benetton and then six times with Ferrari – at the Circuit Gilles Villeneuve and this helped Ferrari to become the team that has won the most frequently here, with a tally of 10 triumphs. McLaren and Williams also have a strong record at the Canadian circuit, having claimed seven wins here apiece.

Above **Ferrari leads the way:** Michael Schumacher wasn't Ferrari's only winner in Montreal, as Jean Alesi had his day of days here in 1995 when he scored his only grand prix victory then rode back to parc ferme on Schumacher's Benetton.

INTERLAGOS

Although rough around the edges, Interlagos remains one of the world's great racing circuits, with its dipping, twisting lap providing scope for the brave to overtake. Often a late-season race, Interalgos has been made all the more exciting by hosting some classic title shoot-outs.

THE WORST WEATHER

When rain arrives in Brazil, as it often has throughout the history of the Brazilian GP, it hits hard. In 1993, the water lay so deep at some points on the circuit that drivers struggled not to aquaplane. Aguri Suzuki spun on the start/finish straight and even multiple World Champion Alain Prost rotated when he came upon the scene of Christian Fittipaldi's spun Minardi. Ayrton Senna overcame a stop-go penalty to win on this very wet day.

THE FAST AND THE SLOW

Bad weather and accidents are the main reasons for speeds being kept in check

at Interlagos. The slowest Brazilian GP held at this undulating circuit was won by Jordan's Giancarlo Fisichella in 2003 at an average winning speed of 95.009mph.

after the race spent its first eight laps behind a safety car. Conversely, the fastest grand prix here was won by Ferrari's Michael Schumacher in 2004 at an average of 129.566mph.

HALF A SECOND, TWO BROTHERS

The closest finish to a Brazilian GP at Interlagos was when Michael Schumacher won in 2002 ahead of his brother Ralf whose Williams had chased him home, losing out by just 0.588s. It was the first outing for the Ferrari F2002 and although Ralf could close in on the Ferrari he simply couldn't find a way past, perhaps wisely being wary as Michael had

clashed with Ralf's team-mate Juan Pablo Montoya on lap 1.

FEW ACHIEVE DOMINANCE

One unusual feature of Interlagos's history is that no driver has ever won at the circuit in the São Paulo suburbs more than two years in a row. Emerson Fittipaldi won in 1973 and 1974, then Michael Schumacher in 1994 and 1995, Mika Hakkinen in 1998 and 1999 and Juan Pablo Montoya in 2004 and 2005. Two teams have won three in a row, though: Ferrari from 2006 to 2008, then Red Bull from 2009 to 2011.

Left **Half a second, two brothers:** Michael Schumacher (left) was chased to the finish in 2002 by brother Ralf.

Above **Track facts:** The circuit sits in a natural amphitheatre as is clear when viewing from above the Curva do Sol and looking back towards the Senna S.

TRACK FACTS

Opened: 1940

Country: Brazil

Location: 9 miles south of Sao Paulo

Active in F1: 1973–77, 1979–80, 1990 on

Most wins/driver: Michael Schumacher, 4 (1994, 1995, 2000, 2002)

Most wins/team: Ferrari, 8 (1976, 1977, 1990, 2000, 2002, 2006, 2007, 2008) & McLaren (1974, 1991, 1993, 1998–99, 2001, 2005, 2012)

Lap length: 2.667 miles

Lap record: 1m11.473s, 134.837mph, Juan Pablo Montoya (Williams), 2004

Below right **A popular home win:** Emerson Fittipaldi leads away from pole position to score for Lotus in the 1973 Brazilian GP.

FERRADURA

There is gradient change aplenty at the home of the Brazilian GP, and Ferradura is one of the trickiest of these. It's approached up the climb from Descida do Lago, then the track arcs gently to the right, but it's made difficult by the fact that it's at the crest of this hill before a level run from its exit to the next turn, Laranja. Taken in fifth gear, it's easy for drivers to carry too much speed in and spin.

RUNNING TO FORM

Even the quickest of examinations of a Formula 1 history book will reveal that Michael Schumacher is way out clear in the number of grand prix victories, with 91, so it's likely that he will be the driver with the most wins at any of the contemporary circuits. Interlagos is no different and his tally of four wins is the greatest. Likewise, Ferrari and McLaren, the teams at the top of the victories chart here, have eight wins each.

BETWEEN THE LAKES

The name Interlagos means 'between the lakes' and the original 4.946-mile circuit lay-out crossed the lake at the foot of its hillside site twice. The shorter track, introduced in 1990 crosses the lake only once, at Descida do Lago.

- - - - - - - - - - - - - - - - -

Below **Ferradura:** This long righthander with its uphill entry and downhill exit remains a true test of driving skill.

A POPULAR HOME WIN

After holding a non-championship race in 1972, a Brazilian GP at Interlagos had World Championship blessing for 1973. Emerson Fittipaldi was the nation's hope and he qualified second behind his Lotus team-mate Ronnie Peterson. Fittipaldi took the lead at the start and fellow Brazilian Carlos Pace leapt into second in his Surtees, but was soon demoted. Fittipaldi was untouchable though and his was a popular win.

SENNA, BUT ONLY JUST

Ayrton Senna had won plenty of races but never at home, and it was starting to get to him. Having won 1991's opening race in Phoenix, he put his McLaren on pole at Interlagos (as he had in the three preceding years). Senna made the race truly memorable for the home fans as he led every lap, until he hit gearbox trouble and had to run the final seven laps in sixth gear, just holding off Riccardo Patrese's Williams.

CIRCUIT DE CATALUNYA

Spain's relationship with Formula One was hit and miss but the opening of the Circuit de Catalunya gave teams a real reason to go there, primarily to test. The arrival of Fernando Alonso has now given the Spanish a hero to cheer and he has the crowds pouring in.

TRACK FACTS

Opened: 1991
Country: Spain
Location: 15 miles north of Barcelona
Active years in F1: 1991 onwards
Most wins/driver: Michael Schumacher, 6 (1995, 1996, 2001, 2002, 2003, 2004)
Most wins/team: Ferrari, 7 (1996, 2001, 2002, 2003, 2004, 2007, 2008)
Lap length: 2.892 miles
Number of turns: 16
Lap record: 1m21.670s, 127.500mph, Kimi Raikkonen (Ferrari), 2008

ONE CITY, FOUR CIRCUITS

Most countries that have hosted a grand prix have moved their race around the country. However, although Spain has spread its grand prix between five venues, four of these have been in or around Barcelona. Pedralbes was the first, with its around-the-houses circuit, used between 1951 and 1954. The race returned to Barcelona in 1969 when a track was laid out around Montjuich Park in the centre of town. After spectators were killed there in 1975, the city had to wait until 1991 for the race to return, to the purpose-built Circuit de Catalunya, north of the city. The number of Barcelona-based venues reaches four if pre-World Championship circuits are included, with the Sitges oval south of the city hosting the 1923 Spanish GP.

A THRILLING DEBUT

The first Spanish GP held at the Circuit de Catalunya in 1991 is remembered for Nigel Mansell's scrap with Ayrton Senna. Gerhard Berger led for McLaren, with Senna second, but Mansell was on a charge in his Williams and pulled alongside the Brazilian's McLaren as they passed the pits. They were inches apart at 180mph and Senna refused to cede, but Mansell was on the inside line and so took the place and went on to win.

Above **Track facts:** The end of the lap, as it was before a chicane was introduced in 2007. *Right* **A thrilling debut:** Nigel Mansell pulls his Williams alongside Ayrton Senna's McLaren during the track's 1991 debut.

MALDONADO ENDS DROUGHT

Despite having had its cars win the Spanish GP five times in the first seven visits to the Circuit de Catalunya, Williams had to wait a further 15 years until it could celebrate there again. This victory in 2012 came against the form book, but the team understood their Pirelli tyres' behaviour better than any rivals and the mistake-prone Pastor Maldonado held off Fernando Alonso's Ferrari to the flag.

SCHUEY'S SEXTET

A sextet of Michael Schumacher's record 91 grand prix wins came at the Circuit de Catalunya. The seven-time World Champion won for Benetton in 1995, Ferrari in 1996 and then again each year from 2001 to 2004. Mika Hakkinen is next on the list, with three wins.

FOUR IN A ROW

Since the Spanish GP moved to the Circuit de Catalunya in 1991, it has developed a habit of being won by one team for several years in succession. Williams won through Nigel Mansell (twice), Alain Prost and Damon Hill. Then McLaren took three in a row from 1998 and should have made that four in 2001, but Mika Hakkinen was denied. The team that grabbed that win, Ferrari, then won again in 2002, 2003 and 2004, with Michael Schumacher at the wheel each time.

WET WEATHER MASTERCLASS

Every now and again a driver proves why he is one of the greats by producing a drive that makes his rivals look ordinary. Michael Schumacher, already a double World Champion, produced just such a drive in Spain in 1996 when exceedingly heavy rain turned the circuit into a lake. Yet he sailed clear effortlessly to win by 45s. This was his first of many wins for Ferrari.

HAKKINEN THWARTED

Losing a win through mechanical failure is gutting. Yet, to lose out on the final lap is the cruellest cut of all. This is what befell Mika Hakkinen in 2001 when his quest to make it four wins in a row for McLaren came unstuck when his engine tightened as he flashed past the pits for the final time. By Turn 3, it was all over, his tactical win plucked away and handed to Michael Schumacher.

ELF

||||||||||||||||||||||||||||||||||||||||||

Overtaking isn't easy at the Circuit de Catalunya and one of the most reliable spots for passing moves is the first turn, Elf. Approached at around 190mph in seventh gear down the long, sloping start/finish straight, this corner is a 90-degree righthander. Late braking can be rewarded if a driver can still haul his car right to get onto the optimum line for Turn 2, making the sequence of corners almost an 'S'.

A HOME WIN AT LAST

For decades, Spanish fans had to look to their motorcycle racers for any glory, with the nation's car racing trophy cabinet remaining empty. Alfonso de Portago showed promise but was killed in 1957. The wait went on until Fernando Alonso came along. His first few attempts came to nothing, but this was put right when he landed a drive with Renault and won the Spanish GP in 2006, ushering in thousands of new fans who wanted to see a home win, which they got again in 2013.

Above **A home win at last:** Fernando Alonso has the marshals waving their flags in celebration in 2006 after becoming the first Spaniard to win the Spanish GP. *Below* **Elf:** Mercedes GP's Nico Rosberg leads the field out Elf into Turn 2 at the start in 2013.

SUZUKA

Suzuka stands out as one of an elite group of circuits that provide the drivers with a real challenge. With some occasionally extreme weather plus its scheduled date towards the business end of the season, this Japanese venue has hosted some memorable races, with the great Ayrton Senna becoming a real fans' favourite here.

STARTING WITH A BANG

The first World Championship round held at Suzuka was in 1987 – the only two previous Japanese GPs had been held at the Fuji Speedway in 1976 and 1977. The 1987 race saw drama as early as qualifying when Nigel Mansell crashed and ended his title challenge by injuring his back. This took the pressure off his Williams teammate Nelson Piquet, who was cruising to fourth place when his Renault engine failed. Victory was taken by Gerhard Berger for Ferrari, with Ayrton Senna second for Lotus.

BACK IN THE BEGINNING

The first Japanese GP was held back in 1963, at Suzuka, just a year after the circuit was opened. It wasn't a Formula One event, but a sportscar one, with victory being taken by the best of a field of European drivers brought over to Japan to bolster the race entry. The winner was British driver Peter Warr in a Lotus 23 who went on to become Lotus founder Colin Chapman's righthand man and, after Chapman's death in 1982, the team principal.

HIGHS AND LOWS

Ayrton Senna was supported with a passion by Japanese fans, but his all-attack attitude that they loved led not only to victories in 1988 and 1993, but disqualification after winning in 1989, penalized for his McLaren having received a pushstart from the marshals as it sat across the track after being hit by Alain Prost. He extracted revenge on Prost a year later and drove the Ferrari driver off the circuit at the first corner.

TRACK FACTS

Opened: 1962
Country: Japan
Location: 30 miles south-west of Nagoya
Active years in F1: 1987-2006, 2009 onwards
Most wins/driver: Michael Schumacher, 6 (1995, 1997, 2000, 2001, 2002, 2004)
Most wins/team: Ferrari, 7 (1987, 1997, 2000, 2001, 2002, 2003, 2004)
Lap length: 3.608 miles
Number of turns: 18
Lap record: 1m31.540s, 141.904mph, Kimi Räikkönen (McLaren), 2005

Above **Track facts:** Suzuka is the only F1 circuit overlooked by a Ferris wheel, and this is the view to the starting grid. *Left* **Highs and lows:** Ayrton Senna waves to his besotted fans after winning in 1993, but other years weren't so kind.

SHINING AT HOME

No Japanese driver has yet won a round of the World Championship, and only twice has a Japanese driver finished on the podium. So, it was with a strong sense of occasion that Aguri Suzuki guided his Larrousse to third place in the 1990 Japanese GP, advancing from 10th on the grid. Takuma Sato finished fifth at Suzuka for Jordan in 2002 and then improved on that by finishing third for BAR at Indianapolis in 2004, while Kamui Kobayashi had a spectacular charge up the order to seventh for Sauber at Suzuka in 2010.

S-CURVES

||||||||||||||||||||||||||||||||||||||||||

Suzuka is an extremely difficult circuit, but the S-Curves are rated as being even more technically difficult than fabled, high-speed 130R bend. This stretch of track early in the lap includes two left-hand bends and two rights, alternating, on a steepening upward slope as the track climbs the hillside beyond a pair of lakes behind the paddock.

The final corner of the sequence, the second right-hander, is the tightest of all and the nature of the layout is such that any mistake is magnified through each of the corners as it becomes ever harder to get back onto the racing line.

FINN FLIES FASTEST

Kimi Räikkönen holds the lap record, setting the fastest ever race lap around this sinuous circuit in 2005 when he threw his McLaren around the 3.608-mile lap in 1m31.540s, for an average speed of 141.904mph. The Finn's drive in that race was magnificent, as he had to make up ground having started from 17th on the grid after rain hit qualifying as he was making his one-at-a-time run. He only made it back into the lead after a late-race pitstop by passing Giancarlo Fisichella's Renault on the way down the hill past the pits into the final lap.

Above **Finn flies fastest:** Kimi Räikkönen attacks Suzuka's bends in 2005, where his amazing turn of speed earned him a race lap record.

SEVERE WEATHER

Japan in autumn can be hit by major storms and the 2010 Japanese GP came close to being called off when a typhoon passed through, delaying qualifying until the Sunday morning when, mercifully, it turned out dry. Sixteen years before that, the race was started in the wet, had a safety car come out when drivers aquaplaned off the track and then had to be called to a halt after 15 laps when Martin Brundle hit a marshal attending a crashed car. It was restarted 20 minutes later.

MIGHTY MICHAEL

Michael Schumacher holds the record for scoring the most grand prix wins at Suzuka, with six victories from his first, for Benetton in 1995, to his most recent, for Ferrari in 2004. Emphasising his prowess, Michael was right in the mix in 1994 before being beaten by Damon Hill in a very wet race. In 1998, he started from the back of the grid after stalling on pole position and raced up to third before pulling off with a puncture, enabling Mika Hakkinen to land the drivers' title. In 2006, he retired with engine failure while leading. He finished second in 1994, 1996 and 1999.

Below **S-Curves:** Nelson Piquet guides his Williams FW11B through Dunlop Curve on F1's first visit in 1987, with the twisting S-Curves shown clearly in his wake.

FORMULA 1 STATISTICS

Michael Schumacher's phenomenal Formula 1 career propelled him at the top of pretty much every table of driver records and it has also helped Ferrari to top the constructors' tables too. However, the statistics reveal some perhaps forgotten names, emphasising how the world's most spectacular sport has ebbed and flowed over the decades as teams and drivers have shone brightly then waned or, sadly, been extinguished. **Note:** Statistics correct to the start of 2016.

DRIVER RECORDS

STARTS

325	Rubens Barrichello	163	Thierry Boutsen
308	Michael Schumacher	162	Mika Hakkinen
285	Jenson Button		Johnny Herbert
256	Riccardo Patrese	161	Ayrton Senna
	Jarno Trulli	159	Heinz-Harald Frentzen
254	Fernando Alonso	158	Martin Brundle
247	David Coulthard		Olivier Panis
232	Kimi Räikkönen		Sebastian Vettel
230	Giancarlo Fisichella	152	John Watson
	Felipe Massa	149	Rene Arnoux
216	Mark Webber	147	Eddie Irvine
210	Gerhard Berger		Derek Warwick
208	Andrea de Cesaris	146	Carlos Reutemann
204	Nelson Piquet	144	Emerson Fittipaldi
201	Jean Alesi	135	Jean-Pierre Jarier
199	Alain Prost	132	Eddie Cheever
194	Michele Alboreto		Clay Regazzoni
187	Nigel Mansell	128	Mario Andretti
185	Nick Heidfeld	126	Jack Brabham
	Nico Rosberg	123	Ronnie Peterson
180	Ralf Schumacher	119	Pierluigi Martini
176	Graham Hill	116	Damon Hill
175	Jacques Laffite		Jacky Ickx
171	Niki Lauda		Alan Jones
167	Lewis Hamilton	114	Keke Rosberg
165	Jacques Villeneuve		Patrick Tambay

WINS

91	Michael Schumacher	12	Mario Andretti
51	Alain Prost		Alan Jones
43	Lewis Hamilton		Carlos Reutemann
42	Sebastian Vettel	11	Rubens Barrichello
41	Ayrton Senna		Felipe Massa
32	Fernando Alonso		Jacques Villeneuve
31	Nigel Mansell	10	Gerhard Berger
27	Jackie Stewart		James Hunt
25	Jim Clark		Ronnie Peterson
	Niki Lauda		Jody Scheckter
24	Juan Manuel Fangio	9	Mark Webber
23	Nelson Piquet	8	Denny Hulme
22	Damon Hill		Jacky Ickx
20	Mika Hakkinen	7	Rene Arnoux
	Kimi Räikkönen		Juan Pablo Montoya
16	Stirling Moss	6	Tony Brooks
15	Jenson Button		Jacques Laffite
14	Jack Brabham		Riccardo Patrese
	Emerson Fittipaldi		Jochen Rindt
	Graham Hill		Ralf Schumacher
	Nico Rosberg		John Surtees
13	Alberto Ascari		Gilles Villeneuve
	David Coulthard		

Left **Starts:** Making more than 100 grand prix starts doesn't guarantee you a win, as Jean-Pierre Jarier discovered, although he had looked all set to hit that target early in his F1 career when he dominated at Interlagos for Shadow but retired.

Above **Wins:** Michael Schumacher celebrates winning the 2006 Chinese GP for Ferrari, not knowing that this record 91st Formula 1 victory would be his last.

WINS IN ONE SEASON

13	Michael Schumacher	2004
	Sebastian Vettel	2013
11	Lewis Hamilton	2014
	Michael Schumacher	2002
	Sebastian Vettel	2011
10	Lewis Hamilton	2015
9	Nigel Mansell	1992
	Michael Schumacher	1995
	Michael Schumacher	2000
	Michael Schumacher	2001
8	Mika Hakkinen	1998
	Damon Hill	1996
	Michael Schumacher	1994
	Ayrton Senna	1988
7	Fernando Alonso	2005
	Fernando Alonso	2006
	Jim Clark	1963
	Alain Prost	1984, 1988 & 1993
	Kimi Räikkönen	2005
	Ayrton Senna	1991
	Jacques Villeneuve	1997
6	Mario Andretti	1978
	Alberto Ascari	1952
	Jim Clark	1965
	Juan Manuel Fangio	1954
	Damon Hill	1994
	James Hunt	1976
	Nigel Mansell	1987
	Kimi Räikkönen	2007
	Michael Schumacher	1998
	Michael Schumacher	2003
	Michael Schumacher	2006
	Ayrton Senna	1989 & 1990

POLE POSITIONS

68	Michael Schumacher
65	Ayrton Senna
49	Lewis Hamilton
46	Sebastian Vettel
33	Jim Clark
	Alain Prost
32	Nigel Mansell
29	Juan Manuel Fangio
26	Mika Hakkinen
24	Niki Lauda
	Nelson Piquet
22	Fernando Alonso
	Nico Rosberg
20	Damon Hill
18	Mario Andretti
	Rene Arnoux
17	Jackie Stewart
16	Felipe Massa
	Stirling Moss
	Kimi Räikkönen
14	Alberto Ascari
	Rubens Barrichello
	James Hunt
	Ronnie Peterson
13	Jack Brabham
	Graham Hill
	Jacky Ickx
	Juan Pablo Montoya
	Jacques Villeneuve
	Mark Webber
12	Gerhard Berger
	David Coulthard
10	Jochen Rindt

FASTEST LAPS

76	Michael Schumacher
42	Kimi Räikkönen
41	Alain Prost
30	Nigel Mansell
28	Jim Clark
	Lewis Hamilton
25	Mika Hakkinen
	Sebastian Vettel
24	Niki Lauda
23	Juan Manuel Fangio
	Nelson Piquet
21	Fernando Alonso
	Gerhard Berger
19	Damon Hill
	Stirling Moss
	Ayrton Senna
	Mark Webber
18	David Coulthard
17	Rubens Barrichello
16	Felipe Massa
15	Clay Regazzoni
	Jackie Stewart
14	Jacky Ickx
	Nico Rosberg
13	Alberto Ascari
	Alan Jones
	Riccardo Patrese

Above **Wins in one season:**
James Hunt had a tumultuous
1976 campaign for McLaren, but
his six wins proved to be just
enough to overhaul Niki Lauda.

TITLES

7	Michael Schumacher
5	Juan Manuel Fangio
4	Alain Prost
	Sebastian Vettel
3	Jack Brabham
	Lewis Hamilton
	Niki Lauda
	Nelson Piquet
	Ayrton Senna
	Jackie Stewart
2	Fernando Alonso*
	Alberto Ascari
	Jim Clark
	Emerson Fittipaldi
	Mika Hakkinen
	Graham Hill
1	Mario Andretti
	Jenson Button
	Giuseppe Farina
	Mike Hawthorn
	Damon Hill
	Phil Hill
	Denis Hulme
	James Hunt
	Alan Jones
	Nigel Mansell
	Kimi Räikkönen
	Jochen Rindt
	Keke Rosberg
	Jody Scheckter
	John Surtees
	Jacques Villeneuve

POINTS*

1896	Sebastian Vettel
1867	Lewis Hamilton
1778	Fernando Alonso
1566	Michael Schumacher
1214	Jenson Button
1209.5	Nico Rosberg
1174	Kimi Räikkönen
1071	Felipe Massa
1047.5	Mark Webber
798.5	Alain Prost
658	Rubens Barrichello
614	Ayrton Senna
535	David Coulthard
485.5	Nelson Piquet
482	Nigel Mansell
420.5	Niki Lauda
420	Mika Hakkinen
385	Gerhard Berger
360	Damon Hill
	Daniel Ricciardo
	Jackie Stewart
329	Ralf Schumacher
326	Valtteri Bottas
310	Carlos Reutemann
307	Juan Pablo Montoya
290	Nico Hulkenberg
289	Graham Hill
287	Romain Grosjean
281	Emerson Fittipaldi
	Riccardo Patrese
277.5	Juan Manuel Fangio
275	Giancarlo Fisichella
274	Jim Clark
273	Robert Kubica
266	Sergio Perez

* This figure is gross tally,
ie. including scores that
were later dropped.

CONSTRUCTOR RECORDS

STARTS

- 908 Ferrari
- 781 McLaren
- 700 Williams
- 572 Renault* (nee Toleman then Benetton then Renault* then Lotus II)
- 526 Toro Rosso (+ Minardi)
- 492 Lotus
- 435 Force India (+ Jordan then Midland then Spyker)
- 418 Tyrrell
- 409 Prost (+ Ligier)
- 402 Sauber (+ BMW Sauber)
- 394 Brabham
- 383 Arrows
- 338 Red Bull (+ Stewart + Jaguar Racing)
- 303 Mercedes GP (+ BAR + Honda Racing + Brawn)

NB. The Lotus stats are based on the team that ran from 1958 to 1994, whereas those listed as Renault* are for the team that started as Toleman in 1981, became Benetton in 1986 then Renault in 2002 and ran as Lotus 2012-15. The Renault listings are from its first spell in F1 between 1977 and 1985. The stats for Red Bull Racing include those of the Stewart GP and Jaguar Racing teams from which it evolved. Likewise, Force India's stats include those of Jordan and Midland plus Spyker; and Scuderia Toro Rosso those of Minardi.

WINS

- 224 Ferrari
- 181 McLaren
- 114 Williams
- 79 Lotus
- 51 Red Bull (+ Stewart)
- 49 Renault*
- 45 Mercedes GP (+ Honda Racing + Brawn GP)
- 35 Brabham
- 23 Tyrrell
- 17 BRM
- 16 Cooper
- 15 Renault
- 10 Alfa Romeo
- 9 Ligier
    - Maserati
    - Matra
    - Mercedes
    - Vanwall
- 4 Jordan
- 3 March
    - Wolf
- 2 Honda
- 1 BMW Sauber
    - Eagle
    - Hesketh
    - Penske
    - Porsche
    - Shadow
    - Toro Rosso

WINS IN ONE SEASON

16	Mercedes GP	2014		Williams	1987
	Mercedes GP	2015	8	Benetton	1994
15	Ferrari	2002 & '04		Brawn GP	2009
	McLaren	1988		Ferrari	2003
13	Red Bull	2013		Lotus	1978
12	McLaren	1984		McLaren	1991
	Red Bull	2011		McLaren	2007
	Williams	1996		McLaren	2012
11	Benetton	1995		Renault	2005
10	Ferrari	2000		Renault	2006
	McLaren	2005		Williams	1997
	McLaren	1989	7	Ferrari	1952 & '53
	Williams	1992		Ferrari	2008
	Williams	1993		Lotus	1963 & '73
9	Ferrari	2001		McLaren	1999
	Ferrari	2006		McLaren	2000
	Ferrari	2007		McLaren	2012
	McLaren	1998		Red Bull	2012
	Red Bull	2010		Tyrrell	1971
	Williams	1986		Williams	1991 & '94

POLE POSITIONS

208	Ferrari	11	BRM	
154	McLaren		Cooper	
128	Williams	10	Maserati	
107	Lotus	9	Ligier	
58	Red Bull (+ Jaguar)	8	Mercedes	
53	Mercedes GP (+ Honda Racing & Brawn GP)	7	Vanwall	
		5	March	
39	Brabham	4	Matra	
34	Renault* (+ Toleman + Benetton + Lotus II)	3	Force India (+ Jordan)	
			Shadow	
31	Renault		Toyota	
14	Tyrrell	2	Lancia	
12	Alfa Romeo	1	BMW Sauber	
			Toro Rosso	

FASTEST LAPS

232 Ferrari
152 McLaren
133 Williams
71 Lotus
54 Renault* (+ Toleman + Benetton + Lotus II)
47 Red Bull
40 Brabham
37 Mercedes GP (+ Brawn GP)
22 Tyrrell
18 Renault
15 BRM
   Maserati
14 Alfa Romeo
13 Cooper
12 Matra
11 Prost
9 Mercedes
7 March
6 Vanwall
5 Force India (+ Jordan)
3 Sauber
   Surtees
   Toyota

POINTS

6244.5 Ferrari
5017.5 McLaren
3338 Williams
3140.5 Red Bull (+ Stewart + Jaguar Racing)
2788 Mercedes GP (+ BAR + Honda Racing + Brawn GP)
2545.5 Renault* (+Toleman, + Benetton + Lotus II)
1514 Lotus
919 Force India (+ Jordan + Midland + Spyker)
854 Brabham
803 Sauber
617 Tyrrell
439 BRM
424 Prost (+ Ligier)
333 Cooper
312 Renault
304 Toro Rosso
278.5 Toyota
171.5 March

TITLES

15 Ferrari
9 Williams
8 McLaren
7 Lotus
4 Red Bull
2 Brabham
   Cooper
   Mercedes GP
   Renault
1 Benetton
   Brawn
   BRM
   Matra
   Tyrrell
   Vanwall

ONE-TWOS FINISHES

1	Ferrari	78
2	McLaren	47
3	Williams	32
4	Mercedes GP	23
4	Red Bull	15
6	Brabham	8
	Tyrrell	8
8	Lotus	7
9	BRM	5
	Mercedes	5
11	Alfa Romeo	4
	Brawn	4
13	Benetton	2
	Cooper	2
	Matra	2
	Renault	2
17	BMW Sauber	1
	Jordan	1
	Ligier	1
	Maserati	1

Opposite left **Wins:** Alain Prost blasts his McLaren past polesitter Nelson Piquet in the 1984 Portuguese GP, but his seventh win of the year left him just half a point away from the title.

Opposite right **Pole positions:** Nico Rosberg celebrates his 11th 2014 pole position for Mercedes in Abu Dhabi.

Below **One-two finishes:** The sustained excellence of Sebastian Vettel and Mark Webber for Red Bull Racing has propelled the team to fifth.

PICTURE CREDITS

The publishers would like to thank the following sources for their kind permission to reproduce the pictures in this book. The page numbers for each of the photographs are listed below, giving the page on which they appear in the book and any location indicator (C-centre, T-top, B-bottom, L-left, R-right).

Claudio Ceria: 184L

Getty Images: /Allsport: 170R; /Mike Cooper: 98T; /Klemantaski Collection: 22T; /Vladimir Rys Photography: 124-125; /Rainer W Schlegelmilch: 62C, 171B; /Sascha Schuermann/AFP: 176

LAT Photographic: 4-5B, 4R, 12-13, 14T, 14B, 16B, 17R, 18T, 18B, 21R, 21B, 22B, 23C, 23B, 24B, 25TR, 25L, 26T, 26B, 27T, 27C, 30R, 31T, 32C, 32B, 33T, 35B, 38T, 38B, 39C, 39B, 40T, 40B, 41B, 44C, 45T, 46, 47B, 48BL, 49C, 49B, 50T, 51R, 52L, 52R, 54T, 54B, 56T, 56BR, 57L, 58TR, 58B, 60T, 63R, 66TL, 67T, 67B, 68T, 68B, 69B, 70R, 71T, 71BR, 72R, 72B, 73C, 73B, 75TR, 75B, 82R, 82B, 84-85, 86, 87T, 87L, 87BR, 88-89, 90TL, 90B, 91T, 91B, 92-93, 94L, 94BR, 95C, 95B, 96-97, 98B, 99T, 99L, 99R, 100-101, 102TL, 102R, 102B, 103, 104-105, 106, 107T, 107L, 107C, 110TL, 110B, 111T, 111C, 111BR, 128, 129T, 129B, 132B, 133TL, 133TR, 133B, 140B, 141T, 141C, 142-143, 144T, 144L, 144B, 145C, 145B, 148BL, 150-151, 153B, 156TL, 156C, 156BR, 157T, 157B, 158-159, 160TL, 160R, 161T, 161B, 162-163, 164TR, 164BL, 164BR, 165T, 165B, 168R, 169T, 172B, 173B, 174, 175TR, 175R, 175B, 177T, 178B, 179B, 180C, 180B, 181B, 182C, 183R, 184R, 186R, 186B, 187B, 189, 190BL; / Lorenzo Bellanca: 83BR, 114B, 148C, 169B; /Charles Coates: 4BC, 6-7, 30B, 34L, 37BR, 59TL, 60B, 69T, 74T, 123B, 134-135, 137L, 140T, 152B, 182B, 187T; /Glenn Dunbar: 2, 5L, 10-11, 19T, 20R, 28T, 29B, 53R, 66B, 119B, 123TR, 130-131, 149TL, 153T, 188T; /Steve Etherington: 9, 31B, 33B, 41TR, 42-43, 48R, 70B, 77T, 78-79, 80-81, 112-113, 114T, 118T, 122TL, 132T, 136B, 138-139, 146-147, 152C, 154-155, 171T, 185T; /Andrew Ferraro: 20B, 34BR, 36B, 37R, 45C, 47T, 55R, 77R, 77BL, 115L, 116-117, 118B, 120-121, 137B, 185B, 190R; /Andy Hone: 37T, 64-65, 76R, 166-167; /Jed Leicester: 173R, 191; /Colin McMaster: 172R; /Peter Spinney: 136T; /Alastair Staley: 47TL, 126-127, 149B; /Steven Tee: 5, 83TR, 115B, 119TR, 122BL, 170BL, 179T, 183B

Press Association Images: /AP: 53B; /Victor R. Caivano/AP: 63B; /Antonio Calanni/AP: 74B; /DPA: 17B, 28B, 45B, 73T; /David Davies: 35C, 59BR; /Tom Hevezi/PA Archive: 62B; /John Marsh/Empics Sport: 16T, 36T, 51B, 53T, 55TR, 61R, 76B; /PA Archive: 15T; /Alberto Pellaschiar/AP: 50B; /Martin Rickett/PA Archive: 27B; /Daniel Roland/AP: 178R; /S&G and Barratts/Empics Sport: 19B; /Michael Sohn/AP: 61T; /Peter Steffen/DPA: 24T; / Sutton Motorsport: 15B, 29T, 56BL, 57B

Sutton Motorsport Images: 55BR, 108-109, 168B, 177B, 181T, 188B

Topfoto.co.uk: 44B

Every effort has been made to acknowledge correctly and contact the source and/or copyright holder of each picture and Carlton Books Limited apologises for any unintentional errors or omissions that will be corrected in future editions of this book.

ABOUT THE AUTHOR

||||||||||||||||||||||||||||||||||

Bruce Jones has been covering motor racing for more than a quarter of a century. He has written countless books on the subject, from Formula 1 to the broadest spectrum of world motor sport, with titles aimed at all ages. As a journalist he worked on *Autosport* in the mid-1980s, a magazine acknowledged as the voice of motor sport the world over, going on to be Editor in the mid-1990s.

In addition to his writing, Bruce has been a pitlane interviewer for FOM Television, also conducting the official post-race TV interviews. Branching into event commentary, he regularly broadcasts at the Le Mans 24 Hours and, his favourite event of the year, the Goodwood Revival historic race meeting.

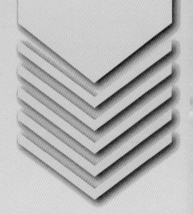